3

JOHN UPDIKE

A Study of the Short Fiction

Also available in Twayne's Studies in Short Fiction Series

Twayne's Studies in Short Fiction

Gordon Weaver, General Editor
Oklahoma State University

JOHN UPDIKE
Courtesy of Hana Hamplová

JOHN UPDIKE

A Study of the Short Fiction

Robert M. Luscher
Catawba College

TWAYNE PUBLISHERS · NEW YORK
Maxwell Macmillan Canada · Toronto
Maxwell Macmillan International · New York Oxford Singapore Sydney

Twayne's Studies in Short Fiction Series, No. 43

Copyright © 1993 by Twayne Publishers

Twayne Publishers	Maxwell Macmillan Canada, Inc.
Macmillan Publishing Company	1200 Eglinton Avenue East
866 Third Avenue	Suite 200
New York, New York 10022	Don Mills, Ontario M3C 3N1

Macmillan Publishing Company is part of the Maxwell Communication Group of Companies.

Library of Congress Cataloging-in-Publication Data

Luscher, Robert M., 1954–
    John Updike : a study of the short fiction / Robert M. Luscher.
        p.   cm. — (Twayne's studies in short fiction : no. 43)
    Includes bibliographical references and index.
    ISBN 0-8057-0850-2 (alk. paper)
    1. Updike, John—Criticism and interpretation. 2. Short story.
I. Title. II. Series.
PS3571.P4Z76   1993
813'.54—dc20   92-43160
                                             CIP

10 9 8 7 6 5 4 3 2 1

Printed in the United States of America

Contents

Contents

Preface

Prolific in a variety of genres, John Updike is without question one of North America's premier men of letters; regularly alternating novels, poetry, short fiction, and volumes of assorted prose, he has currently published over 30 volumes—averaging nearly a book a year over the course of his career. In addition, he regularly reviews a wide variety of literature for the *New Yorker*, his earliest home as a writer. A recent *Esquire* article mapping the cosmos of contemporary writers ranks Updike among the brightest stars because of his sustained brilliance: "Year after year, the highest average in the majors," comment the editors.[1] Unfortunately, most assessments of Updike's literary reputation—as well as those of other authors—tend to focus on novels, equating length with difficulty, privileging the extended narrative as a superior achievement, and disparaging short stories as a way to warm up for or fill time between novels. Yet Updike is more than a novelist who writes stories on the side; he is a seriously committed craftsman of the exacting shorter form, with 10 collections and over 200 stories to his credit. While consistently advancing the level of his craft, he has contributed actively to the genre's current revitalization through formal experimentation and stylistic excellence. Few authors of short fiction have been so widely anthologized and featured with such frequency in *Best American Short Stories* and *Prize Stories: The O'Henry Awards.*[2]

Updike's stature as a short story writer, however, is perpetually shadowed by his impressive novelistic achievements: the Rabbit tetralogy, which follows Rabbit Angstrom's flight through the past four decades; the trilogy of modern offshoots of Nathaniel Hawthorne's *The Scarlet Letter* (*S.*, *Roger's Version*, and *A Month of Sundays*); *The Centaur*, blending the mythic with the mundane; and *The Coup*, unique in its capture of the ravings of a deposed African dictator. Still, like his New England forebear Hawthorne, Updike has exhibited a sustained mastery of the short story form throughout his career, shaping a canon of short fiction that merits critical attention apart from the novels. "Updike reaches his highest range of accomplishment in this medium," states Rachel Burchard. "In the short stories he presents all of his major themes with intensity and artistic discipline more refined than that of his novels, with poetry more eloquent than that in 'The Great Scarf of Birds,' and with religious *empressement* to compare with that of the Psalms."[3] Nonetheless, despite such high praise, Burchard relegates her study of the short fiction to the final chapter; similarly, most other critics either offer limited commentary on the short stories or discuss them in passing within chapters on the novels. Robert Detweiler's Twayne volume, *John Updike*, and Donald Greiner's *The Other John Updike* devote the most extended and serious attention to Updike's short fiction, but no single volume concentrating solely on Updike's achievements in the genre has appeared.

The majority of Updike's stories focus on loss and the ongoing struggle against time's diminishment. While both sexual and spiritual yearnings animate Updike's characters in their searches for fulfillment and provide some respite, art and memory ultimately afford the most enduring agents for arresting loss. With the quality of a collective elegy for the Protestant middle class, Updike's canon of short fiction captures the changing historical background, the shifting social mores, and the personal responses to the altered sociocultural circumstances that have heightened spiritual uncertainty, social unrest, sexual freedom, and domestic tension. Together, the stories chronicle the metamorphosis of middle-class domesticity from the security of the post–World War II era through the subsequent skepticism and moral upheaval of the sixties and seventies to the contemporary apprehension of the need for renewed trust.

With the chronological progression of Updike's protagonists, the thematic focus of his stories shifts accordingly. The early emphasis on "unexpected gifts" that grace the protected realm of childhood, for instance, gives way to studies in the difficulty of rescuing and preserving the remembered past in young adulthood. Correspondingly, the depiction of different phases of experience often spurs experimentation with fictional technique: the lyric story, which recounts a character's sustained plunge into the past, and the montage story, which assembles fragments of memory in a search for pattern and wholeness, both emerge as new forms when Updike's characters become conscious of loss and actively struggle to counter its potential ravages. From the beginning of Updike's career, however, his stories have consistently subordinated the traditional emphasis on plot and dramatic action, privileging instead reflection and the rhythmic dimension created by rich figurative language and imagery. Updike's talents in the comic realm emerge in a slightly different variety of story: the picaresque tales of Henry Bech, his Jewish literary alter ego, which also provide the opportunity to satirize the contemporary publishing industry. Still, Bech's erotic exertions and his struggle to rescue experience through art, as well as the stories' ironic tone and the semi-autobiographical connection to Updike's own travels, provide continuity with the rest of the canon.

Updike's career as a writer of short fiction began with his flight from his position at the *New Yorker* and his subsequent commitment to exploring his own roots and to transmuting his own experience into fiction. Nonetheless, as a roving reporter who wrote occasional pieces for the magazine's "Talk of the Town" column, Updike was afforded ample opportunity for honing his skills in vignette-like narratives and cultivating the talent for "silent spying" that would serve him so well as a resident chronicler of the suburban milieu; the pieces detailing visits to exhibitions and other events, Updike remarks, may have been partially responsible for the permanent overdevelopment of his "gift of metaphorical elaboration."[4] Although his fictional apprenticeship occurred while he wrote for the *Harvard Lampoon*, Updike's departure from New York to the small town of Ipswich, Massachusetts, established the distance that allowed him to create his literary niche; nonetheless, the *New Yorker* has served as the most frequent outlet for his short fiction, although Updike gradually has begun to place stories in more varied locations. His training in the visual arts (he once aspired to be a cartoonist for either Walt Disney or the *New Yorker*) also proved invaluable for a career as a writer, providing aesthetic practice transferable to fiction by helping him "to visualize his scenes, even to construct his personalities and to shape the invisible contentions and branchings of plot."[5]

Illustrating the same proclivity for realistic texture that animates his fiction, Updike's comments on his aesthetic interests explain his departure from the literary center: "My success was based . . . on my cultivated fondness for exploring corners—the space beneath the Shillington dining table, where the nap of the rug was still thick; the back stairs, where the rubber galoshes lived; the cave the wicker armchairs made when turned upside down against the rain on the porch. I had left heavily trafficked literary turfs to others and stayed in my corner of New England to give its domestic news."[6] Early in his career, Updike sold stories to the *New Yorker* with the aim of supporting himself in a more congenial environment for writing fiction and raising a family, but since that time, with the changes in the publishing industry, the novels (and film rights) have become his major source of income. While Updike feels that he should compensate Knopf, his longstanding publisher, for the less lucrative collections of short stories, poems, and assorted prose by making every other book a novel, his commitment to the short story has remained constant because it provides a congenial form for capturing critical moments of crisis and perception. If his novels serve as extended "moral debates" with his readers, his short stories challenge assumptions about the "ordinariness" of daily experience and foster greater awareness of the particulars that subtly alter life's direction.

With an unwavering commitment to realism, Updike has remained determined to illuminate life's corners and reveal the inherent mystery of the ordinary. His work has remained at the center of the post-Joycean evolution of the short story, so much so that his trademark internal dramas, with their terminal epiphanies and deemphasis on plot, are nowadays taken for granted as one paradigm of the short story. Although Updike has consigned the volumes of his contemporaries to his basement shelves, he has nonetheless absorbed many of their lessons and remains open to experimentation. He professes that J. D. Salinger's formless stories were a "revelation,"[7] impressive not only for their sharp dialogue but also because they "were very open to tender invasions."[8] John Cheever's depictions of suburban manners and Vladimir Nabokov's resplendent style also proved influential in illustrating fictional possibilities. Updike notes that he has "learned quite a lot from [Donald] Barthelme's short stories without getting or liking every one. I do think he catches a rhythm, a kind of hollowness, and a fitful energy that is part of our contemporary experience."[9] A few of his stories even contain Barthelme-like illustrations. Updike's most distinctive formal contributions to the art of short fiction, however, have been his sustained lyric pieces and his montage stories, related vignettes driven less by plot than by a coalescing network of incidents and images. In addition, his four short story sequences—unified, coherent collections of independent stories—stand out among a growing canon of contemporary works that find this paradoxical form aesthetically and thematically suitable.

While focused on many of the same thematic concerns that dominate Updike's novels, the short stories must be appreciated on their own terms rather than as scaled-down echoes of the longer works. Indeed, Updike's talents as a writer may be more naturally suited to the short story than to the novel. His lustrous stylistic precision, meticulous attention to detail, control of dialogue, and intuitive sense of form all serve him well in the crucible of the short story form, which demands careful crafting of nuance and compression of character and event.

Notable early in his career for the sustained lyric flights of characters seeking to recapture a lost past, Updike has lately reined his tendency toward lavish description; nevertheless, against the starker backdrop of recent voguish minimalism, his more elaborate prose style remains distinctive. Although Updike often unifies his stories with a network of imagery, his short fiction is not laced with detail for the pleasure of the symbol hunter. In both novels and short stories, Updike's commitment to realism stems from his belief in the world's capacity to yield hard-earned insight. As the narrator of "The Blessed Man of Boston, My Grandmother's Thimble, and Fanning Island" states, "Details are the giant's fingers. He seizes the stick and strips the bark and shows, burning beneath, the moist white wood of joy."[10] Unlike the recent school of brand-name realism that seeks to immerse readers in the trivia of popular culture, Updike embeds selective detail not only for historical backdrop but out of a deep-seated belief that quotidian life teems with objects and experiences that have the potential to evoke wider perception.

Throughout his career, Updike has been dogged by critics' suspicions that his gem-like prose disguises a failure to tackle "larger subjects" with a more political, urban, or tragic slant. The most extreme form of this complaint is that Updike has little to say and expends his considerable verbal gifts on trivial matters. While Updike does move outside the range of suburban experience more than he receives credit for, such criticisms begin with the premise that everyday experience is devoid of significant sorrows and joys—the very assumption which his fiction seeks to combat in choosing to place domestic life in the foreground. Updike has assumed the challenge of revealing the depths of beauty and sadness in the mundane world; he celebrates the intensity of the ordinary, while simultaneously bemoaning its transitoriness and the gap between our spiritual yearnings and the external consolations for which we strive. Early in his career, in his essay "The Dogwood Tree: A Boyhood," Updike articulated the rationale behind his art that continues to serve as the basis for his fictional aesthetic:

> I reasoned thus: just as the paper is the basis for the marks upon it, might not events be contingent upon a never-expressed (because featureless) ground? Is the true marvel of the Sunday skaters the pattern of their pirouettes or the fact that they are silently upheld? Blankness is not emptiness; we may skate upon an intense radiance we do not see because we see nothing else. And in fact there is a color, a quiet but tireless goodness that things at rest, like a brick wall or a

small stone, seem to affirm. A wordless reassurance these things are pressing to give. An hallucination? To transcribe middleness with all its grits, bumps, and anonymities, in its fullness of satisfaction and mystery: is it possible or, in view of the suffering that violently colors the periphery and that at all moments threatens to move into the center, worth doing?[11]

His commitment to "middleness," made with a consciousness of the world's surrounding violence and potential blankness, is not in itself a shunning of life's great calamities and sorrows but rather a recognition of the conscious maneuvers to keep them at bay. As a result, Updike is most compassionate toward his characters, even when his depiction is tinged with irony; although they often arrive at some insight into their compromised situations, many remain dislocated or unable to act upon their insights.

While Updike's short fiction deals with human universals, it contains a strong regional slant, with most of his stories firmly placed in the northeast—either the rural Pennsylvania milieu of his youth or suburban New England communities. Whatever the setting, however, Updike's main concern is with charting the emotional geography of middle-class American domestic life. The passage from rural Olinger to suburban Tarbox and similar communities (which occurs between *Pigeon Feathers* and *The Music School*) represents the movement from youth to the complexities of maturity and the subsequent crises of middle-age; only Henry Bech makes a counter movement, fleeing the suburbs to return to the familiar life in New York City from which marriage has separated him. As Updike's stories have accrued, his status as an astute cultural observer whose fiction contains a record of nearly a half century of dramatically changing American social mores has begun to be recognized. While the great social calamities may loom in the background, as does a consciousness of the void that the remnants of his characters' religious faith seeks to breach, Updike focuses on how the inherent fissures of relationships are exacerbated by the era's brisk social change. While his characters invariably cast fond backward glances to happier times before loss and separation, Updike transcends mere nostalgic indulgence in his depictions of their yearnings to rescue meaningful portions of the past as they attempt to discover strategies of accommodation to the waning of memory, relationships, and life itself.

As Updike has remarked in an interview with Charles Samuels, he has written because the "rhythm of my life and oeuvre demanded it, not to placate hallucinatory critical voices."[12] Part 1 of this work explores this rhythm by examining the short fiction chronologically, concentrating on the common thematic concerns and fictional techniques that are highlighted by Updike's neat packaging of his own canon. Updike's early stories featuring adolescents and young marrieds concern the dilemmas of maturity and memory that accompany crossing the threshold of youth or assuming marital responsibilities. The stories in *The Same Door* and *Pigeon Feathers* most often employ a Joycean epiphany to heighten the revelations of everyday experience or the grace-like gifts of Olinger. Yet even these affirmations are not without an irony that becomes increasingly apparent as happiness recedes from easy grasp: insight often occurs only as the protagonists begin to establish the distance that will ultimately separate them from security. Updike effectively brings this phase of his career to a close with *Olinger Stories*, the short story sequence that arranges the stories occurring in this locale into a Bildungsroman that sketches a literary departure to less secure territory, where access to memory is more problematic and spiritual inquiry yields only provisional answers.

Updike's early work begins his persistent portrayal of the struggle with the enigma of loss—whether of youth and rural protectiveness, of domestic bliss and the consolations of sex, or of the veneer erected to mask the void. In the realm of *The Music School* and beyond, into the increased weariness depicted in *Museums and Women*, greater effort and discipline are required to capture life's more elusive satisfactions and to weave the more disparate notes of the past, present, and future into a coherent whole. Both the briefly sustained lyric plunge into memory and the short sketch epitomize the transitory attempts of Updike's suburbanites to grasp some authentic bit of reality, unearthing artifacts of their pasts that sometimes only increase puzzlement and dissatisfaction; whatever epiphanies occur usually lead to more painful realizations of loss or spiritual uncertainty, though Updike's artist figures occasionally achieve rare moments of connection.

Before the self-proclaimed midpoint of his career (marked by his long poem *Midpoint*), Updike created Henry Bech, the blocked Jewish writer, and Joan and Richard Maple, the perpetually separating couple—characters whose recurrence later led to the publication of three more short story sequences. The only exception to chronology occurs with the Bech books, which were published twelve years apart; since both feature the same character and focus on the American writer's situation, they are discussed in the same chapter. With their dry humor and picaresque quality, the Bech stories stand out from Updike's epiphanic and lyric stories, although they touch similar anxieties about loss, using the contemporary artist's diminished stature in a mass media-based culture. More favorably reviewed than any of Updike's other collections, the Bech books serve as the analogue in short fiction to the Rabbit tetralogy. When Updike does not feel the necessity to alter fictional masks, as with Bech and the Maples, the resultant story sequences rank among his best work. More closely autobiographical than the Beck books, the stories of Joan and Richard Maple collected in *Too Far to Go* are among Updike's more traditional ones; together they embody a poignant study of the cycles of attachment and detachment that occur with the stresses of contemporary marriage.

Problems and *Trust Me*, examining marital separation and the territory beyond, round out the currently collected Updike canon of short fiction. Although Updike hit the ground running as a writer, he appears to have found his stride in his latest fiction—not by abandoning the experimentalism of mid-career but rather by incorporating lyricism and a muted irony into the epiphanic form that he has never totally forsaken. The inevitable burden of guilt Updike's middle-aged characters carry spills over into new relationships, despite the callouses which their souls have grown to protect them from betrayal—both others' and their own.

Part 2 presents a selection of Updike's commentary on his career as a writer and on the art of fiction. Some of this material is gleaned from Updike's reviews of other writers, but the main sources of this commentary are interviews, Updike's memoirs, and literary essays. Part 3 contains a sampling of the prevailing winds in Updike criticism. It was difficult to include a varied sampling of academic criticism because of length considerations. Some attempt, however, has been made to represent crucial articles that cannot be found in one of the three collections of critical essays on Updike.[13] Space limitations prevent full representation of the spectrum of critical opinion on each collection; instead the excerpts from reviews included here attempt to echo the consistent chords that span reviewers' assessments of Updike's works over the course of his long and distinguished career.

Notes

1. "The Universe Today," *Esquire* August 1987: 52.
2. Updike's stories have been featured a total of 22 times in the two major yearly anthologies: 10 times in *Best American Short Stores* and 12 times in *Prize*

Stories: The O'Henry Awards (receiving two First Prizes). A complete listing of these stories is contained within the chronology.

    3. Rachel C. Burchard, *John Updike: Yea Sayings* (Carbondale: Southern Illinois UP, 1971), 133.

    4. John Updike, *Hugging the Shore* (New York: Knopf, 1983), 847; hereafter cited in the text as *HS*.

    5. John Updike, "The Illustrative Itch," *New York Review of Books* 10 April 1986, 35.

    6. John Updike, *Self-Consciousness* (New York: Knopf, 1989), 143; hereafter cited in the text as *SC*.

    7. Robert Boyers, et al., "An Evening with John Updike," *Salmagundi* 57 (1982), 42.

    8. Frank Gado, "A Conversation with John Updike," *The Idol* 47 (1971), 7.

    9. Richard Burgin, "A Conversation with John Updike," *John Updike Newsletter* 10, 11 (Spring–Summer 1979), 1.

    10. John Updike, *Pigeon Feathers and Other Stories* (New York: Knopf, 1962), 245; hereafter cited in the text as *PF*.

    11. John Updike, *Assorted Prose* (New York: Knopf, 1965), 185–86; hereafter cited in the text as *AP*.

    12. Charles Samuels, "John Updike," *Writers at Work: The Paris Review Interviews*, 4 (New York: Viking, 1976), 440.

    13. The three volumes devoted exclusively to reprinting criticism on Updike's work are: David Thorburn and Howard Eiland, eds., *John Updike: A Collection of Critical Essays* (Englewood Cliffs, NJ: Prentice Hall, 1979); William R. Macnaughton, ed., *Critical Essays on John Updike* (Boston: G. K. Hall, 1982); and Harold Bloom, ed., *John Updike* (New York: Chelsea House, 1987).

Acknowledgments

For permission to quote from Updike's collections of short fiction and prose I am indebted to Updike's longstanding publisher, Alfred A. Knopf. Permission to reprint items in Parts 2 and 3 was granted by: Viking/ Penguin and the *Paris Review*; Charles E. Reilly; Alfred A. Knopf; Houghton Mifflin, the *New York Review of Books*, University of Alabama Press; the English Department of Syracuse University; *Studies in Short Fiction*—Newberry College; University Press of Kentucky and Harvester-Wheatsheaf; the *New Republic*; the *Virginia Quarterly Review*; and Martin Secker & Warburg Ltd.

In large part, the preparation of this manuscript has been a solitary endeavor, but without the support and assistance of my colleagues at Catawba College its long-delayed completion would never have been possible. I would especially like to thank Dr. Charles Turney and Dr. Cheryl Peevy for reading portions of the manuscript; Ms. Jackie Simms for her diligent searches for fugitive items; and Ms. Melanie Bookout for her clerical assistance. Gordon Weaver's patience and supportive responses as the chapters accumulated was also invaluable. Thanks also to Liz Traynor Fowler, former Twayne editor whom this manuscript outlasted, for her encouragement and faith. I am also grateful to Catawba College for the summer grants that helped me secure the freedom I needed to write and research. Finally, I am indebted to my family—Diana, Aurora, and Julia—without whose understanding, love and support this work would have been impossible. This book is dedicated to Diana: she endured.

Part 1

The Short Fiction: A Critical Analysis

Poised on the Threshold: *The Same Door*

The stories in Updike's first collection, *The Same Door*, all passed originally through the same portal: the *New Yorker*, which published his first story, "Friends from Philadelphia," in 1954. Updike had harbored ambitions to appear in its pages since the age of 13, during his days on the family farm in Plowville, when he yearned to escape the life that he later realized "was to become my material and message."[1] Yet he notes that acceptance of his first story, written in a Vermont cabin on a borrowed typewriter the summer after graduating from Harvard, produced an "uneasy, apologetic sense of having blundered through the wrong door."[2] Nonetheless, steady employment waited beyond, and from 1955 to 1957, he supported himself and his family by writing "Talk of the Town" columns for the magazine, which continued to publish his fiction as well. Thus the *New Yorker* became the means through which Updike was ultimately to realize his ambitions, transcend his past, and depart from the source of so much of his early fiction.

Paradoxically, the door swung both ways—out of the past and back into it. Updike has remarked that writing "The Happiest I've Been," a story set in Olinger—the fictionalized version of his hometown, Shillington, Pennsylvania—elicited a "simultaneous sense of loss and recapture"[3] as he entered the past to create a tribute memorializing its loss. Of the 16 stories in the collection, however, only 5 take place in or near Olinger. The majority are set in New York City, a less nostalgic and hospitable locale, and feature young married couples. Updike's protagonists thus occupy both sides of the passage that leads from their youthful origins to the beginning of mature independence, but in both cases they usually are not far from the threshold in between.

Although he admits to adapting his own experiences freely, Updike does not intend his fiction to be "thinly disguised memoir."[4] Whatever correspondence his stories may have to his experience, Updike, like any artist, transmutes memory into fiction. Having crossed the threshold from life to art, the stories generated by his memories are of another order than non-fiction such as "The Dogwood Tree: A Boyhood." As Updike has remarked: "I feel no obligation to the remembered past;

what I create on paper must, and for me does, soar free of whatever the facts were. . . . I disavow any essential connection between my life and whatever I write" (Samuels, 433–34). As creations of a particular artistic sensibility, the stories share a common style and stance; in this sense, the book's title is also appropriate, as the reader seems to pass through the same door in each successive story. While some critics see such consistency as a drawback, in a first collection it indicates an admirable certainty of voice and mastery of form. During Updike's short apprenticeship on the *Harvard Lampoon*, he cultivated the skills that would characterize his subsequent efforts in short fiction: framing actions, chains of association, stylistic flights of descriptive prose, and, most importantly, the intentional ambiguity of the conclusion that tilts rather than carries the reader in the right direction.[5]

As many early commentators on Updike's fiction note, however, the influence of the *New Yorker* is dominant. Most stories were revised somewhat before book publication, but all share the well-known *New Yorker* flavor: light on plot and action, with an emphasis on mood and detail instead. While some critics bemoan the magazine's influence on Updike's style and technique,[6] his admiration of its artists and writers has not lead to a slavish emulation of stories often criticized as slick, polished, and lacking substance. Although Updike keenly captures contemporary fashions, his achievement transcends much of the other fiction published in the same pages because of his delicate compassion for his characters and the studied portraits of the ambiguity of their conditions. What Updike has extracted from the *New Yorker* is a commitment to realism and to the search for significance in daily events; his stories rise above urbane social satire to sympathetic insights into the compromises and regrets of the modern world.

Lending the collection technical unity is Updike's adaptation of the Joycean epiphany as a concluding device. James Joyce first used the term to describe the type of incident that the young artist Stephen Hero pondered collecting for a book: "By an epiphany he meant a sudden spiritual manifestation, whether in the vulgarity of speech or of gesture or in a memorable phase of the mind itself."[7] Now loosely applied by critics to refer to a character's moment of insight, for Joyce, an epiphany could be any event that shimmers with significance. While a character's insight is certainly "a memorable phase of the mind," there are many others that an artist might depict; utterances and gestures, even continued delusions, might also constitute epiphanies. Thus, Arthur's "luminous thought" in "Sunday Teasing"—"You don't know anything"—

embodies the more traditionally recognized epiphany; however, Ace's dance of distraction, Freddy Platt's French chatter, and the ironic return of happiness in "A Gift from the City" all present epiphanies that demand a recognition beyond the surface of things.

A more contemporary influence than Joyce is J. D. Salinger, whose stories, many of which also were published in the *New Yorker*, depict similar open-ended moments that involve significant bits of dialogue, revealing gestures or actions, and muted moments of illumination. Updike's early efforts at developing the understated conclusion exhibit an instinctive understanding that a story's ending is its most crucial feature; 25 years later, in his introduction to *Best American Short Stories 1984*, Updike uses the image of the door to describe the successful short story's conclusion as the most appropriate exit from a narrative with many false doors (*BASS*, xvii). Even in his first collection, not one of the exits we take is forced or unnatural, and all share a similar design: a diffuse moment that throws the reader back onto the story, giving it in retrospect a logical and anticipated sense of completeness.

The repeated technical similarity signals a thematic one: most characters exit into a temporal rather than an eternal realm. While few seek answers to spiritual doubts as explicitly as David Kern later does in "Pigeon Feathers," most look for some type of accommodation or redeeming moments in daily living. Discussing his later compilation of *Olinger Stories*, Updike states: "The point, to me, is plain, and is the point, more or less, of all these Olinger stories. *We are rewarded unexpectedly.* The muddled and inconsequent surface of things now and then parts to yield to us a gift" (*OS*, viii). Though the "gift" may often take the form of a moment of knowledge or even grace, these rewards are often ambiguous blessings. Still, even if these moments of clarity fail to resolve his characters' dilemmas or complicate their lives in new ways, the temporal world need not be a vicious circle.

Though Updike stands on the threshold of his productive career in *The Same Door*, his first volume of short stories (his third published book) is hardly the work of a novice, though the stories in the latter half of the book (arranged in order of composition) exhibit some technical advances, a greater stylistic confidence, and a willingness to experiment. On the whole, however, Updike shows himself to be an adept craftsman of the short story, carrying forward the Joycean tradition but beginning to refine the form. Stories such as "Who Made Yellow Roses Yellow?" capture nuances of character in dialogue; others, such as "Toward Evening," rely more heavily on imagery to convey mood and theme, but the most successful stories blend these techniques. While not yet directly confronting the spiritual crises treated explicitly in later works, Updike's early stories nonetheless explore the problems of loss and memory and the discovery of ordinary life's spiritual essence.

The collection's two epigraphs—one from Henri Bergson, the other from T. S. Eliot—both concern pleasures, and the reticence encountered when attempting to examine and articulate them. The epigraphs reveal two of Updike's persistent concerns—memory and domestic life—and signal that both can open out to reveal unexpected gifts. In "The Dogwood Tree: A Boyhood," Updike describes pleasant memories and family love as experiences that constitute the calm center of his subjective geography, having "the neutral color of my own soul" (*AP*, 170). Yet recapturing past pleasures, or casting the unarticulated love within a family into a fictive light, is a difficult task, riddled with problems of subjectivity. The characters, dwelling on the threshold between a youthful past and a diminishing present, struggle to see clearly, often unaware of how to savor ephemeral pleasures or domestic love.

Although Updike may have made no special effort to do so, the collection is structured so that the Olinger stories frame the rest, which, except for "Dentistry and Doubt," feature young married protagonists. Yet the Olinger stories are by no means isolated nostalgic excursions, disjunct from the rest; the volume's second and third stories, concerning postadolescent characters (Ace Anderson and Mark Prosser, respectively), link the two groups.[8] Furthermore, the character of John Nordholm appears in the first and last stories, aged four years and poised on the threshold of maturity at the volume's end. Memory thus becomes the route by which the reader enters and exits the collection, suggesting that some inadequacy of their present existence sends the characters continually questing into the past. The notion of the "unexpected gift," however, applies equally to all the volume's stories; in both Olinger and New York City, beauty and significance may inhere in the commonplace.

"Friends from Philadelphia," Updike's first published story, opens with John Nordholm glimpsing a thigh below a half-drawn shade—an appropriately arresting detail for an author whose fiction often examines American sexual mores. That view of Thelma Lutz's leg, however, may be the only unambiguous gift that John receives in the course of the story. Though welcome in the Lutz home, he must endure Thelma's pretenses and mocking remarks while waiting for her father to arrive home to help him accomplish his errand: purchasing a bottle of wine for John's parents and their dinner guests from Philadelphia. Mr. Lutz, slightly inebriated, lets John drive his new car to the liquor store and buys an expensive bottle of wine costing well over the two dollars John gives him, and even sends over a dollar's change home.

Lutz's persistent remarks about his prosperity and the more educated Nordholm's lack of it cast a shadow, however, on his apparent generosity. The tone of his comments, at least initially, "wasn't nasty, but soft and full of wonder"; still, Lutz repeatedly observes that intelligence is not rewarded by material prosperity, marking its value suspect. Praising John for his quick mastery of the gears, for instance, he remarks to Thelma, "He's a smart boy. He'll never own a new car."[9] John, on the other hand, is painfully aware of his parents' economic inferiority, so much so that he pretends not to know how old their used 1940 Plymouth is. Still, he becomes Lutz's unwitting messenger when he returns home with the wine and the change; though the guests undoubtedly will be impressed with the vintage, the Nordholms should understand Lutz's mixed motives.

The interaction between Thelma and John, both uncertain adolescents in the process of defining their social roles, also reveals the pervasiveness of the values Lutz holds. Thelma greets John with a "hostesslike gesture," but her sarcasm toward him in front of her mother and her affected New York City accent are attempts at assuming a sophisticated role. John, whose family now lives on a farm outside of town, is an outsider seeking social acceptance. While he behaves politely toward Mrs. Lutz, Thelma treats him ironically, almost as a social inferior; however, she acts embarrassed by her father's derogatory remarks about John and coaches John when he is unsure about how to start the car. The two adolescents spar with each other, but they are able to put aside their roles for moments of honesty and directness. John's success at driving and turning a few good metaphoric phrases builds his confidence and inflates his ego. Thelma, however, bluntly informs him of his vanity when he admires his hand—on which he, like the young Updike, hopes to "ride the fine thin pencil line" out of his hometown to success. In return, John alerts her that plucking her eyebrows and calling him "Jan" are unattractive mannerisms. Their conflict thus continues, but on a constructive and more honest level. Still, as John steps out of the Lutz's car, he attempts to reassert his superiority by reminding her to remember his advice; but at the same time his status as the unwitting bearer of the ironic gift reveals to us his vulnerability and silently undercuts his aura of maturity.

While John has not yet crossed the threshold to the responsibilities of adulthood, Ace Anderson has—physically, not emotionally—in "Ace in the Hole," an exploration of the incomplete transition between youth and maturity. A former basketball star who has just lost his job, Ace— now literally "in the hole"—is an early version of Rabbit Angstrom, the more fully developed protagonist of Updike's novelistic tetralogy, but the short story does not allow him much space to run. Ace would rather hide his head, ostrich-like, than face his wife Evey with the news of his unemployment. When the inevitable confrontation occurs, he is able to deflect her criticisms by turning on the radio and grabbing her to dance.

Updike frames the story with music, Ace's temporary means of escape. The opening line informs the reader that "Ace needed the radio, especially today"; like John Nordholm, he seeks something to make him feel "so sure inside" and galvanize the self-confidence that can raise him above the mundane world. Although this confidence manifests itself in a flippant, adolescent fashion, Ace is capable of (but not comfortable with) assuming a more mature role. As he waits for the radio to warm up, his remarks reveal both sides of his personality: first, using a youthful idiom, he proclaims, "Jesus. She'll pop her lid"; then, irked by his voice's thin and scratchy quality, he adds in a more resonant tone and formal idiom, "She'll murder me." More adept at alternating than reconciling his adolescent tendencies with his mature ones, Ace is pulled both ways, conscious that his youth is receding and the tensions of marital responsibility are overtaking him. Despite his escapist tendencies, he is mature enough to realize that some compromise is inevitable, even as he tries to postpone it.

For Ace, the basketball court, like Hemingway's bullring, provided an opportunity to exhibit grace under pressure; such glory can be recaptured only in scattered moments—winning the drag race, running home instead of driving—but not without repercussions. Although not much older than the two boys he races, they call him "Dad," suggesting a wider gulf than age difference alone creates. Ace empathizes with their emotional state—"young and mean and shy"—but later regrets his own meanness in calling one a "miserable wop." In running the short distance home from his parents' house, he follows his old coach's advice, but inadvertently rouses his infant daughter and thus provokes derisive remarks from Evey. Even the newspaper's mention of his former record remaining unbroken arouses mixed emotions because the article calls him by his given name instead of by his youthful nickname. When Evey later shoves the paper in the trash, he makes no protest. While Ace exhibits a cavalier attitude to Evey about losing his job, he counters his mother's indulgent sympathy with a more resigned consciousness about life's realities and a defense of his wife. Ace recognizes that his mother's indulgence has left him unprepared to deal with life's exigencies, but confronted with Evey's pragmatism and burdened by his own guilt, he can only respond with evasions, using music and his charm as his "ace in the hole" when all else fails. Committed to marriage, Ace will not flee, but domestic tension makes him feel crowded. No longer is he scoring baskets surrounded by cheering fans, staving off anxiety; now, during marital skirmishes, the "tight feeling" is more difficult to vanquish.

The story's symmetrical construction, signaled by the almost exact repetition of the words "In the moment before the tubes warmed up" preceding a dialogue marker, shows that Ace has come full circle. The story ends as it begins, with Ace in motion, though this time he is spinning rather than going forward. Both Ace and Evey know that their problems remain, but Evey's rationality is finally no match for her husband's evasiveness. As the radio's music surges from the speaker, Updike's prose tunes up as well: "The music ate through his skin and mixed with the nerves and small veins; he seemed to be great again, and all the other kids were around them, in a ring, clapping time" (*SD*, 26). This vision is Ace's charmed circle, an "unexpected gift" of past vitality arresting the conflict of the present, but it moves him no closer to resolving his problems and crossing the threshold into maturity.

Mark Prosser, the high school teacher in "Tomorrow and Tomorrow and So Forth," is a younger version of George Caldwell in *The Centaur*, sharing his compassion to a degree but more aloof from his students and not as deeply wounded by his work, although he is not immune to feeling that his life creeps along with the same "petty pace" mentioned in the Macbeth soliloquy that his students seem unable or unwilling to understand. Few in Mark's restless class want to grapple with the deeper implications that he attempts to explain. His soliloquy on Shakespeare's dark sentiments about life's fraudulence only bores them. Even his best student doodles indifferently while Mark attempts to sketch how Shakespeare transcended this despair to reach a "redeeming truth . . . as if he had pierced through the ugly facts and reached a realm where the facts are again beautiful" (*SD*, 31)—the same goal for which Updike's characters strive. As yet unaware of what lies beyond "the bright bold surface" they perceive in Shakespeare's comedies, his students maintain "the quality of glide": the desire to "slip along, always in rhythm, always cool, the little wheels humming under you, going nowhere special" (*SD*, 39)—the same sensation Ace finds so difficult to maintain past adolescence.

Mark struggles against easy cynicism and feelings that his life is a fraud, that his classes are mere "sound and fury, signifying nothing" to his students. His sexual attraction to Gloria Angstrom is another weakness, but when he intercepts the flattering note about him, he reacts with integrity, although he chooses to remain deluded about his appeal to her. Instead of ridiculing her or making advances, he gently lectures her after class on the abuse of the language of love, extracting an unexpected apology. Yet even when he later learns that Gloria has passed similar notes in other classes, he refuses to let this damning fact change his belief that she was genuinely moved and repentant: "The girl had been almost crying; he was sure of that." Although the reader is not as sure, the honesty of Gloria's remorse is finally not the issue. More importantly, Mark avoids cheap humor and denies himself easy cynicism. While his male pride affects his perception, he clings to a redeeming belief that in certain moments one can rise above life's petty pace.

A less tenuous moment of transcendence is depicted in "Dentistry and Doubt," the one story which seems anomalous in a volume otherwise concerned with Olinger residents and young married people. Although the protagonist is a native Pennsylvanian, the story takes place in England, where Updike spent a year studying art. The tone as well as the locale differ from the other stories. Updike explicitly addresses problems of faith for the first time in this story, embedding an ordinary incident with spiritual significance by conjoining an American divinity student's crisis of faith and visit to the dentist, both of which seem to have been postponed as long as possible. The work performed on the student's eyeteeth indirectly helps restore his spiritual vision, as well as his dental health.

"Toward Evening," a curiously neglected story, shows Updike consciously beginning to experiment with a looser short story form, juxtaposing images with action to create a counterpointing symbolic dimension. Unlike "Friends from Philadelphia," which develops character and conflict almost exclusively through dialogue, "Toward Evening" chronicles incidents and images through Rafe, the protagonist and central consciousness. Only six snippets of dialogue punctuate the story, making Rafe's comment to his wife on his day's activities all the more poignant an attempt to escape his silent isolation: "I saw some funny gloves today," (*SD*, 66) he remarks, reducing his active imaginative engagement with the surrounding world to mere observation of the unusual, and eliciting no response. Yet "Toward Evening" is no random catalogue of images; Rafe's perceptions of and reactions to his environment reveal a character travelling wearily through the incipient wasteland of modern life. The image with which the story opens—a woman "apparently paralyzed" on the bus steps in front of Rafe—suggests the paralysis that plagues Joyce's Dublin, though Rafe assists with her ascension so that he can board the bus to begin his journey home. Updike's periodic use of bird imagery serves as a counterpoint to such images of stasis: once the woman is lifted, for instance, Rafe's freed hands feel "as if birds had flown from them"; in addition, the bus doors are compared to pterodactyl wings and Rafe carries a mobile of rubber birds for his child. In a world dominated by demolished buildings and advertising, such intimations of flight become appropriate emblems of transcendence.

In a "dreamy" mood on his journey homeward, Rafe's imagination casts about his surroundings, seeking sustenance wherever it can. On Broadway, his active mind attaches historical significance to the ascending building numbers: "1832, 1836, 1846, 1850 (Wordsworth dies), 1880 (great Nihilist trial in St. Petersburg), 1900 (Rafe's father born in Trenton), 1902 (Braque leaves LaHavre to begin to study painting in Paris), 1914 (Joyce begins *Ulysses*; war begins in Europe), 1926 (Rafe's parents marry in Ithaca), 1936 (Rafe is four years old). Where the present should have stood, a block was torn down, and the numbering began again with 2000, a boring progressive edifice" (*SD*, 63–64). Significantly, these events begin with the death of Romanticism's central figure and intersperse Rafe's origins with the beginnings of modernism: nihilism, war, and artistic attempts to create a new order amid the chaos. The block corresponding to the present lacks renovated structures or replacements for those torn down—no fragments to shore against the ruins—while the future offers a bland promise in its progressive architecture. More promising is the proximity of interesting women on the bus; though physically unattainable, they engage Rafe's eye and invite his imagination to roam in sexual speculation. The first, with two blue streaks dyed in her "oloroso-colored hair" and a copy of Proust, rises above the world of work and domestic life by her sensuality and abstraction. The other exotic woman, a "young Negress" wearing blue half-gloves, has "the hint of grotesquensess needed to make Rafe lustful." After indulging his imagination in these temporary diversions that suggest a life beyond his, Rafe reflects, "The pure life of the mind, for all its quick distances, is soon tedious. . . . Dress women in sea and sand or pencil lines, they were chapters on the same subject, no more unlike than St. Paul and Paul Tillich" (*SD*, 65). Ennui has overtake Rafe to such a degree that even his momentary flights of fancy end quickly and provide no satisfactory escape.

Equally arresting, it seems, are the ingenious creations of modern advertising, testimony to the displaced creativity which should be erecting new structures in the vacancy of the present. The Jomar Coffee advertisement on the bus, like the neon Spry sign that concludes the story, uses the gimmick of alternating messages to attract attention. Rafe's position is such, however, that he cannot resolve the doubleness produced by the corrugated cardboard design into two separate pictures, neither of which is completely intelligible. Such double images punctuate the story, creating perceptual problems in reconciling the real and the imaginative into a coherent vision. Both pictures in the coffee ad depict satisfaction, but in Rafe's case it seems that the surface of things rarely presents him with the necessary fulfillment to be attained by reconciling imagination and reality.

While a Sartrean nausea arises from his contemplation of the Jomar ad, his resigned contemplation of the Spry sign at the story's conclusion accomplishes a momentary imaginative leap. As twilight descends, Rafe stares mutely out the window, focusing on the sign instead of talking with his wife. Though he and his wife are not newlyweds, their relatively young marriage has been eclipsed by a premature twilight of discontent. At home, he breathes "that invisible gas, goodness," but his favorite meal becomes an anticlimax after his wife's disappointment over his failure to purchase a "genuine Calder" mobile for the baby; instead, Rafe has purchased a bird mobile more expressive of his own longings to soar above the mundane. As he gazes out the window at the city, the Spry sign, emblem of the spiritually empty world of advertising, dominates his view, much as the eyes of T. J. Eckelburg preside over the valley of ashes in *The Great Gatsby*. Yet Rafe attempts to humanize the sign by imagining the labor involved in its creation, so that its neon and metal become equated with images of peace: rivers, trees, babies, and sleep. His epiphany, while an unexpected gift, is nonetheless an ambiguous replacement for lost marital bliss.

The final cluster of images suggests the opaque surface of reality and the submerged life into which Rafe has retreated. While the Spry sign dominates the darkened sky, the Hudson River, in the foreground, represents the more immediately present blackness of the buried consciousness: "Reflections sunk in it existed dimly, minutely wrinkled, below the surface" (*SD*, 68). If the story itself seems unresolved, its enigmatic quality reflects the state of affairs it depicts, calling attention to the tension of disconnectedness that demands recognition. Although not quite a montage of reflections like the final two stories in *Pigeon Feathers*, "Toward Evening" anticipates this technique, especially in its final pages.

A closer couple, Richard and Joan Maple, whose marriage has not yet reached such an impasse, also show signs of marital tension in "Snowing in Greenwich Village," the first of a series of stories concerning these recurrent protagonists. Marital tensions are also evident in "Ace in the Hole" and "Toward Evening," but in the first of the Maples stories, nascent marital problems take center stage. On the surface, the story sketches Rebecca Cune's visit to the Maples' new apartment and an abortive encounter that occurs after Richard walks her home, but the dialogue and the narration are rich in implication. Like the Jomar Coffee sign in the previous story, action and communication convey multiple messages that shift with the angle of vision: "'We have some hard stuff if you'd rather,' Joan said to Rebecca; from Richard's viewpoint the remark, like those advertisements which from varying angles read differently, contained the quite legible declaration that this time *he* would have to mix the Old Fashioneds" (*SD*, 71). Joan and Richard may communicate on a plane of familiarity inaccessible to Rebecca; on the other hand, this subliminal message may arise from Richard's self-consciousness about his shortcomings as a host. As he tries to impress Rebecca and demonstrate competence to Joan, his showy gestures reveal his insecurity.

Rebecca, with her "gift for odd things," impresses Richard with more than her talent for storytelling; the sexual component of some of the odd incidents she relates hints at a freer, more vital world outside of marriage. As Greiner has noted, her name is sufficiently close to the word "cunt" to suggest the crude fashion in which Richard may envision her.[10] Rebecca has lived with an unmarried couple who broke up after she moved out, and has dated a teacher who enjoys pretending to be a headwaiter or the Devil. As she relates her last story, this tension between the two women becomes evident, as Joan keeps questioning her, petulance entering her voice as she begins "egging her on." If there is a subtle battle for Richard's attentions occurring, Joan, suffering from an extended cold, has the better hand. Not only does her illness elicit his "genuine concern," but her spontaneous outburst of affection when the mounted police pass taps the intimacy they possess. Yet seen from Rebecca's angle of vision, Richard later realizes, such action might be rendered as sentimental, even grotesque, in one of her amusing stories.

For Joan, Rebecca may be one of "the inextricable elements of one enchanting moment"; for Richard, however, she represents temptation from the start. Efficiently disposing of her coat on their bed may demonstrate his competence as a host, but it also seems "as if he were with great tact delivering a disappointing message." That message, though ambiguous, may be that only her coat, and not her body, will grace his bed. After he walks Rebecca home, however, the prominent bed in her apartment does not receive her coat, which she keeps on, perhaps to signal he is not welcome; on the other hand, she may be waiting for him to remove it as he has done previously, a gesture that would be loaded with sexual overtones in this new locale. When Rebecca announces that her apartment is "hot as Hell," her swearing may hint at a certain looseness, but Richard draws back from pursuing any opportunity that her close proximity in the doorway might invite. Rebecca's ambiguous actions, as Greiner notes, pin Richard in a corner: he may either hypocritically cheat on his sick and affectionate wife or appear foolish to Rebecca, and perhaps become the butt of an amusing anecdote, by failing to act when opportunity presented itself (Greiner, 75). If she is not leading him on, he will seem doubly foolish in his lust if he makes an advance.

Whatever the case, Richard's successful escape from her apartment, accomplished through an awkward joke, restores order but reveals his vulnerability. Whether he can stand in the same door again and maintain his position has been opened to question. His victory here is somewhat hollow, as his monosyllabic response as he departs—"night"—merely notes the existence of the darkness that he, like the young boy at the end of Joyce's "Araby," must travel through to return home. Yet as the conclusion reveals, his passions still burn. Richard's final lines ("Oh but they were close") echo the story's opening, but in this new context they signify an awareness of the sexual component in their physical proximity. Perhaps deluding himself in his belief that he and Rebecca are "close" (or were close to having sex), Richard seems to express wistful longing rather than regret.

"Who Made Yellow Roses Yellow?" is closer in spirit to a J. D. Salinger story than any other in the volume, though Freddy Platt, the pretentious, cosmopolitan protagonist, is more the object of satire rather than compassion. As former undergraduate editor of the college humor magazine *Quaff*, Freddy is an imaginative extrapolation from Updike's days as editor of the *Harvard Lampoon*, although, unlike Updike, little maturation or advancement of talent appears to have taken place. Freddy, in fact, is a blueblooded, more intellectual version of Ace Anderson, striving to keep his youthful glory alive. Yet Ace, unlike Freddy, is more aware of the necessity of moral compromise and more poignant in his struggle against it. Like Arthur in "Sunday Teasing," Freddy is paralyzed by his own perceptivity, which renders the world of works and days ridiculous to him, even while he seeks a job offer from his more conventional former classmate.

The reflective and somewhat passive Rafe in "Toward Evening" evolves into the more actively unkind husband, Arthur, whose morning lethargy in "Sunday Teasing" begins a complacent routine that echoes the opening of Wallace Stevens's "Sunday Morning"; for Arthur and his wife Macy, however, the day remains like "wide water," with no reawakening of spiritual vitality. Disillusioned with church, Arthur prefers to read the Bible at home, but his interest in sin and remorse is purely intellectual, as he exhibits little—if any—remorse for the petty cruelties he commits almost unconsciously toward Macy throughout the day. Although he later attempts to salve the wounds by being a dutiful husband and cleaning up the apartment, the order he restores is only physical, and does little to atone for the emotional injury inflicted by his teasing. Arthur resembles the "perceptive man caged in his own weak character" from the French short story he analyzes for Macy, who cannot understand his sympathy for a character who is "so awful to his wife." Arthur's earlier assertion that "man should be lonely" receives ironic fulfillment as he stands alone at the sink, finally beginning to glimpse his own ignorance.

"Incest" is a daring, though indirect, treatment of a sexual taboo, concerning, in part, "the dark side of a father's adoration of his infant daughter," as A. C. Spectorsky observes (15). The sexual dreams which frame the story—one recounted by Lee to his wife, the other entered directly by the reader—invite Freudian interpretation, though not until the story's conclusion is it clear that the girl in both dreams potentially represents his daughter Jane. Yet to comb the story for hints of incest ultimately reduces its wider implications; certainly, the fact that both Lee's wife and daughter are named Jane might foreshadow a later "confusion," or a yearning for a younger version of his wife. More importantly, however, Lee's dreams and the story as a whole concern the displacement of sexual desire that inevitably accompanies married life, full of days "when you sow and not reap" (*SD*, 160).

Magic circles are the dominant image in "A Gift from the City," one of the collection's more developed and ironic stories. In another story, "His Finest Hour," a couple receives an unexpected gift from their neighbors that provides a memory that will sustain them on foreign soil; the gift that James and Liz believe they have received is the return of their safety and happiness, a freedom from the disturbing elements beyond their comfortable lives. "Like most happy people," the story opens, "they came from inland," quickly suggesting not only the city's inability to breed happy people but also the insularity of these transplants. Such charmed isolation, however, ultimately cuts them off from the city's more unexpected gifts. On one level, the story concerns the limitations of charity, but Updike also explores the personal costs of a security that attempts to banish conflict and thus diminishes receptivity to periodic infusions of grace.

Their somewhat embarrassed charity to the black man begins in both compassion and fear when Liz gives him ten dollars, ostensibly to help his family set up housekeeping in the city. James is ripe for such an incident to occur; somewhat troubled by his easy success, he acts as if the city, like a pagan god, must receive tribute, lest his good fortune cease: "James's suspicion increased that the city itself, with its steep Babylonian surfaces, its black noon shadows, its godless millions, was poised to strike. He placated the circumambient menace in the only way he knew—by giving to beggars" (*SD*, 167). Yet such anonymous, almost superstitious alms are of a different order than the charity that the black man seeks. The threat of his return clouds their weekend activities; though the connection is never explicitly drawn, the man's dark skin comes to represent to them the shadowy fears that symbolically haunt their landscape: the city, the playground, and even Liz's picture, *Swans and Shadows*.

Although the Negro's story is inconsistent and garbled, James dumps 20 dollars and a pocketful of change on him. But James's true feelings are revealed in his abruptness and rude asides; he has dehumanized the man to such an extent that he can compare him to a shaver he designed. After showering this man with money and groceries, however, when it comes time to pay Janice, the babysitter, they become penurious, silently refusing to pay her for the time she remained while they dealt with the Negro. They can only bestow charity on an unknown stranger, paying him off to escape him, but when it comes to a case closer to home, they are unable to be truly charitable despite their knowledge of Janice's need.

The Negro's persistence forces James to reexamine his charmed circle; to remain safely inside, he realizes, "only a sin could be placed there as a barrier." Liz, however, must commit that sin of refusing charity, as James hypocritically retreats to his office; there, his "personal constellation" of white tacks and undisturbed work encourage "the illusion that each passage of life was on a separate sheet, and cold be dropped into the wastebasket, and destroyed by someone else in the night" (*SD*, 191). In essence, Liz becomes the one who figuratively empties the garbage, as the Negro becomes "her problem." Exhibiting a healthy independence, she successfully extricates herself from the situation James has exacerbated. James, however, has developed a selfish, uncharitable attitude toward his wife, using weariness with being the protector as an excuse to "let her draw her own circles." In relation to the city, the couple still remains insulated from the real human gifts it might contain. The story structure itself is circular, with the threat banished and happiness returned, yet the comedic form belies the tragic implications of the sense of diminishment and the shifts that have occurred within that circle.

In "Intercession," Paul may not be successful in his first golf game, but he does achieve understanding and acceptance of his current role in life. Like James, he has surrendered some of his dreams to achieve financial success; despite his childhood ambition to draw, he has become an "idea man," writing the plot for a syndicated adventure strip that someone else illustrates. Somewhat defensive about his position and dissatisfied with his removal from the strip's actual production, Paul seeks a new challenge in golf. Initially, the game represents time stolen from his work and family, and his poor performance only frustrates him and exacerbates his guilt. Nonetheless, Paul confronts the game on its own terms, unlike the brash teenager he meets, a self-styled expert who nicknames himself "Professor Shaw." He too is a novice, but in his youthful impatience he cavalierly ignores the rules, hitting a number of balls for each shot and playing the best one. In Shaw, Paul sees a reflection of his younger self; the summer drought fosters the illusion "that the warps of the course had confronted him with himself of ten years ago" (*SD*, 204). Greiner sees Paul's annoyance with Shaw as an uncharitable rejection of a soul in need of companionship, and concludes that Paul's behavior shows him to be "a pilgrim who has failed the test" on the modern road to Damascus (Greiner, 85). Yet Paul's angry challenge to play by the rules only brings out into the open the fundamental difference in their games and in their lives. Paul endures Shaw's impudent comments and coaching, but his distaste for "this fat-lipped, daddy-loving brat" whom he feels has patronized and evaded him represents a rejection of his old self and a resolve not to idealize youth but to accept maturity.

During the ensuing conflict of styles, Paul's successful drive seems to be the miracle he hoped for, the payoff for his honest effort: "This luck gave him afflatus. He had outplayed the boy here; he was, when you came right down to it, the better golfer, being the older man, a resident of real life" (*SD*, 207). This epiphany is his unexpected reward: a banishing of guilt, an unashamed acceptance of his age, and an understanding that real life—not unencumbered, lawless youth—contains its own intrinsic satisfaction. Thus, when his next shot disappears without a trace, "as if a glass arm from Heaven had reached down and grabbed it," he can contentedly shoulder his bag and return home, crossing the barren landscape being graded for construction. This slice, not the successful drive, is where the true intercession occurs, since it interrupts Paul's progress toward the fifth green which he has envisioned as "paradisiacal." As Updike concludes a later story, "The Ideal Village," "Man was not meant to live in paradise"[11]—a truth which Paul's struggles on the golf course have illustrated. "You're alone," the woman selling score cards told him before he began, and the landscape he must cross, desolate with abandoned machines, seems to illustrate this fact: "In all the landscape no human being was visible, and a fatiguing curse seemed laid on everything" (*SD*, 209). The illusions which open the story have been replaced by harsh truths, but these are not punishments for uncharitable behavior of personal failure; rather, they constitute the sad realities of a fallen world, from which golf is a temporary, though sometimes ineffectual, escape.

The return to Olinger for the volume's conclusion might seem like a retreat from the "fatiguing curse" that concludes "Intercession," but even the childhood world of "The Alligators" contains disappointments. Like "Araby," it is a tale of a young boy "driven and derided by vanity"; young Charlie stands outside the door that grants social access, frustrated in his attempt to realize his vision of love. Although it seems that his dream about Joan Edison among the alligators is a revelation and a directive, Charlie discovers that he is too late in initiating contact with her and that he has been blind to the rituals of social acceptance. Joan, transferring into Charlie's fifth grade class in midsemester after moving from Baltimore, antagonizes both her classmates and the teacher with her snobbish pretensions. Miss Fritz's peeved response to Joan's attack on the Olinger school's inferiority—"All good things come in time, Joan, to patient little girls"—implicitly foreshadows Joan's eventual social acceptance after enduring the class's ritual persecution.

In his dream, Charlie misinterprets this initiation rite as the behavior of a pack of alligators, and casts himself in the role of rescuer. Yet in his own quest for acceptance, Charlie has also been an alligator—"worse," the narrator states, "because what the others did because they felt like it, he did out of a plan, to make himself more popular" (*SD*, 212). The heroic Tarzan-type rescue he envisions in his melodramatic dream, however, becomes only a shy, fumbling approach in real life. What should be his finest hour is spoiled by the realization that Joan has adapted, been assimilated, and become "queen of the class." The revelation of Charlie's folly and blindness hardly approaches the more tragic consciousness of more mature characters such as Paul or Rafe, yet the story shows that even as a youth in Olinger one is not immune to incipient alienation.

John Nordholm, who reappears as narrator of the final story, "The Happiest I've Been," presides over the reader's symmetrical entrance to and exit from the volume. While John is not unhappy in the volume's initial story, his naive self-assurance exists on a plane well below the ironies being conducted on the adult level. In this nostalgic narration, however, John's happiness takes place with full awareness of the pain and complexity accompanying maturity. He witnesses changes in himself and in others at the New Year's Eve party that has been an annual tradition since his youth, but maintains a serenity quite unlike the insularity that marks the restored order in "A Gift from the City." Indeed, the very consciousness of change and duality, of successfully reaching a point of transition, is what produces John's most transcendent happiness.

Though the only first person narration in the book, "The Happiest I've Been" is a successful experiment for Updike, who crosses from personal reminiscence into the realm of meditative fiction. Nonetheless, Updike accurately preserves the "sudden simultaneous sense of loss and recapture" that he comments he experienced in his own winter memories of his high school crowd's New Year's reunion parties—the impetus behind the story.[12] The narration has a muted, controlled tone and a cinematic quality, presenting a series of loosely flowing events spliced together, with lengthy shots of key memories, before moving on to the next scene. Occasionally, Nordholm interrupts the narration, momentarily breaking the illusion by adding some detail learned later or making a comparison to the present: "Girls hate boys' doubts; they amount to insults. Gentleness is for married women to appreciate. (This is my thinking then.)" (*SD*, 223), he remarks at one point. Thus the reader is subtly reminded of John's changed perspective: he now has greater insight into both himself and the events, but as the parenthetical present tense indicates, the narrative generally attempts to ignore that temporal distance and keep the past alive in the present. Through his narration, John attempts to counteract the process sketched in the Bergson epigraph: fleshing out, not reducing, past pleasures as he revives memories in his artistic re-creation of the happiness he feels while poised on the threshold between youth and maturity.

The events appropriately begin at John's house and conclude on the expressway, leaving Olinger and heading into "tunnel country." As in some of Updike's later short fiction, however, mood becomes more important than event: the concrete particulars evoke a transitional milieu that exists almost suspended in time. The annual party John and his college classmate and boyhood friend Neil attend, though it marks movement to a new year, also embodies a type of continuity. For John, these events coalesce with those of previous celebrations to form what he calls "my life's party"—an accumulation of layered memories. Nonetheless, signals of change and unhappiness emerge at this celebration: Neil sulks in another room about his bad luck in love, a couple cries on the stairwell, and Margaret, the host's jilted girlfriend, alternates between frenzied dancing and getting sick. As John notes the increased hardness of the women and greater brutality of the men, he feels a "warm keen dishevelment, as if there were real tears in my eyes. Had things been less unchanged they would have seemed less tragic" (*SD*, 228). Amid the subtle metamorphoses, the first marriage within the group stands out as one of the most significant changes. At midnight, all the men want to kiss Emmy, the married girl, in what Detweiler sees as a ritual sampling of the marital state that will soon be theirs as well (Detweiler, 17). Yet such behavior also has the flavor of a self-consciously roguish gesture, playfully undercutting the marital bond even as they acknowledge that they may soon embrace it.

In contrast to Neil, John soberly drifts from room to room, seemingly immune to extremes of feeling. Indeed, throughout the entire story, he feels "this sensation of my being picked up and carried." Though John seems a passive observer, his receptivity to and mental engagement in the events signal a maturing consciousness confronting reality in another fashion. After he and Neil leave the party to take Margaret and her friend home, John serves as Margaret's sounding board, exploring past memories, present sorrows, and vain hopes with her while Neil and her friend grope behind the sofa. Instead of taking sexual advantage of Margaret, John becomes her headrest as she falls asleep on his shoulder—one more welcome delay in their departure. Although John is ready to return to his girlfriend in Chicago and resume college, he experiences pleasure in lingering on the threshold.

The story's conclusion provides the volume with a coincidental imagistic symmetry: in "Friends from Philadelphia," John drives and then surrenders the wheel to Mr. Lutz; here, he is driven out of Olinger by Neil and then takes the wheel at the end, in control of his passage. As the story concludes, he has not reached his destination, but is making a symbolic descent into "tunnel country," from a plateau of happiness that he may never again attain as youthful irresponsibility receives its last "blessing" in the early sunlight. Even in such moments, however, there exists a built-in consciousness of time's passage; before cataloguing the reasons for his happiness, John observes: "A second after the scratch of his match occurred the moment of which each following moment was a slight diminution" (*SD*, 241). While he has developed a new awareness of time's inevitable diminishment, he has, in compensation, received trust, the mark of increasing responsibility. With satisfaction both ahead and behind him, Nordholm conveys an overall sense of a smooth passage undergone by a renewed person who has travelled for the last time through the same door, but tries to keep it propped open to memory's access.

Ceremonies of Farewell: *Pigeon Feathers*

Pigeon Feathers, perhaps Updike's most versatile collection, demonstrates a masterful command of language and technique. In only his second collection, Updike is sufficiently comfortable with the short story form to experiment with a variety of narrative strategies, especially variations on first person narration such as the epistolary story, the lyrical meditation, and the montage. The most notable of these forms, the lyrical meditation, is especially suited to Updike's talent for capturing the detailed texture of experience.[13] The prose equivalent of Robert Browning's dramatic monologues, the lyric story allows Updike to dramatize the mind's search through the darkening past for some vital spark that might illuminate the present and guide his characters onward through the increasing complexities of mature life. The montage, dependent on the principle of juxtaposition, essentially fuses three or more separate lyrics which might at first glance seem disjunct; on closer examination, however, these stories reveal a surprising aesthetic unity that comments formally on the possibilities for reassembling past experience.

Updike's "local boy," who assumes an independent existence as the composite protagonist in *Olinger Stories*, recurs at various intervals, but his characters again include an increasing number of young married couples; Jack and Clare reappear three times, at different stages in their relationship, though they are displaced in subsequent volumes by the Maples (later revealed to be the unnamed couple in "Wife-Wooing") as Updike's focal suburban couple. Excluding the eternal archangel, these protagonists range in age from 10 to their late twenties, roughly the same span as those featured in *The Same Door*. However, the characters in *Pigeon Feathers* are slipping deeper into themselves, grappling more with doubt, and pondering the narrowing of their lives. While the preservation of memory still assumes great importance as the past recedes, in *Pigeon Feathers* there is a greater urgency to the struggle against loss and a more explicit metaphysical dimension to the quest. Accompanying worries about rescuing the diminishing past, the religious element—

particularly the concern with immortality—widens the implications of the theme of loss.

Pigeon Feathers and his first three novels, Updike states, are dominated by "a central image of flight or escape or loss, the way we flee from the past" (Samuels, 434). In equating these three ideas, he indicates the ambivalence inherent in the departure from Olinger's equilibrium and relative simplicity. Flight may be liberating, but it also destroys certain cherished items in the process. Thus, while some of the younger characters flee *from* the past, those who have crossed or linger on the threshold between adolescence and maturity flee *toward* the past, wrestling with its details and yearning to recapture its mysteries. Captured memories may temporarily invigorate the present or stave off uncertainty, but, as Updike observes in his poem "Shillington, "The having and the leaving go on together."[14] Ambiguous ceremonies of farewell dominate *Pigeon Feathers*, as maturing characters begin to realize how far they have receded from the past and strive to accommodate themselves to the present.

In the collection's strikingly appropriate epigraph from "A Report to an Academy," Kafka's narrator characterizes the problems of the past's closing door, which is not a cosmic trick but rather the result of the individual assuming a comfortable niche in the world. Though unable to derive enough momentum from the slackened winds of youth, the characters discover that its elusive breezes can contain essences which provide intangible resources for survival in the present. Yet reentering the past is a painful process, because the opening that allows access "has grown so small that, even if my strength and willpower sufficed to get me back to it, I should have to scrape the very skin from my body to crawl through." The painful cost of forcefully retrieving something enduring from the flux, however, is suffered willingly by many of Updike's characters in their retrospective flights. Looking backward often produces an insatiable desire for an imaginary Eden, a mythic realm of continuous blessing that stirs discontent even more. Thus, the realism acquired in the process of escape is countered by the romantic longings for greater security. Most successful in establishing some stay against confusion are Updike's artist figures, whose struggle seems more productive than those who attempt to relive or reconstruct their past. The redemptive possibilities of art thus stand out as one path that leads beyond sheer nostalgia and regret.

Although the effort to recall a name from the past may seem a trivial exercise in memory in "Walter Briggs," the opening story, failure to do so has disturbing implications for Jack. Such maddening memory lapses are common, but they confirm his fears that his grip on the past is fading; in addition, he is disturbed because his competitive nature will not allow him to be content with his wife Clare's superior performance in the memory game they play on the way home from a cocktail party. Their positions in the car indicate the current state of their marriage and one potential source of dissatisfaction: Jack drives and Clare sits in back, separated by their two children while they converse across the seat to occupy this "enforced time together."

Their remembrance of things past—specifically their first months of marriage as employees at a YMCA camp—proves more fruitful than their review of the present. Much to her husband's irritation, Clare proves to be the custodian of shared memories. Just as she could hear the faraway breakfast bell at camp, so her memory stretches across the wide range of their past, "calling into color vast tracts of that distant experience." Although Jack becomes frustrated when he is unable to remember the name of a particular man, Clare's more playful attitude banishes the spirit of competition and results in an unexpected reward; in discovering "such a good game for the car just when he thought there were no more games for them," they temporarily transcend their marital impasse in a mutual excursion into their shared past.

Such moments, however, do not endure. Later that evening, Jack, bothered by his "unsatisfactory showing," guiltily wonders whether the past is more precious to Clare. As he lies awake, his earlier quest for the elusive name is unexpectedly fulfilled; various scenes of their summer at the YMCA camp cinematically unfold, and the name "Briggs" culminates his memories. Updike's ending is not without numerous ironies that undercut Jack's achievement in retrieving this now seemingly insignificant detail. What motivates Jack's chain of memories is his revived jealousy of a young German boy whom Clare recalled fondly. Furthermore, in whispering the remembered name to his sleeping wife, Jack is savoring victory, not simply sharing success; subconsciously, his reach into the past resembles that of the white pines he personifies as "stretched to a cruel height by long competition," an unpromising image of the course their marriage could take if Jack's competitive ethic overshadows the cooperative one. Undeniably, his recall of the name represents a victory over time and loss, but more important for Jack is his triumph over Clare. At best, the concluding epiphany is an ambiguous achievement, positive in its recall of their honeymoon days and *Don Quixote*'s idealism, but negative in the insecurity Jack exhibits and in the forebodings of a future dominated not by the spirit of shared happiness but by the persistence of competitive desire.

Clyde Behn's declaration that "Happiness isn't everything," in "The Persistence of Desire" invites comparison with another Olinger story, "The Happiest I've Been." If John Nordholm's prolonged farewell to Olinger at the end of *The Same Door* represents a high point in happiness for Updike's sensitive young protagonist, Clyde's remark rationalizes the inability to reattain that plateau. Outwardly possessing all the trappings of happiness—a stable marriage, children, a career—Clyde is still bothered by a persistent desire for a more passionate life, though such satisfactions are elusive and unstable. Ostensibly, he returns to Olinger to seek a cure for misdiagnosed eye problems, but in reality he searches for some lost essence. He latches onto an old flame, Janet, as the emblem of past joy through whom he hopes to recover lost opportunities. Yet Clyde's sojourn in Olinger, despite his apparent success in setting up a liaison with Janet, may raise more discontent than it will ultimately satisfy.

As Clyde stares at the checkered floor in Dr. Pennypacker's familiar office, he becomes "crisscrossed by a double sense of himself," finally realizing his persistent imaginative yearnings to turn back the clock. While waiting, he reads the reassuring fact that the body's cells replace themselves every seven years, but the two clocks in the lobby stand as reminders of time's passage. On the face of the new digital clock, time literally slips away as each number becomes "another drop into the brimming void"; the grandfather clock from which he seeks the comfort of the familiar has stopped, suggesting that the arrested past may not remain viable in the present. Still, through Janet, Clyde seeks "his splendid perishable self" in a second chance to capture the joy that eluded them.

Unlike Allen Dow and William Young, two younger versions of Clyde featured in subsequent Olinger stories, he appears to win the object of his desire, although Updike's portrayal of his final vision of renewal is tinged with irony. At one point, Clyde, his eyes blurred by drops, is unable to see his fingerprint whorls, suggesting that his current hold on his identity is slipping. While Clyde receives an unexpected gift in the form of Janet's note—presumably containing permission to contact her—one should question the clarity of the vision it engenders: with the note in his pocket like "armor" against unhappiness, Clyde "became a child again in this town, where life was a distant adventure, a rumor, an always imminent joy." Whatever satisfactions Clyde may experience in

Olinger—sexual or otherwise—they are still "imminent," mere promises of desire fulfilled. Janet's writing is a familiar and hopeful hieroglyph, yet Clyde is unable to discern an exact message. As Updike remarks, "optically bothered Clyde Behn seems to me to be a late refraction of the child Ben [in "You'll Never Know, Dear"] who flees the carnival with 'tinted globes confusing his eyelashes'" (*OS*, ix). Both are affected by blurred vision, but while Ben is held back unwillingly by a benevolent world, Clyde wants to believe that he is welcomed back into it. When Pennypacker dismisses him into "a tainted world that evaded focus," the eyedrops temporarily allow him to indulge in an illusory escape from the present into an idealized realm of memory.

The title of "Still Life" serves as a clever metaphor for the lack of progress in a romance between two art students of different nationalities, yet it might also characterize the problems with this story: like his protagonists, Updike has assembled all the elements for his composition, but they never quite cohere. Many of Updike's stories, in which perception rather than action assumes primary importance, could be likened to still lifes, but this tale finally lacks the pressure of memory, the more dynamic tensions of domestic life, and the interplay of ideas that impel Updike's better stories, such as "Flight," the volume's first retrospective first-person narration, in which Allen Dow reexamines a crucial emotional separation from Olinger—his mother in particular—as he struggles to understand the burdens of the past. Mrs. Dow resembles a refined and stronger version of *Winesburg, Ohio*'s Elizabeth Willard, Sherwood Anderson's repressed and dreaming mother figure who hopes to have her son enact the escape from the village that she was unable to accomplish. Allen's mother, with her flair for the dramatic, creates the self-fulfilling prophecy of her son's flight, a communal myth that he simultaneously rebels against and strives to make his own while he inhabits the middle ground between the ordinary life of Olinger to which he is attracted and her persistent vision of transcendence. She nurtures his dream and stifles his rebellion so that he will, like a phoenix rising from the ashes of her past, redeem her failure.

Allen resists his special destiny because he perceives that in leaving Olinger, he will merely fulfill the expectations of the very community he wishes to defy. Simultaneously flattered and rejected by the town, he feels trapped in everyone else's dream, as if he "were a sport that the ghostly elders of Olinger had segregated from the rest of the livestock and agreed to donate in time to the air." Paradoxically, in her attempt to steer him to freedom, his mother must restrict his options; in contrast,

Allen's courtship of Molly Bingaman represents his attempt to shape his own destiny. While an oedipal reading of the conflict between Allen and his mother is certainly possible, Mrs. Dow's bitter hostility toward Molly arises from her fear that such an Olinger-bred "little woman" will keep Allen close to the ground; despite her personal barbs and the grudge she harbors from Mrs. Bingaman's past snub, Mrs. Dow fights not so much against Molly as against what she represents. Ironically, in her desire to see Allen soar beyond Olinger, she assumes a domineering, dictatorial role similar to one her father took when he forbade her to leave Olinger for New York. Yet Allen cannot typecast his mother as a villain in this story. In retrospect, he must face the unpleasant truth about his past behavior: he too has emotionally abused Molly, who, caught in the middle of their struggle, nonetheless returns unconditional love.

In striving to understand his mother, Allen seeks the sources of his present self; in the process, he touches her suffering and sacrifice, as well as the ambivalence of her relationship with her father. Updike singles out Allen's epiphany as an exceptional moment of insight: "chafing to escape . . . and a bit more of a man but not quite enough," Allen becomes attuned not only to his own feelings but also to the dreams of his mother and grandfather. "There has never been anything in my life quiet as compressed, simultaneously as communicative to me of my own power and worth and of the irremediable grief in just living, in just going on" (Samuels, 434). Though Allen is casting off from his mother, she has indeed won the crucial battle, forcing him to be independent of both her and Molly: "the chair ceased to be felt under me, and the walls and furniture of the room fell away" (*PF*, 72–73). As the supports of Olinger vanish from beneath his feet, he begins the flight away from boyhood. In his sensitized state, Allen reaches a rare comprehension of the ambivalent life beyond Olinger, of "the suppressed pain, with the amount of sacrifice I suppose that middle–class life demands" (Samuels, 434). Such insight, not the mere physical departure from Olinger, is perhaps the true flight he achieves in the story.

Beyond the confines of his native Olinger, Allen is nevertheless bound to his origins. Telling the story does not free him from the past; paradoxically, his narrative flight there and back only strengthens the ambivalent connection and highlights his loss. The mature Allen who narrates the story has progressed beyond the self-conscious and conceited adolescent who speaks of himself in the third person, as if his life were a novel in the making. Examining his former self across the distance of years rather than minutes, he discovers, proves to be a more complex operation, "just as it might be hard for a movie projector, given life, to see the shadows its eye of light is casting." Thus, in order to understand himself, he replays the lives of the preceding generations, and discovers in their struggles the source of his own ambivalent love and the meaning of his flight. "A Sense of Shelter," an obvious companion piece to "Flight" (which it directly follows in *Olinger Stories*), features a slightly older protagonist who has no such longings to soar. Instead, William Young retreats temporarily into the warm, insular environment of Olinger High, envisioning a secure, predictable, future stretching like a "long tube" from its halls, insulated from the cold world outside. Essentially, the story replays the foiled romance of "The Alligators" using older characters, with similar irony resulting from the suitor's dismissal and realization of his sheltered vision's deficiencies.

Updike's unobtrusive use of the frame tale in "Should Wizard Hit Mommy?" raises a seemingly simple bedtime tale to a serious examination of the ongoing conflict between the pragmatic and imaginative sides of human nature and its effects on marriage. The story picks up Jack and Clare, the protagonists of "Walter Briggs," two years later, expecting their third child and engaged in home improvement, their relationship plagued by the tensions of compromise and Jack's resentments. While "Walter Briggs" could be used as a context for explaining Jack's final sulking withdrawal, sufficient clues within the frame narrative and Jack's nap-time tale for four-year-old Jo provide the context necessary for understanding the story's enigmatic conclusion.

Upstairs, Jack uses storytime as a temporary escape into a world of fantasy and romance; downstairs, Clare continues to paint, her scraping chair a reminder of shared domestic responsibilities and her pregnancy. Yet even his small but guilty indulgence in the world of art has become somewhat routine for Jack, since Jo now anticipates the plots of his "Roger Creature" stories, in which an animal with some problem receives a magical cure from a benign wizard. Varying the pattern of romantic fantasy, however, has unforseen consequences. Like the wizard in his story, Jack's artistry creates problems rather than solves them: it not only brings out latent feelings of resentment in Jo but also places Jack in what he perceives as "an ugly middle position" between mother and child. Through the story, he taps his own discontent with his wife's pragmatism, but finds it necessary to defend realism and maternal authority in front of his daughter. With this inner conflict raging, he returns to work, and the story concludes in an epiphany of brooding passive resistance.

Ironically, Jack's attempt to be creative brings him closer to the familiar world than he wants to be. His initial twist is an innocent one: Jo's choice of a skunk as protagonist leads Jack into a personal connection between the story and certain childhood humiliations he experienced; thus his identification with Roger Skunk's social ostracism creates an emotional investment in the story's outcome. The second twist occurs less innocently, arising from Jack's cruel desire for attention and control: Jo's impatience stirs his general resentment of women who take things (like him) for granted and of Clare in particular. To revive Jo's attention, he alters the conclusion by making the situation more complex and introducing a note of realism into the fantasy.

Displeased with the wizard's tampering with her offspring's natural odor, the mother skunk demands that his smell—his essence—be restored. Like the mother in "Flight," she asserts that her offspring is qualitatively different from his peers and should remain that way, despite his wishes to the contrary; the social problems Roger's difference causes must be solved naturally, through time. Though entering a realistic phase, Jo is not quite ready to accept such a conclusion; she is more accustomed to problems being solved with a wave of the wizard's wand. Jo senses the ending's truth, but the mother's challenge to the wizard's authority is scandalous to her; she would rather that the wizard fight back, an unharmonious ending which Jack, anxious to maintain authority over his fictive world, will not allow. His defense of Roger's mother comes across as an apology for the status quo. While the story's overt message may be an affirmation of motherly love, in context such love seems an authoritarian voice of realism. Jack catches himself in the middle: to allow the wizard's magic to triumph as Jo wishes would condone resentment of her mother, yet the more realistic ending denies the transforming power of art and, ironically, of his own wizardry.

As a result, Jack's descent into the mundane world and his responsibilities occurs with a heightened consciousness of his own ineffectuality and of the cage love has built. Both the house they labor to beautify and the unborn child for which he is responsible suggest displaced creative energy that will eventually increase his entrapment. As Albert Griffith notes, Jack's final words—"Poor kid"—are a lament not only for Jo, the child in the middle, but also for the vanishing child within himself.[15] Yet Jack's passivity and brooding self-pity are somewhat immature responses, and he only exacerbates his isolation by not communicating his feelings to Clare.

Updike's later inclusion of "Wife-Wooing" as one of the early Maples stories in *Too Far to Go* confirms that the couple in this story will eventually separate; considered alone, however, the story possesses a more hopeful resolution. "Wife-Wooing" begins with the narrator's Joycean celebration of his wife's erotic attraction, quickly adopts a more wounded, defensive tone after his oversubtle seduction fails, and concludes with a surprising testament to her insight and instinctiveness. Robert Frost's description of a poem as a work that "begins in delight and ends in wisdom" applies well to the figure this story makes as its narrator retraces the contours of his experience. Updike's portrayal of an anxious, striving male psyche is a revealing and accurate one. Not only the narrator's prurient calculations but also his zealous pursuit of the object of his desire are laid out for examination in this somewhat self-satiric dramatic monologue addressed to his wife. Although finally sympathetic, the narrator betrays his egotism as he recounts his erotic musings and sublimated frustration. While the scathingly objective assessment of his wife the morning after she rebuffs his overtures may be as accurate as it is uncharitable, his own shortcomings become more evident as the story unfolds. After his wife unexpectedly satisfies his thwarted sexual desire, he gains perspective on the experience and exposes his own foibles in the course of the retrospective narration.

The story's Joycean wordplay and alliterative vitality celebrate "the magical life language leads within itself," yet while the narrator's words capture his erotic feelings and tune up his ardor, they fail to generate corresponding emotions in his wife. His ornate words dance in his mind, but their play of sound and sense is finally a self-contained magic, unable to overcome his wife's disinterest. At times, his prose is so purposely exaggerated that it verges on self-conscious parody. When he describes their family meal in terms of a primitive gathering around the hearth and casts himself as the brave masculine provider, for instance, he clearly indulges in self-satire; his fantasy serves to highlight the gap between the sedate purchase of a take-out meal and the primal struggle for subsistence. Preoccupied with the erotic conquest instead of hunting and gathering, the narrator channels his energy toward seduction. He knows that "Courting a wife takes tenfold the strength of winning an ignorant girl," and his words and actions comprise an elaborate courting ritual which is transparent to his wife. Buying Sunday dinner is a ploy to conserve her energy for "a more ecstatic spending"; his exhibition of paternal patience is likewise part of the scheme overtly begun when he evokes memories of their honeymoon and the rose window, which he previously refers to as a vaginal symbol. His innuendos, however, are ignored as his wife opts for a book on Nixon and falls asleep, leaving him replete with lust, haunted by the memory of the rose window and its interlocked shadows, an emblem of the sexual fulfillment that has eluded him.

Recounting his uncharitable thoughts the next morning, the narrator exposes a residue of anger and pettiness; his earlier meditations on "smackwarm" garters give way to a scathing and vengeful study of time's ravages on his wife and a masculine satisfaction with going to work in the city, the realm of stone, to escape the soft "domestic muddle." Absorbed in his work, he hopes to insulate himself from frustration and sublimate his desire, yet this pose is no more genuine than his identification with the primitive man. His love life finally turns out to be similar to the problem he carries home from work: no matter how much he "pushes," the door to resolution remains closed, and his mind circles aimlessly. As his wife's brief, impromptu wooing shatters his defenses, he learns that only when he ceases striving will his unexpected reward occur. The obvious but "momentous moral" she teaches him—"an expected gift is not worth giving"—is a corollary to the idea Updike has articulated as the "point" of *Olinger Stories*: *"We are rewarded unexpectedly. The muddled and inconsequent surface of things now and then parts to yield us a gift"* (*OS*, vii). Forcing that surface apart, as those receding from the simpler times of Olinger are apt to try, inevitably creates frustration. Though the narrator's pride is wounded during this lesson, he is nonetheless attentive to its humor, and attempts to defuse the lesson's sting with playful verbal wit in a portrait that both anatomizes his flaws and affirms his love.

In "Pigeon Feathers," the volume's most explicated story, physical separation and metaphysical doubt suddenly widen the distance from Olinger for 14-year-old David Kern. His movement away from the familiar milieu marks an abrupt change in everything from the furniture arrangement to reading habits, so that his life becomes "upset, displaced, rearranged," much as Updike's own was when his family moved from Shillington to reclaim the family farm in nearby Plowville (of which Firetown is the story's fictional equivalent). After reading H. G. Wells's denial of Christ's divinity, David's beliefs are similarly disturbed, so much so that he experiences "an exact vision of death" that shakes the foundations of his formerly unquestioned childhood faith.

Qualitatively different from the tiny hole in Ben's identity the lost dime makes in "You'll Never Know, Dear," this vivid premonition of extinction sends David desperately in search of some solid foundation on which to erect a "fortress against death." Neither his mother's pantheism, his father's perfunctory Protestantism, nor Reverend Dobson's vague analogies can provide a satisfactory defense against David's persistent "invitations to dread." Particularly frustrating is the minister's inability to address his questions: Dobson's evasive comparison of the soul's continued existence to the way Lincoln's goodness endures fails to provide the definite reassurance of resurrection he craves. His parents present a divided rather than united front, as their argument about whether the land possesses a soul shows. Immersed more in the duties than the mysteries of faith, Mr. Kern seems a "distant ally." To David, his almost dogmatic orthodoxy seems unattainable, though their trips into Olinger at least provide temporary escape from the rural vacancy in which his mother mystically revels. Her perception of nature's miraculousness bears some similarity to David's final insight, yet he cannot accept her transcendental vision of nature's indwelling deity. "God has to be different," he asserts, or else nature becomes "an ocean of horror," beyond whose commingling of beauty and death nothing else exists.

Only after he kills the pigeons that have soiled the old Olinger furniture in the barn does David receive an affirmation from an unlikely source: the dead pigeons' intricate beauty "robed him in this certainty: that the God who had lavished such craft upon these worthless birds would not destroy his whole creation by refusing to let David live forever." His closest approach to this vision beforehand occurs when he studies his dog Copper's physical intricacies. Copper's "wealth of embellishments" contain intimations of God's hand, but the earthy smell of the dog's fur prevents David from making the leap of certitude that he does when he examines the pigeon's wings.

Despite David's concluding leap of faith, the reader should, as Robert Detweiler suggests, be attentive "to the possible irony in the whole performance" (Detweiler, 150). His affirmation of God's existence, a rudimentary version of the theological argument from design, is more important as a strategy to cope with his fear of death rather than as a genuine religious commitment. As Updike's early placement of "Pigeon Feathers" in *Olinger Stories* indicates, David is only one step beyond the pure Olinger child; the faith he grasps is provisional, and in need of supplemental support as he recedes further in time and space from Olinger. In "Flight," for instance, Allen Dow recalls "steep waves of fearing death" as a cyclical phenomenon, occurring about once every three years, confirming that the crisis in this story, though particularly intense in David's adolescent mind, is not settled but part of an ongoing struggle.

"Archangel," a dramatic monologue in which the heavenly narrator promises an abundance of treasures "as specific as they are everlasting," concerns the revelatory moments of daily experience. While the angel asks only for love and praise in return, either the price of commitment is too high or the auditor doubts his promises. Updike seems to be daring the reader to treat the angel as an unreliable narrator, and, like the listener within the story, dismiss his promises. Thus the auditor's refusal, not the angel's gifts, may be the key to Updike's theme. As Alice and Kenneth Hamilton note, the angel's language at one point echoes Christ's invitation to Thomas to touch his side, which would give tangible proof of his divinity.[16] Yet human experience in the world outside Olinger, where change and loss become increasingly prevalent, belies easy acceptance of the angel's offer, though his patient repetition hints that the opportunity is not lost with this refusal of earthly delights transposed into a finer key. "These glimmers I will widen to rivers," the angel promises, in language reminiscent of the artist's task. The artist too strives to generate a receptivity to the world's richness and to facilitate the recapture of the past's fleeting treasures. His perceptive eye can likewise uncover the glimmering beauty inherent in memories or in the details of everyday existence.

In "You'll Never Know, Dear, How Much I Love You," 10-year-old Ben's attempt to lose his 50 cents at the local carnival calls forth Olinger's inherent protectiveness. Initially, Ben is lured to the carnival as a communal ritual, fearing "only he will be left behind, on empty darkening streets"—an echo of Joyce's "Araby." Yet unlike Joyce's narrator, Ben, who immediately sees through the commercial facade, wants to become this world's willing victim. His innocence becomes a commodity to be spent; like the 50 cent piece, it "must be broken, shattered into tinkling fragments, to merge in the tinsel and splinters of strewn straw." The contrast with "Araby" is revealing: Joyce's story involves a youth who fails in a quest to retrieve a fragment of a formerly mystical bazaar and climaxes in an epiphany that retrospectively reveals his vanity, while Updike's features a child frustrated in his desire to lose his innocence at a tawdry affair and culminates in his confused retreat.

Like an astronomer gazing at the night sky, Walter, the narrator of "The Astronomer," surveys an incident from his past, which he compares to a "vast sheet of darkness in which a few moments, pricked apparently at random, shine." Yet the bright moment on which he focuses his gaze, notable for its religious affirmation and the reassertion of his ego, hardly seems random. Before he concludes the story, Walter modestly claims "That is all I remember," as if his recollections were as jumbled an assemblage as the items heaped on the coffee table that he has just described. In actuality, his retrospective narration is carefully crafted, especially in the use of astronomical language for coherence, to show that *his* vision, clearer and more perceptive than that of Bela, the astronomy professor, is the one that pierces through the "clouds of human subjectivity."

At the time of Bela's visit, Walter, a 24-year-old television commercial writer, is undergoing a religious revival in response to a crisis of faith. Reading Kierkegaard's torturous struggles with doubt calms him, as his own anxieties seem tame by comparison. The astronomer's scientific certitude, however, represents a challenge to Walter's uncertain faith, at least until the unforseen discovery that Bela is likewise susceptible to a fear of the void. In Walter's mind, Bela looms as a formidable intellectual foe, a figure of "abnormal density," like the white dwarf companion of Sirius, whose intense gravitational pull affects even the light around it. He is an atheist behind whose eyes are godless "immensities of space and gas," yet the intellect which so boldly plumbs the depths of space never seems to manifest itself during the subdued, almost anticlimactic visit. Intimidated by the astronomer, Walter has endured Bela's condescension in the past; he never takes offense at Bela's flirtatious behavior toward his wife, since he blandly accepts that he "did not have enough presence in his eyes to receive rudeness." This attitude persists into the present, as Bela snidely impugns Walter's choice of reading matter and lumps him with the "poor Madison Avenue men" Harriet mentions.

Pleased with the "small remission of the field of force" that Bela's pseudo-intellectual joke allows, Walter is even more gratified when Bela inadvertently admits experiencing fear in the desert's open spaces. Ironically, the man who surveys the vast darkness of space discovers terror in lighted earthly spaces devoid of vegetation or man's imprint. Seeing such doubt in Bela is an unexpected gift that brings him down to a less celestial plane, so that Walter, in retrospect, realizes their common humanity. His description of the town lights mirrored by the Hudson River serves as an appropriate analogy for the process of reconstructive memory we witness in this story: "These embers were reflected in the black water, and when a boat went dragging its wake up the river the reflections would tremble, double, fragment, and not until long after the shadow of the boat passed reconstruct themselves" (*PF*, 180).

Only as Walter travels again through darkened waters of his past do his reflections reassemble the fragments of that seemingly ordinary evening into a more meaningful event. In the end, Walter uses the story to show that he, not Bela, has the true astronomer's eye, enabling him to reconstruct his apprehensive encounter as a shimmering revelation.

"A & P," Updike's most frequently anthologized piece, is, on the surface, uncharacteristic. Sammy, the brash teenaged narrator, fashions a seamless narrative and fast-moving plot that is structurally distinct from the lyrical mood or the much looser construction generally evident in Updike's short fiction. A closer inspection of "A & P, however, reveals similar thematic concerns and narrative techniques. Ringing up HiHo crackers rather than reading Virgil, Sammy stands apart from the sensitive young men Updike habitually portrays in his Olinger stories; he is closer in spirit to Ace Anderson of Updike's early story "Ace in the Hole." Yet his impulsiveness ultimately gives way to a nascent awareness of the compromises that may be entailed on the other side of the A & P's automatic door once he crosses through for the last time. While the story lacks the ache of nostalgia present in many of the collection's other pieces, Sammy's backward glance at the recent past seeks its full implications. In retelling the story, he refines the experience into a form that will live in his memory, significant in its continuing impact on his life. Like Walter in the preceding story, Sammy must wait until the initial disturbance passes before his creatively enriched memory of the incident becomes one of the first "pricked moments" in the darkening sky of maturity. "A & P" finally turns out to be another story of a character caught in the middle between romance and realism, and beginning to learn the lessons of bittersweet triumph.

Sammy's narrative, one of the nine first-person experiments in the volume, displays a surprising elasticity of tone, from the ungrammatical opening sentence to the adolescent comparison between Queenie's breasts and scoops of vanilla ice cream to more exact and poetic similes that may reveal an embryonic writer (e.g., "shoulder bones like a dented sheet of metal tilted in the light"). Sammy's lively verbal performance seeks to engage our sympathy for his individualistic gesture in a world of sheep-like shoppers and his manager Lengel's prudish conventionalism. Retelling his story, he casts himself in the role of the "unsuspected hero" that he fails to become for Queenie and her friends. Yet in some respects, his bravado reveals the distance he still must travel toward true maturity. Though only 19, Sammy condescendingly refers to one of Queenie's friends as a "kid"; near the end of the story, however, we learn that Sammy's mother still irons his shirts. Nonetheless, he attempts to associate himself in the reader's mind with Stoksie, who is married, independent, and three years his senior; the only difference between them, he asserts, is the two children Stoksie has "chalked up on his fuselage already"—a testimony to his masculinity in Sammy's wishful vision.

In quitting his job, Sammy initially seeks to impress the three girls with a gesture that will establish his heroism as a masculine protector. Yet his attitude toward women is callow and chauvinistic: he likens the female mind to a "little buzz like a bee in a glass jar" and admires Queenie more for her body and social status than for her retort to Lengel. Furthermore, his disproportionate admiration of Queenie's 49-cent jar of Fancy Herring Snacks exhibits a basic social insecurity; to Sammy, this food is an exotic delicacy emblematic of a lifestyle beyond the reach of his parents (whose "racy" parties feature lemonade and Schlitz beer in stenciled glasses)—a lifestyle on which the ordinariness of the A & P has no right impinging. When Queenie speaks, Sammy "slid right down her voice into her living room," but the scene he imagines is a naive projection of his concept of the good life rather than a moment of genuine insight.

Sammy's shortcomings, however, must be weighed against the strides he makes during and after the experience. He may cling to adolescent attitudes and be motivated by the wrong reasons, but losing his job has at least spurred him to reconsider his position. Initially, he joins Stoksie in leering at the trio of girls in bathing suits, but he experiences a turning point in his feelings when, from his slot at the end of the meat counter, he watches McMahon, the butcher "patting his mouth and looking after them sizing up their joints. Poor kids, I began to feel sorry for them, they couldn't help it" (191). Seeing the butcher assessing the girls like so much meat, as he himself was, awakens Sammy's pity and stirs some guilt; he still calls them "kids," but with an incipient awareness of their victimization. Whatever his faults, Sammy has an active imagination, a growing facility with language, and a perceptive eye and ear. While his defense of the girls may be motivated by a combination of lust, admiration for Queenie's social status, and sentimental romanticism, his gesture is not without principle and quickly assumes more serious overtones. His uncharitable assessments of Lengel and the customers show his growing distance from the world of the A & P; quitting merely severs whatever connection remains.

Yet the tenuous link he felt with Queenie and her world vanishes when she crosses the electric eye and Sammy remains to follow through on his actions; though he follows her across the threshold, he ends up alone in the parking lot, suspended between two inaccessible worlds. Instead of his dream girl, he is met with a premonition of the realities of married life: a young mother yelling at her spoiled children. While saved from the "injection of iron" that has made Lengel inflexible, Sammy realizes the truth of his last words: "You'll feel this for the rest of your life." Indeed, Sammy's recounting of the story shows him determined to do so; he refuses to stoop to self-pity and see its denouement as "the sad part," preferring instead to savor the incident's harsh lesson of "how hard the world was going to be on me hereafter" and thus prepare himself for its unforseen repercussions.

"The Doctor's Wife," included in *Prize Stories 1962*, deserves more serious attention than it has been given. Perhaps the atypical Caribbean vacation setting (also featured in the "Churchgoing" segment of the final story) or the subdued drama presents an unpromising surface. Yet the encounter between the doctor's wife and the young married couple, Ralph and Eve, is shown to have menacing depths, like the sea, and places Ralph in an ugly middle position between the two antagonistic women. The vacationers' tropical Eden recalls Olinger's mythic protectiveness: bloom and harvest seem perpetual, and the two main elements, air and water, "seemed tints of a single enveloping benevolence." Yet a pervasive color consciousness turns out to be the serpent in the garden, or, to use the story's dominant metaphor, the shark beneath the sea's surface. Just as the doctor's wife makes him aware of the "big dark fellows" who visit the waters during turtle killing season, so she reveals the darker depths of prejudice hidden beneath the apparent cordiality of the island's residents and her own veneer of tolerance. The two formerly pure elements are now corrupted: the air by the doctor's wife with her sharp teeth of prejudice, the water by his fear of real sharks, an inescapable reminder that both the natural and human realms contain kindred evils. Often faulted by critics for focusing on lost youth and domestic problems, Updike treats a serious social issue in this modern fable of the fall from grace.

Ralph's plunge into the waters of guilt is followed by the egotism of the shore-bound narrator of "Lifeguard," who begins his dramatic monologue by declaring his virtue: "Beyond doubt, I am a splendid fellow." Updike's calculated ambiguity, resulting from the omission of the article from the more idiomatic phrase "beyond a doubt," immediately raises a number of questions, including whether this divinity student who works in the summer as a lifeguard is indeed beyond doubt, whether such a condition of absolute faith is possible, and whether the lifeguard's image of himself as a splendid fellow is an inflated illusion. Describing himself in glowing terms that recall the gifts in "Archangel," the lifeguard would have us believe he is a gift from God; indeed, in his rhetoric he implicitly likens himself to Christ, incarnated as a savior mounted on the tower with the red cross. Yet he inhabits a world of abstraction and prefers to remain aloof from the surrounding world. In this erudite sermon which teaches more about him than about the mysteries of faith, he muses on the nature of his calling and the modern world's problems of faith, but waits in vain to be called by a congregation of indifferent sunworshippers.

After his memorable parable of swimming as a search for faith, however, the promising introduction to his sermon on the modern inability to confront immensity becomes a condescending and sophistic justification of his lust. In an ironic echo of Kierkegaard's ideas about the man above the crowd of untruth, the lifeguard sets himself above his flock, criticizing every age group except the nubile young girls whose bodies make them more eligible candidates for his personal attention. He is merely a novice theologian who intellectualizes his lust and cloaks seduction with the veil of conversion. Indeed, a sexual overture, not a cry from someone who needs help venturing out into the sea of faith, may be the call he waits for in vain. While offered as a consolation to the masses, his final injunction to enjoy "the single ever-present moment that we bring to our lips brimful" stands out amidst his incoherent and self-serving theology as the suggestion of the world's sacramental nature—a message that should perhaps not be dismissed because of the elitism and narcissism of the messenger.

The volume's final two stories present an imaginative process more constructive than any physical return to Olinger: linking the past with the present, their narrators dramatize the process of memory seeking connectedness. Although Updike describes "The Blessed Man of Boston, My Grandmother's Thimble, and Fanning Island" as a "montage of aborted ideas" (*HS*, 851), such a disclaimer should not undercut the story's status as an experimental work that makes artistic use of fragments shored against the ruins of time's passage. Ostensibly, the story chronicles three successive artistic failures, yet this narrative pretense has too often been taken at face value.[17] Using a triptych of images from aborted works, Updike's narrator, a "would-be novelist," successfully fuses them into a coherent work of another order.

His initial "disappointment," an attempt to see into the life of an old Chinese Red Sox fan—"The happy man, the man of unceasing and effortless blessing"—fails to become the "ecstatically uneventful, divinely and defiantly dull" Proustian recounting he desires, as the narrator finds himself unable to project himself far enough into this stranger's life: "From the dew of the few flakes that melt on our faces we cannot reconstruct the snowstorm" (*PF*, 229). He is more successful in resurrecting details from his grandmother's life, after stumbling across her thimble provokes a flood of memories that begins in his own past and projects back into hers. His grandmother, like the one in "Pigeon Feathers," provides a link with the more tranquil days of Olinger, although the narrator, as he holds her thimble, recognizes that such memories are frail: "I felt at my back that night a steep wave about to break over the world and bury us and all our trinkets of survival fathoms down" (*PF*, 241). Still, by recording these memories, the narrator has preserved them from being washed away, and given them a new aesthetic context within the story.

This segment dovetails into the next with a metaphoric link, as the narrator likens his departure from Olinger after his grandmother's death to being "launched out from an island into a wilderness." Similarly, the Polynesian tribesmen of the final segment launch from one island and become castaways on another. This story of an unsuccessful transplant never becomes the "evocation of . . . the green days . . . a story full of joy" which the narrator hopes to produce. The components he assembles, however, transcend the sum of their parts; together, they embody the search for connections that the local boy, launched from the halcyon world of Olinger, must make as he attempts to compensate for the losses of his receding past. What he discovers is that the past can no longer be grasped whole, only reconstructed in fragments that rescue isolated but relatable details and moments of bliss. "Details are the giant's fingers," he concludes, accepting consolation that the minutiae of the past he can grasp will put him in touch with that larger body of memory.

While the narrator of "The Blessed Man" is frustrated by his inability to produce exhaustive literary catalogues, David Kern, reappearing as narrator of "Packed Dirt, Churchgoing, A Dying Cat, A Traded Car," is content with the montage as a way of connecting past and present. Ten years older than in "Pigeon Feathers," and now father of four, Kern has become a writer and moved to New England, but still looks back to Olinger as his spiritual center. His montage of recollections is a cyclical journey, wearing a new path through the obstructive rubble of adult life with forays into his past. In his comments on the story's composition, Updike notes how the accumulation of images enhanced his understanding of "Proust's remark about the essence of the writer's task being the perception of connections between unlike things." This "farraginous narrative," he continues, contains "a good deal of conscious art" in the interweaving of themes that "had long been present to me: paternity and death, earth and faith and cars" (*HS*, 852). As distance in time from Olinger increases, so does the "pressure of memory and worry" which spurs the local boy's similar attempt to draw connections and counter loss. Associative memory allows Kern to retravel past incidents and create a new coherence, one that also weaves together many of the collection's persistent themes. "Packed Dirt" not only harmonizes four diverse elements but also produces an even "bigger, better kind of music" in its echoes of the preceding stories.

All four segments of this story in some way allude to Kern's father or to fatherhood; the final sketch, "A Traded Car," contains what may be his last visit with his sick father. In addition, repeated images of travel and paths form a unifying motif. In the first segment, "Packed Dirt," the path worn by children's feet makes Kern "reassured, nostalgically pleased, even . . . proud"; associated with the small town, youth, and the reassertion of human will on the environment, these "unconsciously humanized intervals of clay" evoke his own childhood, "when one communes with dirt down among the legs, as it were, of presiding fatherly presences" (*PF*, 247). Seeing the children's instinctive reassertion of a path through the dirt piled by machines levelling the house next door is Kern's unexpected reward; their actions not only counter progress but also stir memories that establish continuity with his past and reassert Olinger's characteristic "repose of grace that is beyond willing."

The second segment, "Churchgoing," is overtly tied to the first when Kern compares the "creeds and petitions" of the church service to "paths worn smooth in the raw terrain of our hearts." Faith, as an avenue linking man with the spiritual, is another path that Kern sometimes finds blocked in the modern world. Nonetheless, the church itself offers a "hushed shelter . . . like one of those spots worn bare by a softball game in a weed-filled vacant lot." Churchgoing also evokes memories of shared experience with his dutifully religious father and functions as a conscious expression of "belief [that] builds itself unconsciously," just as the children wear the paths of packed dirt. Attending church keeps at bay the "nihilistic counterpoint beyond the black windows"—the fear of death which plagues him at 14 and in the last segment of this story. Still, his spiritual uplift here comes not from the service itself but from a view of boats gliding on a placid sea.

A reflection about receiving "supernatural mail on foreign soil" provides continuity between "Churchgoing" and "A Dying Cat," which chronicles a weird coincidence of death and birth. Sent home from the British hospital during his wife's prolonged labor, Kern humanely attends to a dying cat, which he initially mistakes for a baby. Like the dead birds in "Pigeon Feathers," the cat relays a message—"Run on home"—which rings appropriate later in life, when he travels home to visit his ailing father. More of a transitional episode, this section evokes the repeated themes of paternity, death, displacement, and the return.

The final section, "A Traded Car," chronicles a more significant "ceremony of farewell": the narrator's final trip in his soon-to-be-traded first car, which is linked symbolically with an epoch of his life. Its trading marks a passage, one that Kern memorializes through a journey back to his old Pennsylvania home. Confronted with the conjunction of a flare-up of adulterous longings, his recurrent fear of death, and his father's illness, he realizes that there is only one answer: "run on home" in a quest to banish his fear of death, just as Clyde Behn returns to Olinger to face his "disconsolate youth" and persistent desire. Before he visits the hospital, Kern passes the Alton museum (the same one Peter Caldwell visits in *The Centaur*), recalling how in his youth "the world then seemed an intricate wonder displayed for my delight with no price asked." Such unguarded accessibility, characteristic of Olinger's "incoherent generosity," has since vanished with maturity and responsibility. In the Alton library, Kern seeks continuity with his past, searching in books for date imprints that might indicate when he read them rather than looking for the books he has written that might eventually guarantee immortality. Ultimately, he draws strength from both the locale and from his father's apparent truce with death. Mr. Kern's faith may have slipped somewhat, but his buoyant spirits still convey reassurance to his son, for whom he remains a "presiding fatherly presence," standing between him and death.

Kern's departure recalls a similar one by John Nordholm in "The Happiest I've Been," but his age and the impending car trade clearly signal a departure in a new key. In contrast to Nordholm's sunrise departure for Chicago at the end of *The Same Door*, twilight descends for Kern at the New Jersey border; although he must return north in darkness, he does so with a new ability to face his own dark forebodings. There is both terror and joy, he reflects, in man's marriage to the world; "we bring to it a nature not our bride's," he notes, reconciled to the source of the transforming impulse that wreaks changes on the landscape in the "Packed Dirt" segment. While Nordholm feels a new sense of control at the wheel, since others are trusting him, Kern trusts the car, soon to be part of his past, to guide him back to his present. At the wheel during the final leg of his trip, Kern, in an intensification of his father's attachment to his cars, undergoes a metaphoric death, losing "first, heart, then head, and finally any sense of my body" as he becomes one with the vehicle. Thus, after its final service is performed, he returns reconciled to change but conscious of the need for some further "ceremony of farewell" to mark the passage. Through his art, he performs this ceremony, recapturing the elusive past and successfully preserving a pathway to it that may be travelled perpetually.

"Packed Dirt, Churchgoing, A Dying Cat, A Traded Car," which Updike intended to be the last of his Pennsylvania stories, says his first in a series of farewells to Olinger; subsequent collections concentrate on older characters, take place in other locales, and portray a widening gulf from the past and within marriage. Yet Updike pays homage to Olinger once again when he gathers seven stories from *Pigeon Feathers*, three from *The Same Door*, and one that later appears in *The Music School* into his short story sequence *Olinger Stories: A Selection*. Though initially reluctant to reharvest previously published material, Updike found aesthetic and personal justification to overcome his doubts: "They succumbed to the hope that a concentration of certain images might generate new light, or at least focus more sharply the light already there. . . . I bind these stories together as one ties up a package of love letters that have been returned" (*OS*, vi). In assembling the scattered stories of his local boy into a Bildungsroman, Updike gave formal unity to his Olinger fiction and closed the book on his recurrent fictional locale.

Like "Packed Dirt," *Olinger Stories* is a "farraginous narrative," composed of a mixture or variety of materials. However, these materials are not confused or jumbled; instead they possess a conscious thematic and imagistic logic. On a smaller and more compressed scale, then, "Packed Dirt" mirrors the structure of *Olinger Stories*, though it seems more composed rather than arranged, with obvious links, such as the repeated motif of the path, embedded to promote coherence. *Olinger Stories*, on the other hand, like the settlement of Fanning Island in "The Blessed Man," relies more on "accidents" as "the generating agency beneath the seemingly achieved surface of things," as we read separately composed stories in a fresh context and construct a new coherence that simultaneously lends Olinger a more tangible existence and endows it with a mythic status.

Transposing the Music of Reminiscence: *The Music School*

In *The Music School,* Updike carries forward many of the same themes treated in previous stories—memory and its redemptive power, the tension between spiritual yearnings and their physical realizations, the ambiguous blessings of domestic life—but transposes them into a new key suited to older characters who are no longer able to linger in memories of adolescence. With the publication of *Olinger Stories,* rural Pennsylvania becomes a "closed book"; Updike's protagonists, now approaching middle age, must contend with the less idyllic world of Tarbox, still in close proximity to nature but clearly separated from Olinger's rural "fields steeped in grace." The atmosphere of Tarbox, filled with decline and unrealized possibilities, threatens to diffuse through the lives of its inhabitants and make memory the most vital part of their existences. In the move from Olinger to Tarbox, the characters have entered a realm whose history is not intimately connected with their past. No longer sustained merely by memory, they struggle to accommodate themselves to the ever-increasing losses that accompany life beyond Olinger.

The marital tensions of earlier stories have now grown into a gulf; the characters lose closeness not only with their pasts but also with their spouses. As Peter Meinke observes, divorce becomes the volume's dominant metaphor, with separation occurring from spouses, youth, the society, and life itself.[18] Like Bech, the writer Updike debuts in "The Bulgarian Poetess," they are often in a state of "romantic vertigo"; in response to such displacement, Bech speculates, man seeks in love an equivalent of the contentment provided by his first landscape.[19] Isolated and grappling with desire, Updike's mature characters discover that Olinger's unexpected gifts are not readily forthcoming; the rewards that substitute are often fleeting and harder earned. Consequently, a persistent note of infidelity begins to echo through the stories, as the yearning for now elusive satisfactions leads characters beyond marriage. Romantic discord and a sense of perplexity thus dominate their lives, yet they

43

continue to struggle against disillusionment and toward the realization of some mature version of the vanished pastoral.

As in Updike's earlier stories, the heightened perceptions of epiphanic moments allow the characters to rise momentarily above life's turmoil, but these epiphanies most often concern the inherent limitations of reviving the past. For many, loss becomes the past's most crucial event, and the present becomes a striving to transmute and recapture that essence, since complete escape, whether into memory or nature, is impossible once self-consciousness dawns. As some of the volume's meditative stories illustrate, retreat into the recent past is a trap, heightening the gap between past and present and leading to a type of paralysis; the retreat to nature that concludes the book also miscarries, leading deeper into alienation. In formulating possible responses, Updike flirts with the Swiss theologian Denis de Rougemont's notion that one can possess an unrealizable love in its greatest perfection only after its physical duration concludes. But the characters who lower their sights slightly and accept the inevitability of change and grief embody the most successful and resonant resolutions. Their goal is to find a satisfactory equilibrium by accepting loss without total resignation and by continuously striving to discover possible compensations; such incorporation of sorrow leads to a wider and more realistic vision that restores a provisional connection with the estranged past and acknowledges mutability. The artistic visions of the narrators of "Leaves," "Harv Is Plowing Now," and the title story thus represent the most harmonious reconciliations possible in the era of uncertainty into which Updike's protagonists have stumbled.

While most of the stories of *The Music School* strike a common thematic chord, they exhibit an impressive variety of technique. The collection's modes range from the traditional linear narrative of "The Rescue" to the meditative or lyric mode of "Leaves" to the Hawthornesque historical sketch of "The Indian" to the epistolary style of the modern mythic adaptation "Four Sides of One Story." As Updike departs from Olinger and the unexpected gifts of youth, he deliberately seems to seek new modes of fiction to capture the differing texture of experience that confronts characters who have crossed into Tarbox and beyond. The lyricism of what Updike calls the "abstract-personal mode" is especially suited to many of their conditions: at some crux in their lives (often the end of a relationship), they are more disposed to reflect than act—a condition perhaps best depicted in a plotless meditation. Nonetheless, even the more experimental stories in *The Music School* have some precedent in Updike's first two collections, creating continuity among Updike's attempts to extend what many critics decry as the limitations of his realism, poetic style, and focus on the middle range of experience.

The collection's headnote, a stanza from Wallace Stevens's "To the One of Fictive Music," accentuates the characteristic paradox of maturity: our essential separation from but continued existence in nature. Consciousness of this gulf, often allied with a perception of mortality, is the impetus to make "fictive music," and to capture, in art's "laborious weaving," a "perfection more serene" than that which is accessible in the present. In *The Music School*, those who endure suffering and learn to compose a fictive music synthesizing the complexities of experience most closely approach the poetic aim Stevens describes in "Of Modern Poetry," since they create tales of "the mind in the act of finding/ What will suffice." Such an attempt is the substance of the opening story, "In Football Season," which weaves an intricately detailed hymn to the past that very nearly belies the narrator's final proclamation of loss by the immediacy of the evocation. With the texture of an extended prose poem, "In Football Season" uses second-person narration to involve the reader more intimately in the nostalgic descent. As the conclusion to *Olinger Stories*, it functions as a coda to the protagonist's retrospectively realized idyll, highlighting the joys and fears of the local boy who grows to transcend his milieu. As the opening to *The Music School*, it serves as an affectionate backward glance, a prelude to music in a new key.

From the perspective of middle age, the narrator evokes a realm of relative innocence whose alien poignancy makes us continually conscious that its season has passed. Despite the sensual immediacy, the story's mood is autumnal; in one last excursion into the season of youth, the narrator memorializes an ephemeral realm, whose seeds of dissolution were sown long before he was conscious of it. Images of dry leaves and darkness held at bay are interwoven with the memories of young girls, communal identity, and paternal protectiveness. The olfactory sense pervades his descriptions; the story's opening, for instance, recalls the "fragrance girls acquire in autumn"—a distillation concentrated in the hollow crescent formed by their books and bodies, "woven of tobacco, powder, lipstick, rinsed hair, and that perhaps imaginary and certainly elusive scent that wool seems to yield." Like this fragrance, the story itself is an amalgam of visual, olfactory, aural, and tactile memories, all assembled in the hollow of the speaker's imagination; like the young girls, the memories are flirted with but ultimately elusive. In a similar montage image, the students tightly packed into the football stadium emit a single essence, "like flowers pressed together to yield to the black sky a concentrated homage, an incense. . . . In a hoarse olfactory shout, the odors ascended"[20]—a communal assertion against seasonal intimations of death.

In retrospect, the chorus of the song with which the narrator and his friends amuse themselves—the first music in *The Music School*—becomes, "a song for eternity," holding back the inevitable dissipation of youth by the adult world's "winds of worry," even while it contains hints of the sexual knowledge that will bring them into this realm. One of the choruses the narrator composes becomes an ironic commentary on the subsequent stories of marital tension and infidelity, as many of the married characters eventually discover that they indeed "can't get to heaven on a motel bed." For the narrator, the present allure of young girls only reminds him of what is now inaccessible, and of the deep chasm between past and present. In Olinger, time was nonthreatening, "a black immensity endlessly supplied"; its waste, he remarks, "had been necessary; it was permitted." Yet the past tense at the story's conclusion signals the dissolution of his temporary suspension of time as he reenters the present, where he can no longer find the "air of permission" so pervasive in his youth. The narrator retains his faith that "fields steeped in grace" still exist, but these vivid and piercing memories are simultaneously a reward and a reminder of his loss.

"The Indian," though one of the weaker pieces in the volume, assumes importance from its placement: following the exit from Olinger enacted by "In Football Season," this sketch marks Updike's transition in locale to Tarbox, the fictional equivalent of Ipswich, Massachusetts, where Updike moved with his family in 1957 in order to concentrate on his fiction. The story's narrator, instead of seeking access to his past, searches for bearings in Tarbox history. New to his milieu, he cannot celebrate its precious qualities in lavish detail, as the narrator of "In Football Season" does; instead, he begins with a history lesson. The town, not the title character (who does not appear until midway into the story), is initially his focus; the narrator's quest for knowledge about the Indian, its major mystery, dominates the second half. This attempt to blend the historical essay with the lyric mode has resulted in dissonant music, as the story lacks the drama of self-examination that characterizes the volume's more successful meditative stories. Still, the backdrop of decline Updike sketches is a crucial context for his subsequent fiction.

Tarbox, originally conceived as a "pastoral plantation," neither realized this vision nor transformed itself into a vibrant modern center.

Although it has acquired a "cosmopolitan garnish" and achieved some urban renewal, it remains "a town apart." Development has not touched the surrounding marsh, a symbol of enduring nature, though the diminishing animal population suggests that nature too is subject to decline. Reinforcing this aura is the nearby beach, with its ice cakes piled "like the rubble of ruined temples." With local history digested into postcards, the town's Indian comes to represent its living connection to the past. The narrator wishes to romanticize him as a noble savage, but the Indian cultivates the appearance of a typical run-down Yankee. Like the town itself, he is a diminished thing, but he endures, mysteriously ageless, waiting in vain for his inheritance to be restored. Indeed, he now seems more part of the town than of any savage past, bypassed by time and consigned to wait on the fringes. Tarbox, Updike has stated, represents "the arena of the Decline of the West,"[21] but in this brief, static sketch it cannot assume the symbolic dimensions of civilization's "dark climax" which emerge more clearly in a novel length work such as *Couples.*

"Giving Blood" marks the return of the Maples, whose marriage has degenerated after nine years into stagnant routine and bitter quarrels. Richard's adulterous desires, which previously flared in the confines of Rebecca Cune's loft in "Snowing in Greenwich Village," are now more openly flaunted at parties where he does the Twist all evening with a neighbor's wife. As the couple drives to Boston to donate blood for Joan's distant relative, they engage in a verbal bloodletting as a prelude: Joan's remarks about his behavior at the party are astute but piercing; Richard, irritable and defensive that Joan perceives his illicit scheming, cuts deeply with his remark that she is smug, stupid, and sexless. The experience of giving blood temporarily restores peace between them and holds out the promise of invigorating their anemic marriage, but the story ends as it began, with Richard cursing and bemoaning his fate. As a result of Richard's immaturity and lack of perspective on married life, the Maples travel a circular route rather than achieve the rejuvenation their union needs.

For Richard, a first-time blood donor, giving blood is first a chore and finally a test of his manhood. Shamed by Joan for his complaining, he approaches the experience feeling childlike, as the parallel he draws between them and Hansel and Gretel shows. His reluctant altruism, however, results in a very adult epiphany, whose full implications are ultimately lost on him. "Newly defined to themselves" when they fill in the forms with their separate and common histories, the Maples become "chastely conjoined" as they lie at right angles on separate tables, "linked to a common loss," their different blood types simultaneously ebbing. In Richard's mind, they merge on a higher plane as they engage in this mutual sacrifice: "he floated and imagined how his soul would float free when all his blood was underneath the bed. His blood and Joan's merged on the floor, and together their spirits glided from crack to crack, from star to star on the ceiling" (*MS*, 27). This perception of a mystical union, transcending marital squabbles and temptations of the flesh, temporarily restores Richard's wonder at life and renews the sacramental essence of marriage within him.

On the return trip, in a more "insubstantial and gentle" mood, he attempts to sustain this condition, and invigorate their romance with more of "the strange, the untried." Together at an unaccustomed place and time, the Maples try to behave as they did in more innocent days, yet their "date," with overtones of an illicit act and the inevitable recall of their earlier argument, concludes with the resurgence of Richard's dissatisfaction when he gallantly attempts to pay the check and discovers only one dollar in his wallet. Their previously established communion is now destroyed by his self-pity over the sacrifices his family demands. While Richard paints himself as a martyr, Joan's perception is more accurate: "We'll both pay," she states, ostensibly referring to the bill, but further implying not only that both partners pay the intangible costs of married life but also that she and Richard, as long as they remain married, will continue to pay for his egocentric, insensitive behavior. Richard unfortunately fails to comprehend that giving blood is a metaphor of giving love: after being relieved of a pint of blood, he states, "I don't really understand this business of giving something away and still somehow having it," foreshadowing his insensitivity to love's dynamic. Concerned only with the cost to himself, Richard will continue to stand outside the mysteries of mutual sacrifice that can replenish rather than diminish the marital union.

"Leaves," like the foliage its narrator keenly studies as he emerges from his inner darkness, is "curiously beautiful"—a tour de force of poetic language and imagery that grows as organically as the grapevines that prompt the musings it contains. Although "Leaves" has been criticized as overly wrought "lace," its verbal art does much more than spin lovely images; in nine paragraphs, it not only lays bare the pain of separation and the self-examined life but also delves into the problematic relationship between man, art, and nature. In a rare defense of his work, Updike states: "if 'Leaves' is lace, it is taut and symmetrical lace, with scarce a loose thread. . . . The way the leaves become the pages, the way the bird becomes his description, the way the bright and multiform world of nature is felt rubbing against the dark world of the trapped ego—all strike me as beautiful, and of the order of 'happiness' that is given rather than attained" (*HS*, 853). Beauty emerges in "Leaves" from the narrator's struggle to overcome guilt and shame about his infidelity—the root of his separation from nature—and from his urge to create a human equivalent to nature's splendor.

Initially, the narrator shies away from explicitly proclaiming the redemptive power of art; though proud of verbally capturing the blue jay, he summarizes his achievement as "a curious trick, possibly useless, but mine." In his struggle to come to terms with his wanton behavior and "unqualified righteousness," he perceives that self-consciousness is the inescapable source of such separation, the essential gulf between the steady, guiltless natural realm and the flux and blame of the human one. Neither metaphor nor the fiction-making process can completely redeem his guilt and retrieve lost innocence: the "whole furious and careless growth pruned by explanation and rooted in history" cannot, like so many dead leaves, be absorbed by nature. At best, such verbal efforts, result in "a sharpening of the edge where we stand" between the two kingdoms rather than in lasting absolution or joy.

Heightened perception, then, is the end result of his fiction, and the story chronicles the healing ritual of a man in temporary retreat from love. "The green persists long into autumn, if we look," he states, affirming his faith in the power of renewal. As he studies the leaves and their shadows in detail, the narrator achieves a temporary epiphany, losing himself in "a serene and burning universe" of color outside his window; at any moment, however, the telephone could break the precarious spell. Still, such intricate beauty cannot provide lasting relief for a troubled consciousness; the spiked shadows of the very leaves in which he loses himself contain "barbaric suggestions" that recall the pain his experience has brought, return him to memories of his wife, and prompt an attempted reconciliation. Ultimately, the pages he writes, not nature, are the leaves that are more effectual in restoring a lasting emotional composure.

Although the leaves provide the path to solace, another emblem of nature, the spider, shows the narrator that the natural and human realms are "contiguous but incompatible." Placed in the "quaint and antique pose of the fabulist seeking to draw a lesson from a spider," he is unable to make fact flower into truth, as Henry David Thoreau might, and discover nature's moral lesson. Walt Whitman's *Leaves of Grass*, which the narrator reads from on his first night in the cabin, contains the poetic realization of such a lesson: "A Noiseless Patient Spider," a fable of the soul tirelessly launching "gossamer thread" that will connect the material and spiritual realms and thus transcend its isolation. Reading Whitman's poetry occasions a "beautiful awakening," yet the leaves of another artist, like nature's leaves, are but a temporary sanctuary. The narrator's own words, the "subjective photosynthesis" that incorporates his world's diverse elements and constructively transmutes them, weave a web more likely to capture enduring happiness. While "Leaves" does not depict a Whitmanesque spiritual flight, it nonetheless enacts the process of recovery and reordering that may be the closest humans can come to nature's more harmonious balance.

The impersonal crowds of Manhattan and unrealized fantasies of reunion with a former lover dominate "The Stare," whose plotless meditative form accentuates the protagonist's self-enclosed condition and poignantly depicts the pain that arises when memory and desire mingle. In "The Morning," another lyric story, only two words break the protagonist's self-enclosed silence: a whispered call for "My nurse," uttered by a man wallowing in his own pain, in need of emotional first-aid only his former lover can administer. Another meditative story, "The Dark," delves into the insomniac consciousness of a terminally ill man rather than a bereaved lover; the temporal movement of the story is from darkness to dawn, yet the morning light brings no epiphanic revelation. In contrast to these dramatizations of intense inner turmoil, "At a Bar in Charlotte Amalie" focuses on externals. This sketch has some qualities of a slight moral fable on the inevitable wavering of innocence and the implications of being "uninhibited" (a word repeated numerous times by the homosexual), but it hardly seems a tale of "a pale young lady dipping one toe into the icy ocean of Evil," as one reviewer characterizes the story.[22] Nonetheless, the story depicts a certain hollowness at the center of things, symbolically signalled in the opening sentence by the blowfish skins above the bar, illuminated by light bulbs within them.

Like the contemplative protagonists of previous stories, the husbands in more traditionally plotted tales such as "Avec la Bébé-sitter" and "Twin Beds in Rome" are self-enclosed, harboring some inner wound that mitigates their attempts to revive their marriages by travelling abroad with their spouses. Veterans of marital strife, the Maples continue their battle in "Twin Beds in Rome." Unable to end the conflict with a decisive reconciliation or separation, they travel to Rome in the hope that escaping their normal routine (and presumably their children, who curiously receive no mention) will finally either "kill or cure" their wounded marriage. Instead of romance, the eternal city presents them with the heaviness of the past and emblems of ruin: the Colosseum is "shaped like a shattered wedding cake"; the Forum, full of broken columns, has been ransacked for building materials by a later age; the church of Santa Maria contains "life-size tomb-reliefs worn nearly featureless by footsteps." While the Maples' marriage has been previously entombed a dozen times and stubbornly refuses to die, these tombs are fitting symbols of their individual personalities, which they have allowed a narrow conception of marriage to wear down; nonetheless, as with the tombs, there seems to be "a vivid soul trying to rise from the all but erased body."

Although Richard has a preconceived death wish for their relationship, the unexpected twin beds in their room are an embarrassing symbol of a separation already decided by circumstance. The tables in "Giving Blood" foreshadow such a symbolic separation, though in the earlier story the Maples lie at right angles, with the possibility of intersection, rather than on parallel beds. Yet the twin beds force them to sacrifice temporarily the most significant feature of their continued relationship. Ironically, Richard sleeps well, although he becomes hostile toward Joan in his sleep and verbally betrays his wish for her to "go away." During their daytime excursions, however, Richard refuses to relax, and insists on maintaining an oppressive "tension of hope." He is astute enough to realize that they cannot recapture the early bloom of their relationship: "I feel we've come very far and have only a little way more to go," he declares. Nonetheless, he cannot let go enough to allow them the space they need to flourish as individuals.

Richard's psychosomatic illness, as elusive in origin as their marital ills, becomes a catharsis for their common troubles. His tension-induced pains are a remnant of his childhood; recalling the test of his courage in "Giving Blood," Richard confesses that he faced pain more bravely as a youth. His half-joking speculation that the continual need to dole out large tips is the source of his pain shows how little his spirit of charity has grown; still uncomfortable with giving, he has yet to overcome his tendency to analyze his "sacrifices" in terms of their cost. After the pain runs its course, both partners seem to be released from the self-conscious burden they have carried to Rome. They behave as they did when courting and begin to enjoy the city, which presents a new face in the

51

"seemingly solid blocks of buildings that parted, under examination, into widely separated slices of style and time." Instead of ruins, they now see emblems of solid and distinctive individuality, a new ideal for their relationship.

Updike is too astute an observer of the ambiguities of married life, however, to sketch such a guilt-free parting, laced with irony as it may be. Although the Maples' marriage "let go like an overgrown vine whose half-hidden stem has been slashed in the dawn by an ancient gardener," Joan's ensuing happiness arouses Richard's possessiveness. His pleasure in her happiness now makes him jealous of her new vivacity and renews his desire to cling to the rootless vine of their marriage, rather than let it die and allow the trees it has entangled to flourish unencumbered. Only the fourth in Updike's series of 17 collected Maples stories, "Twin Beds in Rome" illustrates that they indeed have *Too Far to Go* (as he titles the 1979 volume) before they are ready for a relatively unconstrained parting.

The epistolary form of "Four Sides of One Story" allows Updike to juxtapose the reflections of four isolated characters who act out a modern version of the Tristan and Iseult legend, which recounts how King Mark's royal servant Tristan falls in love with Iseult while bringing her back for the King to marry.[23] As in *The Centaur*, the mythic interpenetrates the actual, most notably in Tristan's insistence that his and Iseult's love originated from a magic potion. Some knowledge of the various legends is crucial for understanding this allusive story fully; still, the theme of love's mutability and the attempt to preserve love, through renunciation, from the ravages of time and daily contact clearly tie it to others in the volume which have been influenced by Updike's reading of Denis de Rougemont's works, especially *Love in the Western World*. Updike observes that in de Rougemont's analysis of the chivalric influence on Western tradition, "Eros is allied with Thanatos rather than Agape; love becomes not a way of accepting and entering the world but a way of defying and escaping it. . . . Love as we experience it *is* love for the Unattainable Lady, the Iseult who is 'ever a stranger, the very essence of what is strange in woman and of all that is eternally fugitive, vanishing, and almost hostile in a fellow-being. . . . She is the woman-from-whom-one-is-parted; to possess her is to lose her' " (*AP*, 285–86).

"Four Sides to One Story," however, is not merely a reworking of de Rougemont's thesis; as the title implies, Tristan's idealized vision of lost love's purity is only one side of a more complex story, which is structured so that the women's letters are framed by the men's, just as their lives have been. Presenting Tristan's sophisticated justification of his escape first and balancing his romantic vision with the pragmatic calculus of Iseult's husband Mark at the end suggests that the elusive truth lies somewhere between extremes. The glimpses into the women's pain widens the perspective, presenting the intellectualized male reactions as a counterpoint to the more emotive female ones. These four visions will never harmonize; despite King Mark's concluding vision of order, the tense strains of an emotionally unresolved situation linger.

While he is an articulate spokesman for de Rougemont's ideals, Updike's modern Tristan comes across as somewhat of a coward, retreating from emotional turmoil as he travels "away, away from the realms of compromise and muddle" that plague ongoing relationships. Tristan takes pains to establish that his writing wavers because the boat rocks, not because he trembles, and that the splotches on the paper are salt spray, not tears; however, he is not immune to emotion, as the mere unfolding of a napkin can revive memories of love's inception. Still, he attempts to make the past into a parcel of "landlocked days," and sustain an idealized love, one remove from that "paradoxical ethical situation" of being "repeatedly wounded by someone *because he or she is beloved*." Although he feels diminished by her absence, their love derives greater purity from being objectified, flourishing more in his mind than it did in experience.

After Tristan spins his romantic rationalization of their parting, his wife, Iseult of the Fair Hand, presents a compelling and realistic vision of the spurned spouse who can never measure up to her husband's lover. From this Iseult's point of view, Tristan's "saintly pained looks" and noble indecision generate unnecessary torment. Dismissing his mythic explanation of his love for the other Iseult as mere metaphor, she seeks its source in other causes. Her common sense and immersion in daily routine, however, both prove ineffectual in coping with her despair. The letter of Iseult the Fair, Tristan's lover, remains unsent because Mark has confiscated it as potential evidence for a lawsuit against the lovers. Tristan's name, fragmentary memories, and phrases held together by dashes comprise her "side," a free associative flow of thought indicative of her precarious mental state. Her attempted cure, the opposite of Tristan's, is to "kill [him] in my heart" rather than sustain herself with idealized love. The fleeing Tristan, as his wife notes, attempts to hang between the two women; however, both seem to be cutting the ropes and advising him to take up with the other. Iseult's vow to dig up the narcissi he planted emphasizes the strength of her desire to eradicate memory of her self-centered lover, who searches for a reflection of himself in her. By the end of the letter she is unable to write more than the first two letters of his name, a sign that he has become too painful to remember; if she succeeds in burying her remaining memories, accepting her diminished life with Mark will be easier.

King Mark, obsessed with retaining control over his wife and kingdom, is easily cast as the villain, but his pragmatic vision has an unfortunate tint of accuracy. While Tristan's only control exists in denying possibilities before the world can squelch them, Mark, with his lawyers and his purloined letter, *is* that world—the tyrant king who refuses to be usurped. Rather than executing the lovers, he banishes Tristan and places Iseult in psychoanalysis—calculated mercy based on legal and political considerations. Mark's letter is a strange conflation of mythic and modern, ranging from dragon slaying to legal battles, yet he too doubts the story of the magic potion (although he puts the royal alchemists to work on an antidote). While he controls the fates of the players, he is clearly not in control of their hearts. Still, whether Tristan's ideal can be a viable one that sustains anyone besides himself in a world dominated by Mark remains an open question.

"The Christian Roommates," based on Updike's experience at Harvard, might seem out of place among the volume's numerous stories concerning marital tensions; the relationship between the roommates, however, is filled with similar conflicts. When Orson Zeigler, the self-assured premed student from a small South Dakota town, first meets his roommate Hub, he realizes that "they were on the verge of a kind of marriage." Smooth friendship between the two, however, is complicated not only by Orson's circumscribed worldview and rigidly defined goals but also by the degree to which Hub differs. Orson already has his future mapped out as the husband of his high school sweetheart and the successor of his father's medical practice. Hub, an older, nonmaterialistic, vegetarian pacifist who weaves and practices Yoga, presents an enigma that threatens his new roommate's security: he not only tears up draft notices but also scoffs at the sciences as a "demonic illusion of human *hubris*."

To Orson, whose viewpoint the narrator enters freely, Hub seemed "hermetically sealed inside one of the gluing machines that had incubated his garbled philosophy"; the reader's viewpoint is similarly limited to what Hub states and does. Hub's knowledge of Greek, his experience as a plywood gluer, and his interest in philosophical inquiry all disturb Orson, whose initial reaction is to feel "cramped in his mind, able neither to stand erect in wholehearted contempt nor lie down in honest admiration" (*MS*, 135–36). Unaccustomed to the ambivalence that has become a staple of the adult lives of Updike's older characters, Orson tries to remain "morbidly clean" and let nothing from Hub stick to him. Ironically, when Orson immerses himself in his studies and becomes Hub's most vigorous opponent, he loses the opportunity for a wider education that Hub embodies.

In the absence of any other commonalities such as those which bond other pairs of roommates, Orson and Hub, as the title announces, are joined by their Christianity—a fact which perhaps neither ever understands fully. Orson continues to focus more on their differences, recognizing that while the other pairs in their dormitory are united by "geography, race, ambition, [or] physical size," he and Hub—a self-proclaimed "Anglican Christian Platonist strongly influenced by Gandhi"—share only this fundamental quality. The nicknames their peers assign them also signal this affinity: Hub is "the saint" because of his ascetic lifestyle, while Orson becomes "the Parson" for his self-righteous criticism of Hub's praying. Yet the shallowness of Orson's faith becomes evident in his final unexpected loss: after religiously pursuing high grades and premed training, Orson has become the person he always expected to be except in one important respect: "a kind of a scar he carries without pain and without any clear memory of amputation. . . . He never prays." His neglect of prayer may reveal the lack of spiritual turmoil that creates a need to pray; whether he realizes that his spirituality is superficial compared to Hub's or whether Hub has somehow tainted religion forever for him, Orson suffers an unplanned diminishment. Just as the narrator of "The Morning" loses the beauty of mornings when the lover associated with them departs, Orson's religious inclinations vanish with Hub, who goes on to combine divinity school and social activism.

In their skirmishes, Orson shows himself to be a perceptive critic who can home in on Hub's contradictions; while the others debate with Hub about the ethics of his vegetarianism, Orson points to the hypocrisy of his leather belongings and receives Hub's harshest rebuke. Orson may be attempting to distance himself from Hub and become one of the group, but he finds himself unable to adopt a simplistic antipathy: "He resented being associated with Hub, and yet felt attacked when Hub was attacked" (*MS*, 145). Plagued by ambivalence, Orson avoids Hub until the tension reaches a breaking point, when, in a cathartic physical scuffle, they battle about the stolen parking meter. At this point, the roommates are, like Updike's married characters, "pilgrims, faltering toward divorce." Like an incompatible couple, they separate after the second semester, despite Hub's mild attempt to compromise.

Although the story focuses on Hub and Orson, Updike sketches the cameo portrait of a generation in the dorm's other residents. Among the diverse group are two New York City Jews from gifted high schools, a child prodigy from Maine, a homesick black student from North Carolina who plays the trumpet, and two writers, one of whom is named Kern and hails from Pennsylvania. While Orson shares Updike's excema, Kern, "a farm boy driven by an unnatural sophistication, riddled with nervous ailments ranging from conjunctivitis to hemorrhoids, [who] smoked and talked incessantly," shares the name of Updike's local boy from Olinger in "Pigeon Feathers." In his portrait of Kern (who ends up working in advertising), Updike perhaps engages in the opportunity for a bit of parody of his youthful self. When the witty and caustic Kern delivers a long, tongue-in-cheek monologue on how the "tragedy of the universe achieves a pinpoint focus" in the mind of the hen whose egg is wrenched from her for human consumption, Updike may be taking a satiric jab at his own tendency to focus on the inherent tragedies of the mundane.

While "My Lover Has Dirty Fingernails" satirizes the perils of submitting one's life to psychological scrutiny, "Harv Is Plowing Now" asserts that "Our lives submit to archeology," and illustrates how the excavation of memory can be approached more constructively. One of the finest stories in the collection, "Harv Is Plowing Now" links art and archeology as it depicts the narrator's meditative descent through the layers of his past: his present cluttered single existence; a bygone relationship that seems willfully buried and oddly barren; and, at bottom, memories of his rural childhood existence that focus on the image of his neighbor Harv, plowing the fields in spring. Although the base layer of his memories harks back to a pastoral realm much like Olinger, the narrator does not retreat to the halcyon past but rather discovers in it metaphors with which to begin the process of recovery that eludes other bereaved characters.

Appropriately, the story begins with the recollection of another recovery, when, as a child with a fever, the narrator kept warm in front of a woodstove; from this scene, he reconstructs a significant piece of early history on his seemingly isolated family farm, which is mirrored across the meadow by another, where Harv and his mother live. The image of Harv plowing embeds itself in the narrator's artistic consciousness as the embodiment of his agrarian roots: "The linked silhouettes of the man and the mule moved back and forth like a slow brush repainting the parched pallor of the winter-faded land with the wet dark color of loam. It seemed to be happening *in me*; and as I age in this century, I hold within myself this memory, this image unearthed from a pastoral epoch predating my birth, this deposit lower than which there is only the mineral void" (*MS*, 177). Harv has sold the farm and moved to Florida, but the actual continuation of Harv's plowing becomes less important than its enduring memory. In his current condition, however, both the persistence and the substance of this memory become important, as the narrator emulates his old neighbor in an act of plowing up the ground of memory left fallow since his recent separation.

Although linked by a logic of metaphor, the story's subsequent plunge into a description of the English excavators at Ur seems to be an abrupt shift until, at midstory, the narrator declares, "My existence seems similarly stratified," and establishes the link between the archeological discoveries and the shape of his past. The three tiers of Sumerian artifacts correspond to three periods in his life: the bottom layer, containing colored pottery shaped by hand, is the "hidden space where Harv . . . eternally plows"; the top layer, characterized by unpainted, wheel-turned pottery, resembles the present, given depth by the multitude of objects; in between lies a thick stratum of clay, mysteriously devoid of artifacts, "the dense vacancy where like an inundation the woman came and went."

Once past midpoint of the story, the narrator engages in his own "dig," carefully treading through the debris cluttering the present. Any of the seemingly insignificant objects in his catalogue of minute particulars could assume retrospective importance, yet, in sum, they seem a fragile palimpsest over a rarely explored portion of the past. This suspiciously empty middle stage—his abortive relationship with a long-haired woman—occupies the narrator's attention most. As in "The Morning," her departure has swept away the substance of these days, leaving only a "hollowness from which her presence can be rebuilt, as wooden artifacts, long rotted to nothing, can be re-created from the impress they have left in clay" (*MS*, 180). The particular memory he unearths re-enacts their parting—or a version of it. The strains of guitar music which frame the scene subtly evoke the collection's title and headnote, yet they serve as a contrast to the more intricate and lasting fictive music which the narrator composes from the span of his personal history.

The epiphany which occurs at the story's conclusion belies the feeling of impermanence that arises from the disconcerting image of the ocean washing away his footprints in the sand. In order to rise out of the depression and paralysis which plague other characters suffering from lost love, the narrator has undergone a painful excavation that places him once again in touch with the fundamental layers of experience and makes renewal possible. "What is bread in the oven becomes Christ in the mouth," he states early in the story, preparing us for the transformation of memory into a moment of beauty that can only be a prelude, he believes, to some sort of resurrection. In his final vision of wholeness, stars, sand, and sea coalesce in a recognition of human insignificance that nonetheless grants us a place in the cosmos. The narrator's comparison of his mind's liberation to insanity should not, of course, be taken literally; at this transcendent moment of cosmic freedom, he understands that redemption must begin in the elemental world: the earth, one's past. Harv's plowing thus becomes a metaphor for preparing the soil of one's soul, tilling all the layers to ready the ground for new growth, of which the narrator's intricate metaphors may be the first yield.

Updike's techniques of dramatic monologues, startling juxtapositions, and metaphoric richness coalesce in "The Music School" to create a complex amalgam of religion, murder, computer programming, infidelity, music, and innocence. The narrator, Alfred Schweigen, whose German name means "silent," may not be able to write the aborted novel he describes, but the short story form enables him to weave a surprisingly coherent web of metaphoric connections—a temporary stay against the confusion and seeming randomness of events in a life where religion and music are relics of the past, and visits to a psychiatrist by both marital partners are necessary to help sort out the confusion. On the written page, Schweigen can silently forge a continuity between the day's disparate events, even though he is unable to make sense of his own disintegrating marriage.

Schweigen begins the story with the declaration that he exists in time—an obvious and indisputable fact that we nonetheless continually attempt to deny in daily attempts to arrest change. Just as the Church's interpretation of Christ's directive about the Eucharist changes, so must Schweigen's life. The host, presently a translucent wafer that melts without effort, will become thicker and chewier so that it must actually be eaten; correspondingly, the effortless period of youth and early marriage is replaced by the more substantial complexities of mature life—among which are his own infidelity and the computer programmer's random death. Amid the percussion of clashing images, Schweigen strains to comprehend life's present dissonance, a struggle that involves "chewing" reality, not just mirroring it.

The programmer and the priest seem as disjunct a pair as one could imagine, yet each is, to Schweigen, "a man of the future," adapting in his own way to the sweeping changes of the social and intellectual landscape. The two disparate characters represent polarities that draw him in different directions, yet he is uncomfortable with both the programmer's cold unbelief and the guitar-playing priest's secularized religion. Schweigen is a creature of the present with an eye toward the past, unwilling to acclimate himself to the tides of change. Like the computer programmer, he has abandoned religion; he has also abandoned music, a discipline now being studied by his daughter, whose efforts remind him of an innocent realm beyond which he has passed forever. His interlude in the music school where she takes lessons, with its memories of youth and its intimations of "a world where angels fumble, pause, and begin again" not only refreshes him but also offers a meaningful pattern of experience. The school inspires his memories of his difficulty learning music and his awe of its mystery: "Vision, timidly, becomes percussion, percussion becomes music, music becomes emotion, emotion becomes—vision." Music, like writing fiction, transposes insight into a form that another can experience, expanding the composer's vision in the process.

Music also "freights each note with a double meaning of position and duration," just as fiction takes objects and actions and endows them with multiple meanings in new contexts. Even the woman's "two backward steps and then again the forward movement" mentioned before the story's coda become a metaphor for his faltering progress through life. The story itself resembles an elaborate musical composition, with repeated motifs recalling a previous movement. Metaphors concerning sustenance run through the story like a rhythmic sequence: the spiritual nourishment of the host (however it is consumed), the "last supper" of the computer programmer (who is shot at the table), his daughter's "filling" music lesson, memories of the refreshment of communion in his youth, and finally the reference to the world as a host that must be chewed. The variety and indeterminacy of language is another leitmotif, referred to in the theologians' debate over Christ's command, in Schweigen's speculation on how the programmer's "binomial percussion" results in the "music of truth," and in the sketch of music's visionary process; ultimately, however, language is the route of Schweigen's triumph over the seemingly random cacophony of events.

"The Music School" is finally another story of infidelity, yet of a very different order than Schweigen's abandoned novel concerning the adulterous computer programmer slated to die from infidelity—"a case of love, guilt, and nervous breakdown, with physiological complications." This unfinished novel—a diminished and parodic version of *Couples*—provides an instructive contrast to Schweigen's achievement in the shorter form. In the scene described (presumably a high point in the plot), adulterous longings converge with the launching of an artificial star; its overwritten melodrama pales by comparison to the more concentrated attempt to portray the intricate interrelationship of ongoing experience. Existing in time, Schweigen finds, though precarious for the fiction writer, can be a subject in and of itself. His novel fails because "the moment in my life it was meant to crystallize dissolved too quickly"; the short story, he discovers, is a more appropriate form to crystallize the moment before it passes and obliterates the continuity of one experience with the next. Unlike his computer programmer, Schweigen is not a "being too fine, translucent, and scrupulous to live in our coarse age"; instead he grapples with the inescapable "paradox of being a thinking animal."

In the end, his daughter's hopeful refreshment and innocence pierces him like the bullet that killed his acquaintance. Music, he realizes, is no longer instinctive for him: "Each moment that I live, I must think where to place my fingers, and press them down with no confidence of hearing a chord." Yet for all he protests about his lack of skill in life, in transcribing it onto a page, he has laboriously achieved that euphony that seems to elude him, as well as the insight that "we are all pilgrims, faltering toward divorce." In addition, he realizes that "the world is the host; it must be chewed," although he may not be chewing the world as vigorously as he wishes. In writing this story, however, he at least attempts to do with reality what he did with the host in his youth—"to embrace and tentatively shape, the wafer with the teeth"—hoping that the reward for his fictive confession is a "refreshment" similar to the sensation that followed public confession in the country church of his youth.

"The Rescue," related by an omniscient narrator through the viewpoint of Caroline Harris, is one of Updike's rare excursions into the female consciousness. Suspecting that her husband Norman is having an affair with Alice, a neighboring divorcée who has accompanied them on a ski trip, Caroline begins to read intimations of his infidelity in "every tilt of circumstance, every smothered swell and deliberate contraindication." The only novice skier in the group, she approaches the slopes with trepidation augmented by her sense that this trip will force her to confront their marital problems. The ski lift, like her suspicions, pulls her in a "dangerous direction" to the "bare altitude" of the mountain peak, where she simultaneously resolves to follow two challenging courses: skiing "Greased Lightning," the expert run, and leaving Norman, whose infidelity seems confirmed by the suspect pair's words and actions. Since Norman and her son have gone ahead, Caroline descends the slope with Alice, suddenly infused with a new poise: "swooping in complementary zigzags, the two women descended a long white waterfall linked as if by love" (*MS*, 196). Updike's image metaphorically captures the pattern of the women's enforced pairing; linked by love of the same man, they may be destined to crisscross on their descent as long as both the Harrises' marriage and the suspected affair continue.

Their pursuit of the men is halted by an accident that unexpectedly presents Caroline with an emblem of her own inner wounds and swings the pendulum of trust in the opposite direction. The woman they encounter, suffering from a broken leg and a broken marriage, elicits Caroline's compassion and foreshadows her own potential "crack-up" and the dangers of divorce, the course she has chosen out of anger and jealousy. Yet focusing on another woman's "universe of misfortune" begins to heal the breach of marital faith that has led her to detect clues of infidelity beneath the surface of everyday events. The same compassion and patience she extends to the injured woman, Caroline realizes, will be successful weapons if she chooses to battle Alice, whose "finicking" behavior finally convinces her that Norman would never be attracted to their neighbor. Although the story's title ostensibly refers to the slightly bungled rescue of the injured skier, Caroline also rescues a provisional confidence in her husband, which may, however, be no more than a pleasant illusion.

The final two stories, both concerned with returns to nature, provide the volume with a perhaps not altogether coincidental symmetry, although this countermovement is ultimately more ironic than triumphant since access to nature proves problematic. Like "The Indian," "The Family Meadow," sketches a still life of an epoch that will soon fall prey to progress and give way to a less desirable one. Its tone is somewhat elegiac, yet for the present, the family keeps its tenuous hold on the meadow that embodies continuity with its rural history. This family, poised on the edge of dissolution, is caught between "the music of reminiscence" and the changes wrought by time and the encroaching transformation of rural country into suburban neighborhoods. The presence of Karen, a half-Italian granddaughter, is the first sign that change is in the offing; not only is she from different stock, but her age and suburban upbringing alienate her somewhat from the communal rites. For her generation, the past and the country do not nourish but rather "island" them from the familiar sources of satisfaction depicted in Updike's transcription of "middleness." The story's waning action occurs, appropriately, after Jesse's warning about the creek's pollution, a foreshadowing of the inevitable change that his stubborn clinging to the property cannot forestall. Seeking to perpetuate the illusion of unspoiled rural solidarity, he frames the family portrait so as to exclude the encroaching ranch houses. Persistent voices of progress may whisper "Sell," but Updike's story poses the implicit response: "at what cost?"

Balancing the opening hymn to the rural Olinger past, "The Hermit" concludes the volume by reconsidering the feasibility of a Thoreauvian retreat into nature. Stanley, a part-time janitor and construction worker, leaves a life of quiet desperation and moves to a decaying cabin on unused land belonging to a steel company. After partially renovating the cabin (his carpentry an unmistakable allusion to Christ), he discovers that being a hermit is the most suitable vocation for a misfit such as himself—a "non-native" of the "heavy damp climate" of humanity. Intrusions by his more conventional brothers, who consider him eccentric, and by his girlfriend Loretta, whom he fears will ransack his private life, only drive him deeper into solitude. Stanley's withdrawal reaches an extreme when he smashes his mirror, determined not to seek reflections of himself either in a looking glass or in others. He senses a potential disciple in a young boy who has been to visit with his brothers' children, yet the boy, on a return visit, becomes frightened after discovering him bathing in the river and flees when the naked hermit pursues him in an attempt to clarify the misunderstanding. The eventual repercussions of this event bring the forces of convention and authority in search of Stanley, abruptly shattering the peace of his sojourn in nature just as the gap between himself and the spiritual essence behind nature appears to be closing.

As Larry Taylor points out, however, Stanley's sojourn is more of a parody of Thoreau's life at Walden than the portrait of an unadulterated idyll; such details as Stanley's bathing in the shallow stream, Taylor argues, constitute "absurd echoes" of Thoreau's transcendental experiences in plumbing the depths of Walden pond and his own character.[24] Stanley practices a type of Thoreauvian economy, but while Thoreau hoes beans, reads classic works, and keeps a journal that he later transforms into *Walden*, the less self-sufficient and intellectually duller Stanley buys canned food, reads an actress's memoirs and a novel of manners, and writes nothing. Unlike the narrator of "Leaves," who verbally captures nature's precision during his retreat to nature in the wake of a divorce, Stanley's withdrawal is not motivated by a disaster in love, or, as his youngest brother initially suspects, for private trysts; nor is he engaged in a philosophical or religious quest. Instead, his plan emerges from an accidental discovery and ends abruptly before his pastoral retreat leads to enlightenment.

Two echoes of the music motif repeated in a number of stories punctuate "The Hermit." When Stanley first discovers the cabin, the exposed floor beams appear "harplike" and his "rhythmic motions" as he steps from one to another evoke a memory of an uncle who played a church organ. This initial scene's joyful music is later transposed into another key, where nature's "finely tuned strata of distinctions, fixed yet pliant, seemed a greater harp, either waiting to be struck or else played so continually that an instant of silence would have boomed in his ears" (*MS*, 254). Stanley hears nature's music, but the end result is merely "a delicately altered sense of actuality" that furthers his estrangement; intuitions honed, he remains locked in nature's silence, unable to articulate any of his experience or withstand any pressure from society. While he does not consciously seek God in the forest, he becomes accustomed to its silence, and begins to sense a presence waiting to be answered. Updike may mean for the reader to take Stanley's imminent religious experience seriously, as a near-epiphany that might eventually have arrived,[25] yet finally "the thing that wants to be answered" turns out not to be God but the outside world, alerted of Stanley's behavior by his would-be disciple.

"The Hermit," however, is not a cynical fable of society's triumph over man's primal instincts, but rather an ironic observation on the failures of both extremes. While Updike does not debunk the pastoral ideal in this story, it appears to be too fragile to sustain an enduring retreat, and, like the past which the narrator of "In Football Season" seeks, perpetually beyond reach. The truest recaptures of these mutable realms in *The Music School* are those accomplished in fictive music—not simple, remembered melodies, but those which blend the different layers of experience and reconcile the inevitable disharmony between youthful expectations and maturity's diminished reality.

Blocked Art and Bygone Ardor: Bech's Burden

"The Bulgarian Poetess," awarded the O. Henry First Prize in 1965, was an early indication that Updike could step outside Olinger and Tarbox and project his imagination into a character sharing his vocation, but quite unlike himself. Creating a Jewish novelist from Manhattan nine years older than himself, Updike observes, "was a way of unpacking the kinds of experience that only a writer has . . . via an alter-ego who wasn't myself."[26] Next to Rabbit Angstrom, with whom he shares a certain restlessness, Bech has proved to be Updike's most enduring character. His exploits comprise two unified volumes of short stories published a dozen years apart, *Bech: A Book* (1970) and *Bech Is Back* (1982), and this literary alter-ego has twice taken on a playfully independent life, irreverently interviewing his creator in the pages of the *New York Times Book Review* upon the publication of the first two sequels to *Rabbit, Run*.[27]

While some critics persist in treating the Bech collections as novels, Updike lists them under the heading "Short Stories" in the publications list included in his other volumes. His continued refusal to adopt the more prestigious label clearly indicates that these works occupy a generic territory somewhere between the novel and the miscellaneous short story collection. Concerning *Bech: A Book*, Updike states, "the whole texture of the book was that of short stories, and I couldn't bring myself to call it a novel" (Reilly, 161). Updike has remarked how this first volume, whose subtitle betrays the difficulty attaching the label "novel," was "conceived piecemeal," using Bech as the vehicle for different sets of impressions that together comprise an extended reflection on the American writer's condition. While most of the stories were published separately, the book's conclusion and a bridging story were written specifically to round out the volume. *Bech Is Back* likewise assembles a number of previously published episodes with unpublished stories. Bech's marriage to Bea (who becomes his mistress in the first volume) and the production of a new novel provide the sequel with more narrative momentum. Still, unlike subsequent chapters in a novel, each "episode" retains the qualities of an independent story: a sense of unity, internal coherence, and closure. Updike has made no effort to edit repeated details, as one composing a novel might; instead, he retains them for cross reference.

The Bech volumes are short story sequences, a form whose fast-growing ranks also include *Olinger Stories* and *Too Far to Go*. In the former, primarily an arrangement of previously collected stories, the local boy undergoes a slow maturation over the course of the book, as he prepares to transcend his rural hometown. In the latter, which involved a harvesting from other collections as well as filling out the book, the Maples recapitulate the same marital struggles on various fronts. In this respect, they bear more of a resemblance to Bech, who is perpetually sidetracked by the trappings accorded to famous authors and unable to move forward in his career. In finally choosing to divorce, the Maples transcend their marital problems in a way that Bech can never escape his trap of celebrity. Unlike his suburban counterpart Rabbit Angstrom, who makes extended runs across the span of four novels, Bech's career is sketched in the discrete but loosely connected segments of the short story sequence.

The incidents in Bech's life never seem to coalesce into a neat casual chain, and such discontinuity may be one of the problems that prevents Bech from duplicating his early success as an artist. Although a temporal progression exists within both volumes, they retain a picaresque quality, with the protagonist undergoing little essential change over the course of events, despite his experience in new locales and whatever crises he has undergone. If anything, Bech's powerlessness to end his drift and to shape his own destiny is exacerbated, although his consciousness of the situation becomes more acute. In the preface to *Bech: A Book*, Bech, playing the role of critic, remarks on this static quality when he characterizes his portrait in Updike's manuscript as that of a "monotonous hero."[28]

Perhaps Bech's exploits seem monotonous to himself, but the Bech books have been critically well-received, a surprise that encouraged Updike (generally the target of at least a few negative reviews) to continue having fun at the expense of his alter-ego. Furthermore, using Bech as a protagonist, Updike states, "permits me to write without holding back, without compensating for the character's mind" (Reilly, 161). As a fellow writer, Bech may be an intellectually kindred spirit who shares some of the professional dilemmas his creator faces, but his fabled block is by no means characteristic of the prolific Updike, who has stated that "a day when I have produced nothing printable, when I have not gotten any words out, is a day lost and damned" (*SC*, 108).

Bech may thus embody a projection of Updike's fears about the diminishment of a printless existence; in addition, Updike admits, he shares the faults that paralyze Bech: "he wants his work to be absolutely right, and he frequently worries that nothing he does is ever quite good enough" (Reilly, 162). Both experience the tribulations of the public life an author must lead and the panic of asking "what next?" after each book, lecture, or award. Nonetheless, given Updike's book-a-year publishing pace, his empathy with a blocked writer is remarkable. Bech, whose travels mirror those of his creator, owes his existence to Updike's desire to find some way to conserve and use to advantage the very experience that Bech is unable to transmute into art.

Yet Bech, unmarried, Jewish, nine years older, and a denizen of Manhattan, purposefully diverges from his creator, who exploits this distance for a number of purposes. Bech provides a mask from behind which Updike can playfully rebuke the literary industry for the writer's current condition. In the preface Bech congratulates Updike for being the first to concern himself with "our oppression, with the silken mechanism whereby America reduces her writers to imbecility and cozenage. Envied like Negroes, disbelieved in like angels, we veer between the harlotry of the lecture platform and the torture of the writing desk" (*BB*, vi). While Bech may feel like an exploited harlot in the writer's public role, he readily accedes to its demands because he is no longer able to discipline himself to the "torture of the writing desk." After reciting an exaggerated litany of grievances against publishers, Bech dramatizes his frustration: "I could mutilate myself like sainted Origen, I could keen like Jeremiah." Updike undeniably uses Bech as an illustration of the debasement of authorship, but establishes a clear distinction between himself and his "victimized" character. Bech may safely mask a certain bitterness, but Updike's oblique attack is balanced by an awareness of the writer's complicity in adopting the celebrity role. Neither Bech book is a jeremiad; both are wry appraisals of the literary world's potentially deleterious effect on its own.

Updike's attitude toward Bech is clearly an ambivalent one. While Bech engages his sympathies as one who suffers at the hands of the modern literary establishment, Updike maintains an ironic distance from his paralyzed hero. Like Melville's Bartelby, Bech "prefers not to" write, but society provides the unproductive author with an approved and lucrative alternative. Quoting Proust in his essay "The Writer Lectures," Updike provides a surprisingly appropriate description of Bech: "How many for this reason turn aside from writing! What tasks do men not take upon themselves in order to evade this task. Every public event . . . furnishes the writer with a fresh excuse for not attempting to decipher this book. . . . But these are mere excuses, the truth being that he has not or no longer has genius, that is to say instinct. For instinct dictates our duty and the intellect supplies us with pretexts for evading it."[29] Although Bech's writerly instinct may suffer in his role as cultural emissary and celebrity, he has consciously chosen this conveniently provided path of evasion. In the same essay, Updike goes on to admit that even the lecture circuit may ultimately serve a valuable purpose: although it may be a public "confession that one has deserted one's post," such appearances satisfy the writer's need to assert his humanity and momentarily allow him to "taste the ancient bardic role" (25).

For Updike, however, the role of literary celebrity is clearly a lesser one than that of the vital artist absorbing experience and creating fiction. Like many of Updike's other characters, Bech craves escape from the complexities of existence. Yet while such evasions can unwittingly lead younger characters to epiphanies which nurture artistic growth or thin the veil of innocence, Bech, the matured artist, continues to drift further from his purpose. He seeks travel and love merely as stimuli, quick fixes for a sagging ego that provide expressive satisfaction yet divert him from art. In the process, however, Bech seems curiously insulated from any real harm. The recurrent romantic disappointments and missed opportunities are shrugged off; even his existential "panic" in *Bech: A Book* somehow recedes in the gap between "Bech Panics" and "Bech Swings?" Indeed, if Bech suffered intently—if he were a pure victim— his character would descend to the level of an ethnic stereotype.[30] The comedy operates on many different levels in both books, but rarely at the complete expense of Bech, who seems conscious that he is becoming a literary creation rather than producing one, but powerless to change his life. No tragic fall occurs in the course of the books—only a struggle within the prison Bech has had a hand in making.

Bech has a direct role in shaping the reader's image of him in *Bech: A Book*, which opens with a preface attributed to the perpetually blocked writer. The only piece he has written in 1969, this preface is a belabored benediction that took nine days to write. Updike—who confesses in an interview that he composed the preface in a day (*PUP*, 506)—solidifies the ruse by having Bech question the exactness of the characterization but admit that "John" has captured his essential qualities. In a passage that Updike uses to anticipate critical response, Bech dissects his portrait to find allusions to Roth, Bellow, Mailer, Singer, and Salinger, as well as "something Waspish, theological, scared, and insulatingly ironical that derives, my wild surmise is, from you" (*BB*, v). Bech also claims to have a hand in the text: a fictional editor's note alerts us that the "list of suggested deletions, falsifications, suppressions, and rewordings" Bech provides have all been "scrupulously incorporated." Through this complex mechanism of authorial distance, Updike anticipates the collection's major theme of the author becoming a self-created character whose life becomes a consumable public fiction.

Both Bech books follow a similar pattern: a section of foreign travels is juxtaposed with a series of adventures at home; the latter concludes the volume and re-establishes a tenuous and ambivalent equilibrium in Bech's life. In addition to the seven stories and the unifying preface, *Bech: A Book* contains a selection from Bech's Russian journal (an abortive story) and a bibliography of Bech's work, both of which lend further plausibility to his existence. In the latter, Updike not only constructs a plausible career but also settles a few literary scores with reviewers such as Norman Podhoretz and John Aldridge who have not treated his works kindly. Ironically enough, some of the same critics who previously castigated Updike for his limitations or for not fulfilling his promise praise the Bech books effusively. Perhaps the liberating sense of satire and the comic veneer that overlays the barbed treatment of the literary establishment set these books apart from Updike's other stories. Yet the themes which Updike treats in *Bech: A Book* are not incongruous with those examined in previous and subsequent work: the panic of imminent mortality; the sense of vocation as the source of self-definition; the ambivalence of attained rewards; the conflict between self-realization and love; and the tension between art and ardor.

The narrator of the opening story, "Rich in Russia," sets the book's tone; ostensibly a college professor presenting a lecture, he begins his class on Bech by dispelling the myth that being a famous author in America guarantees riches. Thus Bech's finances, not his "quixotic virtue," keep him rooted in his grim Manhattan apartment and motivate his participation in an East-West cultural exchange. The intrusive narrative voice calls attention to Bech's status as part of the academic curriculum, resulting in a life open to scrutiny. Although class ends at this story's conclusion, a similar but less overt authoritative voice seems to dominate the others. Only in the fifth story, "Bech Panics," does a narrator step out, though he seems less certain of his account than the lecturer in "Rich in Russia." Calling attention to the narrators reminds readers that literary biography constructs a character—perhaps even a caricature—at least one remove from the subject. Furthermore, the fiction that Bech himself has had a shaping hand in the final product further complicates the question of whether any such endeavor—making a life into a book, or a piece of it into a lecture—might be reductive or distorting, merely a stab in the dark at truth.

Such meditations on the fiction-making process, however, quickly recede into the background as Bech himself takes the stage. "Artistically blocked but socially fluent," Bech is perfectly cast in the role of cultural emissary. When he goes through the required motions of rubbing noses with Russia's literary lions and attending state-sponsored meetings with ministers, critics, and assorted literati, he senses the inherent element of performance. However, his sense of worth suffers when he compares himself to such Russian giants as Yevtushenko, next to whom he feels like "a graying, furtively stylish rat indifferently permitted to gnaw and roam behind the wainscotting of a fire trap about to be demolished anyway" (*BB*, 15). Self-conscious of inadequacy, Bech nonetheless continues to play the part, secretly relishing the status of a minor celebrity in a country that reminds him nostalgically of his neglected Jewish past.

The sudden riches he receives there, however, are an ambivalent blessing. Ironically, its source is the Russian government, which showers him with rubles in the guise of royalties for recent translations of his work, not the American publishing industry, which has taken advantage of Bech's early lack of business sense. Feeling guilty for robbing the proletariat, he determines to spend the money there, enlisting the aid of Kate, his devoted guide and translator. Unfortunately, as Bech discovers, spending large sums of money in a non-consumer-oriented society is difficult. Kate seizes on this quest as a way to pass time with Bech, but spending the rubles develops into an obsession that blinds him to the possibility of any other relationship between them. Except for a visit to Tolstoy's house, Bech, as Kate observes, indulgently treats his visit to Russia "like a picnic."

Although Bech finally succeeds in exhausting his supply of rubles, he has not reaped the full value of Russia's gifts, as he realizes after Kate's moist farewell kiss. Still, his pangs about not sleeping with her are brief and seem to arise more from a lingering sense of missed opportunity rather than from any strong personal feelings. His departure is further complicated when his suitcase, crammed full of furs and Russian translations of his works, bursts open on the runway as he scrambles to catch his plane. While Bech's furs and cracked watches are recovered, he leaves the burdensome books behind. Suitcases heavy with booty, Bech can no longer "travel light" (the title of his first book), but the souvenir books are excess literary baggage of a reputation that weighs him down. Although Kate promises to send them, they never appear; the narrator's concluding speculations about the reasons leave his students to puzzle about indeterminacy.

Wearing the astrakhan hat purchased in Russia, Bech gets some inkling of the types of missed connection that will dominate "Bech in Rumania" when the American Embassy personnel fail to recognize him at the Bucharest airport. Their plan to use Bech to stir up the "hot" underground writers who are supposedly anxious to meet him is obstructed by the head of the Writers' Union, who behaves more like a state puppet than a revolutionary. Ironically, when Bech accidentally meets with one of these writers, a friend of his guide Petrescu, very little exchange takes place, as the two seem "on opposite sides of a wall" of mutual disinterest and alcoholic stupor. In fact, the only words they exchange, concerning their fictional subjects, illustrate a wider gulf: while the Rumanian writes about peasants, Bech's novels focus on the bourgeoisie. Most of their evening together is spent in a Westernized underground nightclub witnessing an endless floor show that degenerates into a parody of American culture for Bech. Upon learning of this meeting, an Embassy official compliments him on a "sensational job"; playing along, Bech satirically compares himself to "a sort of low-flying U-2," obliquely signaling how little human contact has actually transpired.

From the muddle of events, however, he gleans truths of lasting value. Despite the fact that Bech continually mocks Petrescu, the stoic translator helps him relearn "what he was tempted to forget in America, that reading can be the best part of a man's life" (*BB*, 48). The story's subtitle also draws attention to the chauffeur, a laconic Rumanian who drives with reckless speed and incessantly honking horn, ignoring the wishes of his unnerved passenger by pretending not to understand English. The chauffeur embodies the enigma of Rumania, so unlike the "tough and heroic naivete"of Russia; he personifies "something shrugging and effete [that] seemed to leave room for a vein of energetic evil" (*BB*, 39)—in the face of which Bech remains perplexed and powerless. In contrast, Bech notes, Herman Melville (for whom he shares Updike's fondness), "courageously faced our native terror. He went for it right between its wide-set little pig eyes, and it shattered his genius like a lance" (*BB*, 37). When Bech's fear of the chauffeur's Ahab-like madness evokes a memory of a childhood tormenter, he realizes that he is not a noble failure like Melville, but rather a writer who has squandered his gifts in fruitless attempts to recapture such experiences. At the story's conclusion, clouds blot out a country that to Bech has never been clear: Bech's answer in French to a Slavic passenger sums up his trip: I do not understand; I am an American.

While both translators in the first two stories serve Bech in capacities beyond tour guide, Vera Glavanakova, the title character in "The Bulgarian Poetess," has a more profound effect on him. Arriving unexpectedly at what begins as yet another predictable exercise with party officials and undistinguished literati, the poetess embodies a dedication to art with which Bech has lost touch. Deftly constructed, the story begins in media res with this meeting; after circling back to Bech's arrival to fill in the relevant past, Updike unexpectedly returns to the opening line about halfway into the tale. Although the first Bech story written, it still ranks among the best; moreover, its concern with unfulfilled longing ties it closely with the other stories in *The Music School*, where it was first collected.

Bech's arrival hardly seems hopeful. While Rumania seems impenetrable, Bulgaria is experiencing a flare-up of anti-American turmoil, and Bech feels thinly disguised in his astrakhan hat from Moscow, making its third appearance in the book. Retreating into his hotel room, he seeks comfort in reading Hawthorne's "Roger Malvin's Burial," but instead experiences a mild version of the "panic" which becomes the subject of a later story. Alone in an alien land on what coincidentally turns out to be the first day of Hanukkah, Bech is haunted by the image of Malvin's solitary death, sensing that he too is cut off behind the Iron Curtain.

Yet Bulgaria offers more positive experiences than the two previous Communist countries; instead of the taciturn chauffeur, he encounters a talking tree, "a great leafy loudspeaker" symbolic of poetic profusion and inspiration—a counterpoint to the hotel listening devices. While Bech may seem more of a hollow shell in the previous two stories, in "The Bulgarian Poetess" the reader becomes aware of the artist and seeker who has retreated behind the post of weariness and irony after his artistic powers declined and he sank "deeper and deeper into eclectic sexuality and bravura narcissism, as his search for plain truth carried him further and further into treacherous realms of fantasy" (*BB*, 49–50). The Bulgarians lavish praise on his early works, but when their toasts only echo words he has heard previously, Bech's distaste for his posing becomes "focused into a small brown spot on a pear in a bowl so shiningly poised before his eyes." After Vera appears, however, this same pear, formerly botched by its nagging imperfection and promise of inevitable decay, lies halved before him, "golden and moist," revealing an alluring interior waiting to be enjoyed.

Bech realizes he may merely be suffering a type of "romantic vertigo," but revels in the heightened sensitivity. The young girls of the Moscow ballet school, like Vera, embody an enviable poise and a completeness, quite unlike the disjunction he feels between the self who wrote "Travel Light" and the traveling showman who seems to have jettisoned his artistic integrity. Yet Bech's writerly eye still operates, as the scene at Rilke monastery demonstrates: the beauty of the simple scene with the peasant woman and her son evokes a "nameless absence" attached to that "first landscape" that Bech believes to be the quest of all love. Vera stirs up the murky depths of Bech's emotional and intellectual life from which the creative artist draws, but he is finally unable to rededicate himself to art and discipline himself to write.

Unfortunately, Bech's experience ultimately illustrates that "actuality is a running impoverishment of possibility," a lesson not surprising to many of Updike's other characters. He and Vera will eventually separate, like the two cleaved halves of the pear. The Bulgarians and the rest of the Eastern Bloc are ultimately "people behind the mirror" through which Bech cannot cross, unlike the young princess in the ballet who leaps nightly through her mirror to tryst with a wizard. In the end, at a cocktail party that is Bech's last opportunity to see Vera, "the mirror had gone opaque, and gave him back only himself"—the literary celebrity whose reputation blocks the fulfillment of his desires. While Vera may be Bech's soulmate, their brief liaison consists of only three meetings and a quick exchange of inscribed books, in which Bech's somewhat formal expression of regret is exchanged for Vera's chagrined regrets about her English spelling, concluded with a word that "looked like 'leave' but must have been 'love'"—an ambiguity that signals how the two are intertwined. Paradoxically, the love that grows from separation and unfulfilled longing seems to be its purest form, creating the mystery that temporarily revives Bech's dormant ardor and his reverence for art.

In "Bech Takes Pot Luck," the scene shifts back to America, where the restless author, yearning to be fashionable and hoping to be showered with female adulation, joins celebrities and other media figures— some of the very people responsible for that "silken mechanism" whose reductive effect he decries—for vacation on Martha's Vineyard. Bech's trip with his mistress Norma, her recently divorced sister Bea, and Bea's three children takes an unexpected turn when he is recognized by Wendell Morrison, a former student from a creative writing seminar at Columbia who insinuates himself into Bech's entourage, seeking contact with and approval from his admired former teacher. Norma's discovery that Wendell has some LSD only exacerbates her dissatisfaction with Bech and her craving for a drug trip that she hopes will change her static life. Wendell's introduction of marijuana into the group as a "trial run" to determine whether Norma is a candidate for LSD wreaks havoc on their menage. Bech's luck with pot is not good—it makes him ill—but the experience has unexpected consequences: in the aftermath of their experiment, his relationship with Norma comes undone and she is displaced as his mistress by Bea.

Threatened by Wendell's youth and competence, and repulsed by his unruly fiction, Bech takes every opportunity to sideswipe him with irony; in response, Wendell becomes even more worshipful of his "guru." To Bech, Wendell embodies the ascendancy of undisciplined art and the decay of moral standards. Still, afraid of losing Norma as much as he is afraid of being out-of-date, Bech consents to "pot luck," a controlled experiment where Bech, Norma, and Bea provide the dinner, and Wendell brings pot for dessert. Thus Bech becomes the dutiful pupil as Wendell instructs his former teacher how to smoke marijuana; as they smoke, the drug exaggerates certain qualities in each. Norma becomes greedier and more abrasive as she sucks ravenously on the pipe, complaining that she is not getting high and berating Bech as the "safest man in America since they retired Tom Dewey." Guilt about her divorce nagging at her conscience, Bea sees threatening shapes outside the windows. While Wendell becomes an even more worshipful pupil, Bech feels himself swell in size and importance, parading his French and his verbal wit. Ironically, Bech experiences a rare but fleeting clarity of vision before he succumbs to nausea and symbolically vomits up the experience. Thus purged, he feels "a sadness, a terror" that he has been unable to emulate Joyce, "whose humble suppliant Bech had been"; thrown together with Bea, who praises his work, he begins an affair that will eventually shatter his relationship with her sister.

"Bech Panics," the most serious of these comic stories, employs a unique device—a series of slides—to explore the reasons behind the existential dread that overtakes the author during a visit to a Virginia women's college. Related by a narrative voice reminiscent of the lecturer in "Rich in Russia," "Bech Panics" consists of speculations about the events behind and connections between the scenes depicted in the slides; beyond them, "there is semi-darkness, and the oppressive roar of the fan that cools the projector, and the fumbling, snapping noises as the projectionist irritably hunts for slides that are not there" (*BB*, 99). The narrative frame increases consciousness of the fiction-making process at work and highlights the amount of conjecture necessary to fill in the gaps and construct a coherent narrative about this crucial incident in Bech's life. The story's form thus parallels that of the book as a whole, in which the author has provided a series of pictures and the reader must participate in unifying this loosely connected sequence of episodes.

Updike has stated that he composed "Bech Panics" specifically as a "bridge" between "the Bech of the Vineyard story to the somewhat older and rather hallucinating writer of London" (*PUP*, 506). Yet Bech's "hallucinating" may reach its height in this story, when his tenuously balanced world is shaken by a severe panic. As the customary supports of his beliefs begin to crumble, his imagination jettisons them as pleasant fictions and his crisis worsens. This panic may be mildly foreshadowed in the previous story when he feels the momentary "terror" about his inability ever to equal Joyce's achievement. Here, however, the chaos of family life and his uneasiness with Bea in the dual role of lover and mother contribute to Bech's anxiety when he visits suburban Ossining, John Cheever country and site of the infamous prison Sing Sing. Bech panics not merely because he feels in danger of losing his independence within this ready-made family but because of a more serious existential crisis that the texture of family life seems to exacerbate; even his beloved block, he fears, might not survive the ensuing domestication. To put off the inevitable, he eagerly accepts an invitation to speak when he is seduced by a honeyed Southern accent, a large fee, and perhaps, as Bea jealously notes, "the remote chance you can sack out with Scarlett O'Hara."

In Slide One he is surrounded "seraglio style" by young women—an image which, on the surface, might depict the fulfillment of his fantasies. Yet Southern fecundity combines with the coeds' "massed fertility" in a spiritual assault that topples a tenuous balance within him. His outward poise masks extreme self-consciousness of the motions that merely cover up the life's inherent meaninglessness and keep the abyss at a safe distance: "Death hung behind everything, a real skeleton about to leap through a door in these false walls of books. . . . He felt what was expected of him, and felt himself performing it, and felt the fakery of the performance, and knew these levels of perception as the shifting sands of absurdity, nullity, death" (*BB*, 110–11).

Bech maintains surface composure even as reality seems to unravel before him, often in horrific visions that catalogue a microscopic, historical, and/or biological collage of events and processes behind each moment. No wonder that in Slide Two he is unable to sleep and his panic assumes a tangible shape—"It felt pasty and stiff. Mixed with the fear, a kind of coagulant, was shame" (*BB*, 117)—and the insomniac Bech becomes his own worst enemy. Ashamed of this "adolescent religious crisis," Bech becomes his most hostile critic, bemoaning his degeneration into a crowd pleaser, his cold-bloodedness with women, his unloving treatment of his characters, and the flimsiness and insincerity of his work—all valid complaints that a comic simile helps deflect somewhat: "As soon sleep in a cement mixer as amid these revelations."

Bech takes one step further in this story's "compressed religious evolution" during Slide Three, the scene in the forest. At the nadir of his panic, his despair elicits a vague petition: prostrate on the damp earth, he prays to "Someone, Something, for mercy"; overwhelmed by a vivid sense of absence, "He had created God." Lest this epiphanic moment in nature be too pure, however, Updike concludes the interlude with red ants biting Bech's thumb. This small surge of faith is counterpointed during the poetry reading by the resounding certitude of the Sidney Lanier poem that celebrates the "flood-tide" of faith arising at darkest night.

Yet Bech's respite from panic is finally achieved not by poetry or prayer but with the help of Ruth Eichenbaum, the Jewish literature professor from New York who introduces herself in Slide Four. When this Ruth "amid the alien corn" offers herself sexually as a potential minister to Bech's malaise, the formerly unobtrusive narrator steps out and proposes two potential conclusions to this episode. In the first, Bech adamantly refuses her proposition, displaying an admirable determination to conquer his panic himself. In the alternative, which is perhaps more in character with his reputation, Bech and Ruth make love to counteract his dread. The narrator becomes almost Bech-like at the conclusion of this bit of existential pornography as he bemoans the futility of language in describing their experience: "Enough. Like Bech, we reach a point where words seem horrible, maggots on the carcass of reality, feeding, proliferating; we seek peace in silence and reduction" (*BB*, 130). By calling attention to linguistic inadequacy and the speculative element in narrative, both of which subvert any attempt at truth, he suggests yet another cause for panic—one that perhaps sheds some light on Bech's continued block.

The discovery of a misplaced fifth slide depicting the morning after does not clarify prurient curiosity about the evening's conclusion—although it does allow for a neater conclusion to the episode. The reader's urge for closure is satisfied when Bech, spiritually enervated but financially bolstered by the speaker's fee, is restored to New York and his mistress. If Bech's citation to the winner of the poetry contest is any indication of his state of mind (and not empty rhetoric), he has not totally lost faith in the redemptive power of language; although the winner's poems lack polish, he praises them as "gracious toward the world, and in their acceptance of our perishing frailty, downright brave" (*BB*, 131)—an attitude which he can only hope to emulate.

"Bech Swings?" takes Bech abroad once more, not as a cultural ambassador but as part of a promotion for a British collection of his works. Arriving in London as the daffodils begin to bloom, Bech hopes for a corresponding renewal of his creative spirit, which has ebbed to such a point that he writes nothing but reviews and answers his mail with a series of "repellent rubber stamps." Such reclusive crankiness begins to seem less justified to Bech as his artistic fallowness continues. Travel has not provided the impetus to write, and all his loves, including the recent switch of mistresses, have done little to reawaken the artist within. Still, Bech retains some idealism, hoping that perhaps "one more woman, one more leap would bring him safe into that high calm pool of immortality where Proust and Hawthorne and Catullus float, glassy-eyed and belly up" (*BB*, 135).

The leap across the Atlantic, however, does not prove to be the route to such transcendence, despite his British publisher's attempts to lionize him and his brief fling with Merissa, who—as Bech discovers after the fact—writes a gossip column for her father's tabloid. Although she reduces Bech to a small item in her column, Merissa suffuses her account of their "swinging" exploits with a genuine fondness. She temporarily revitalizes Bech's dormant artistic spirit and becomes the prototype of the central character in the new novel that begins to take shape, complete with a title that signals renewed ambition: *Think Big*. The novel in outline reeks of melodrama, but its conception is evidence that Bech the artist survives: despite problems he foresees in adapting Merissa to the American scene, "Already small things from here and there, kept alive by some kink in his forgetting mechanism, had begun to fly together, to fit" (*BB*, 157). While Bech has qualms about transmuting his love affair into fiction, his plans come across as less reprehensible than what Merissa and Tuttle do to him.

Tuttle, an American graduate student who mercilessly interviews Bech over the course of three days, promises *Observer* readers "the real Bech," but ultimately twists Bech's words and uses the article as an opportunity to attack his work, personality, and politics. Much of what Bech says obliquely echoes opinions that have been extracted by Updike's own interviewers, but Updike is more interested in depicting the parasitic nature of the interview process than in airing his own views. As the insatiable Tuttle probes for material, Bech obligingly provides opinions on the theory and practice of fiction, literary critics, Jewish laughter, and American culture, groping for "the lost wristwatch of truth" a writer seems obligated to provide—only to be rudely treated in print when Tuttle uses few of his actual words.

Unfortunately, the final interview curtails the genesis of the novel-in-progress, although Bech desperately attempts to revive the book (and his sexual potency) in Merissa's bedroom. Desperation leads to failure on both counts, as he self-consciously sees himself acting out his passion "in ten-point type, upon the warm white paper of her sliding skin." Merissa's diagnosis is that Bech is unnecessarily impotent as an artist, and she advises him to "learn to replace ardor with art"—a lesson that Bech should know from his literary idols—Joyce and Eliot—and from William Wordsworth, all of whom are quoted in the story. Merissa merely reminds Bech of what he should have learned from the Bulgarian poetess, but his insistence that "art *is* ardor" foreshadows the attitude that he will carry forward to *Think Big* when he finally does write it in *Bech Is Back*; unable to summon the powers of craft, he will attempt to rely on ardor alone to sustain the outbursts of prose necessary to finish the work.

After visiting Leo Tolstoy's estate in "Rich in Russia," Bech admires the physical ascent of Tolstoy's workspace as his career progressed: "*War and Peace* in the cellar, *Anna Karenina* on the first floor, and *Resurrection* upstairs. Do you think he's writing a fourth novel in Heaven?" (*BB*, 16). His comment assumes an ironic slant in the final story, "Bech Enters Heaven," where the luminaries whose achievements have earned them a place in writer's heaven—the literary academy—are well past their prime. Written to round out the book rather than for independent publication, the story is a fitting conclusion to Bech's aimless pilgrimage. What should be a milestone of achievement—admission into an honorary literary society resembling the American Academy of Arts and Letters—ultimately provides the same ambivalent satisfaction as love and travel have; actuality indeed proves to be "the running impoverishment of possibility," as this "haven of lasting accomplishment" which to the young Bech promises transcendence of time looks quite different from the other side.

Although last in the sequence, the story reaches back to the most distant past so far—Bech's adolescence—in order to show how he has come full circle. In the first of two corresponding scenes, Bech's mother, attempting to reorient her precocious adolescent son, occupies the place of the women who guide Bech in the previous stories. She leads him beyond their Jewish enclave to the north Manhattan bastion of literary culture, where he learns "that there were other types of Heaven, less agitated and more elevated than the school, more compact and less tragic than Yankee Stadium" (*BB*, 177). Each member of this artistic pantheon, Bech observes, has suffered the "crystallization of fame," but despite this forewarning, he elevates this haven of art to a Platonic ideal.

When Bech unwittingly reenters the building later in life, he does so through another portal. Not until he is on stage with the other canonized literary figures does he realize that he is on "the other side of the veil" that seemed to separate him from these luminaries in his youth. As in "The Bulgarian Poetess," where the East and the world of art exist on the other side of the mirror, the motif of doubleness informs "Bech Enters Heaven." Yet as a participant rather than a spectator—one who has crossed through the mirror—Bech becomes disillusioned with his former ideal. The awards ceremony more closely resembles a three-ring circus than the solemn occasion he remembers: one member walks out, while another exposes a psychedelic pig painted on his chest. Up close, the literary idols of his youth are exposed as senile, seedy, and inattentive. Induction seems predicated on literary stasis; by implication, Bech may soon reach the dissipated, sterile condition of the literary fossils that inhabit this pantheon. The induction ceremony becomes slightly surreal when Bech momentarily believes that he sees his deceased mother among the audience, reinforcing the metaphoric equation between induction and death. Thus Bech gains admittance not to the heaven of Catullus that he dreamed of in a previous story, but to a two-dimensional "cardboard tableau lent substance only by the credulous." The process of becoming a character by Henry Bech has thus been completed.

In the face of such tarnished ideals and with the stasis of literary canonization looming before him, all Bech can ask at the volume's conclusion is "Now what?" Although recognizing the anticlimax of his induction, the question also leaves open the possibility of a sequel; if

Bech's fate is to transcend being turned into *Bech: A Book*, he must produce a book from the raw materials of life. Obligingly, Updike does not freeze his artist-hero in such a position of dubious fame; after a five-year rest he revived Bech for the beginning of his literary comeback in *Bech Is Back*, a sequel that more broadly examines the perils of success.

Winner of the Melville Medal for the most meaningful silence, Bech still gropes for direction in travel and romantic infatuation. Like Melville, he remains overshadowed by the reputation from his early works, yet after 13 years of silence Bech is no longer a noble holdout.[31] He remains unable to flourish as a creative artist amid the distractions provided by a culture whose media turn writers into minor celebrities. Yet as he increasingly succumbs to demands for public appearances, his defenses begin to crumble on other fronts. Bech marries and temporarily manages to overcome his block to complete the novel he envisioned in "Bech Swings?"; instead of reviving his early promise, he becomes a popular success, pitched toward the best-seller list by the publishing empire that Updike satirizes. While *Bech: A Book* ends in bafflement, this one concludes with Bech's disillusionment, and a new stasis arises, compounded by Bech's further entwinement in the "silken mechanism" awaiting the unwary writer who continues to surrender whatever privacy he has managed to preserve.

Like its predecessor, *Bech Is Back* consists of seven stories loosely strung together in a story sequence; the four previously published stories are joined by three written to complete the book. The pattern differs slightly: Bech's exploits begin on the American lecture circuit, but after the first story his travels take him abroad: first to the Third World and the "safer" English-speaking sisters, Canada and Australia; then on historical visits to the Holy Land and Scotland for a honeymoon; back home, he uproots himself from Manhattan for a sojourn in the suburbs, but in the end he returns, full circle, to the city. The volume as a whole is somewhat uneven, relying on "Bech Wed," the penultimate novella-length work that occupies nearly one-third of the volume, to tie the stories together and provide narrative impetus. Throughout the volume Bech fends off the inevitable as he interacts with a variety of characters who, though memorable, lack the distinction of the guides and women in the previous volume. Like the second Rabbit volume, *Bech Is Back* seems more like a redux; the most recently published Bech story, "Bech in Czech,"[32] however, promises to revive Updike's alter-ego in yet another key.

The opening story, "Three Illuminations in the Life of an American Author," portrays Bech's craving for financial and ego enrichment; seizing upon almost any opportunity for remunerative travel as an escape from writing, he strives to benefit further from the books responsible for the "shuddering shadows" over his career. His illuminations occur when proximity to the products of his own hand leads to disillusion and further diminishment. In the first episode, his spontaneous visit to a book collector's home shatters Bech's imagined vision of his reputation's devoted caretaker. When Bech discovers all the signed volumes Federbusch garnered from him stacked in a closet along with those of other authors, he sees that his signature has been solicited for an investment. Still, Bech becomes more dejected than affronted; in his invasion of Federbusch's domain, he senses that he has intruded on one of life's "dreadfully musty" secrets: "The greedy author, not content with adoration in two dimensions, had offered himself in a fatal third, and maimed his recording angel."[33]

Similarly, when Bech becomes attracted to a mysterious woman who seems like the embodiment of an evolving character in his novel, offering himself in this third dimension produces disenchantment for both: the real author pales by comparison to the image of Bech she has formed from his work; neither can she equal the imaginative vitality of his ideal Lenore, despite her remarkable similarity. Furthermore, the intersection of life and art eclipses his imaginative efforts and halts the momentum of his revived novel; Poe's "Lenore," he seems to have forgotten, springs from the beloved's unattainability. In the final episode, Bech's autograph plays a much larger role than in the first section; instead of signing rare editions of his work for a collector, Bech consents to sign 28,500 tip-in sheets for a special edition of one of his books, lured by the vision of combining easy money and a Caribbean idyll with his ex-mistress Norma. Too close to Norma and to his own signature, Bech becomes uncomfortable with both; he argues with Norma and becomes bogged down by a growing self-consciousness about his signature, whose quirks seem to embody weaknesses of character. Bech must engage in a marathon signing session that culminates in a symbolic impasse in which he becomes the ultimate blocked writer, unable even to sign his name. When Bech and his books intersect, the resultant illuminations highlight corners of his life that might best have been left in the shadows.

The composite form of the first three stories mirrors that of the book as a whole, although at first glance "Bech Third Worlds It" seems merely a chaotic collage. The dizzying juxtaposition of the scenes may reflect Bech's disorientation with such rapid travel, as Detweiler suggests (180), but closer examination of the locales featured in each of the 12 vignettes reveals a regular pattern: every other section occurs in Africa, while the remaining ones alternate between Venezuela and Korea.[34] In almost every location, however, Bech is reminded of the gap between the emerging countries' concern with the writer's political role and America's tamer definition of the artist as one concerned with depicting a personal vision.

Such colliding visions of art's function are signalled in the early vignettes by the weathered African tower, whose purpose is most likely magical, and by the Japanese poet's 112 lyric poems about frogs. The gulf between the American experience and that of developing nations, Bech discovers, defies easy translation and often produces hostility. When he discusses American humor at a Korean conference, for instance, no one but Americans and a crazy Vietnamese participant laughs. His lecture on "The Cultural Situation of the American Writer" (presumably similar to Updike's talk of the same title in its emphasis on the author's need to express his private truths) is challenged by audience questions about the artist's accountability and role as a proponent of social reform; after each confrontation, Bech readjusts his lecture to lessen the scope of his authority as a spokesman.

At the center of the story, in the sixth and seventh sections, two outbursts illustrating the Third World's warring spirits of vitality and repression occur. In both, the protestors—a satiric Korean poet who seems to be screaming some form of poetry and an emotional young Kenyan—are dragged away by police after they attempt to use Bech's talk as a personal forum. Although Bech is warned that the latter is crazy, the Kenyan speaks very sanely about the personal and political inefficacy of language and recognizes modernism's dispassionate lament in his work: "Your books, they are weeping, but there are no tears" (*BIB*, 36). Bech senses that this kindred spirit might have helped him expunge the persistent guilt he feels in the Third World, but his lectures finally do little to bridge the gap and his contact outside the lecture platform is limited to disdainful ambassadors and the elite, who welcome him into their oases of comfort and safety. The arc of Bech's fear grows more pronounced when incendiary leaflets that label him an imperialist enemy are distributed during his talk in Venezuela; worried that he may be killed in a riot, he regrets that he once "meddled with sublime silence" and spoke out in favor of U.S. intervention in Vietnam.[35] Departure finally lifts his dread as he retreats intact into the comforts of a first-class airline passage—yet the opportunistic writer, it turns out, has not been shaken so much that, if invited back, he would uphold his vow not to return.

As Bech's creative powers ebb and his need to exercise his creativity in any way but writing grows, he loses the ability to discriminate among opportunities. His preference for "safe" places, however, especially after the hostility encountered in the Third World, guides him next to "Australia and Canada," both with familiar and "unterrorized" Anglo-Saxon populations. Instead of directly confronting crowds with challenging questions, Bech is beamed across the country on shows such as "Vanessa Views," a Canadian clone of American talk shows featuring a menagerie of disparate guests and a telegenic host with predictable questions.

Like the preceding story, "Australia and Canada" is broken into 12 alternating episodes, each clearly dovetailed with the next so that Bech's experiences in different hemispheres are interwoven into one continuous plot that suggests the sameness of such trips. The tour of Toronto blends into the tour of Sydney; for instance, the verbal echo of Bech's favorable praise of Toronto (calculated to impress Glenda, the producer) fades into similar praise of Sydney. In both cases Bech ends up in the apartment of his female guides, whose involvement with men named Peter provides a rather humorous transition between sections. The odd symmetry of these visits diverges slightly before the story's conclusion, with Bech meeting with success in the sexual arena in Sydney but striking out in Toronto. In the end, however, Bech departs from these safe lands with renewed yearning for the contradictions of home. He misses the danger of New York: Toronto, where he can walk unthreatened at night, lacks the danger and raw vigor of its "race and corruption and pressure and trash." As the story ends, Bech departs after a night with little sleep, feeling his age and the perilousness of such literary travel. The continent hopping in which he has been engaged, he realizes, has diminishing returns; unlike his creator, Bech has not invented a way to transmute these "cloudy episodes" of his travels into fictive capital. However, an alluringly safe alternative is available back in America: Bea, his "suburban softy."

Bech's subsequent travels in the symmetrical pair of stories are not as a media creature or cultural ambassador but as a husband. "The Holy Land" begins with Bech lamenting his choice of marrying Bea (a Christian), while "Macbech" concludes with Bea complaining that marriage to a novelist was a mistake. For Bech, marriage is part of an ongoing quest "to escape his famous former self"; Bea, on the other hand, wants to "improve him" by deepening the qualities he already has—his Jewishness among them. The honeymoon trip to Jerusalem, however, fulfills her longstanding wish, and uncovers a deeply religious streak in her that Bech had not suspected. In Scotland, the land of her ancestry, the tables are turned, when Bech is surprisingly attracted to its history.

Always fearful during his journeys abroad, Bech feels a certain vulnerability when he travels through the war-torn area surrounding Jerusalem in "The Holy Land." On a tour beneath the city's surface, he worries that he might suffocate; the city is symbolically stifling to him, and he instinctively resists Bea's ardent attempt to put him in touch with his diluted ethnicity. "Religiously and archaeologically prepared," the Episcopalian Bea is enchanted with the Holy Land; Bech, whose vision is primarily aesthetic rather than religious, sees the city as "hideously botched" by the overlay of different cultures and the tawdry commercialism. Bogus "hunger artists" such as the candle seller in Christ's tomb hawk their wares at even the most sacred sites; their contrast with Kafka's genuine hunger artist perhaps serves as an emblem of what could become of Bech if he degenerates further into literary celebrity.

To counteract Bea's ardor, Bech maintains a critical stance and refuses to be moved; contrary to what the Jewish literati they dine with predict, Jerusalem will not be the subject of his next novel. Echoing the title of his stalled novel, he attests to his ambition to "think bigger" and transcend his heritage. However, his experience in Israel does produce a mild epiphany; the holy land, he realizes, metaphorically corresponds to "where you accepted being. Middle age was a holy land. Marriage." Like the city of Jerusalem, his marriage is the scene of continuing hostilities as each partner struggles to occupy territory and maintain his/her own identity; in addition, it imposes layers over his character, sometimes producing anomalies such as the church they visit. Though Bech still chafes about the "creeping we" Bea uses when referring to what she perceives as common thoughts, the musing repeated at this story's conclusion—"I should never have married a Christian"—lacks conviction. His somewhat naive "suburban softy" has surprised him with her resilience, and perhaps revealed some soft spots of his own.

"Macbech" recycles Updike's trip to Scotland as Bech's present to Bea on her fortieth birthday. Perversely, Bech takes to the land of Bea's heritage better than he does his own, identifying with the aura of decline and lost causes in a land "built solid on disappointment." Uncomfortable wearing the yarmulke required at the Wailing Wall, Bech affects a tweed coat and a plaid hat as they travel the Scottish countryside.

Determined not to let Bea easily enjoy the sights, he relishes the role of spoiler and derives a perverse satisfaction from her discomfort. As he continually points out the historical atrocities and exploitation behind the scenery, he unconsciously hands out a dose of what he was forced to take in the Third World. When Bea finally becomes fed up with his gloating, she protests that Bech is appropriating her heritage, seemingly unaware that she has done something similar in Israel. With her writer-husband, however, she fears more that her personality is in danger of being digested for literary purposes.

"Bech Wed" not only provides the story sequence with the main source of action but also links the genesis of his new novel with the preceding events. Bech received his first fleeting inspiration in the previous volume, but "Bech Wed" confirms that his fabled block will crumble as the new novel struggles to emerge. In fact, the incident in the opening story concerning the woman who resembles his protagonist turns out to be the third burst of inspiration that punctuates the interims between his trips abroad. His novel, *Think Big*, gains momentum when he discovers his subject: the extensive media empire on whose fringes the celebrity author travels. Yet when he begins populating his book with such a large soap-opera-like cast of characters, he eventually loses sight of what to do with them. Wed to Bea, he finally rediscovers his calling, more as an escape than a vocation; the novel he finally writes compromises his integrity and ends up dissolving rather than strengthening their relationship. While publication represents the fulfillment of Bea's deferred wishes, for Bech, actuality once again proves to be "the running impoverishment of possibility."

Bech's discomfort in Bea's Ossining house, a suburban outpost loaded with new responsibilities, spurs him to reconstruct a "surreal distillation of his cloistered forsaken apartment" in Manhattan on the unfinished third floor. Retreating from domestic confusion in this garret, he is eventually forced to forsake whatever household concerns he might use as an excuse not to write and to enter into the world of his characters. In her efforts to squeeze a novel out of her unproductive, sidetracked husband, Bea condescendingly instructs him in common sense and the Protestant work ethic: instead of perpetually courting the muse, he must simply produce something each day. Thus, she drives him upstairs into memories of Manhattan and wistful recollection of his life before literary celebrity. Engaged in such personal archeology, Bech rediscovers how to connect life and art; in a metaphor that evokes his underground excursions in two previous stories, the narrator notes that he enters the "catacombs of private life" and "retrieved that vast subterrain detail by detail and interwove the overheard music of a tranced time with the greedy confusion his characters bred" (*BIB*, 118).

Ironically, the WASPish suburbs, not the Holy Land, help Bech retrieve a consciousness of his Jewishness. Physically and imaginatively elevated above the mundane, Bech casts a critical eye on those around him; in the suburbs, he feels like a spy amidst the *goyim*, whose complacent lives seem preoccupied with narrow, self-centered pursuits that are readily transfigured into the struggles within his imagined media empire. After hearing pieces of the work in progress, Bea protests that his book is unfair to WASPs and should be retitled "Jews and Jerks," yet Bech ignores her complaint and continues to use his novel to lash out at her and the Christian world whose "collective chill" he feels. The short preview of the evolving novel the narrator offers, as well as the brief excerpts to which he alludes, demonstrates that Bech's work, whatever its intentions, is plagued by sensationalism and artificiality. In his fixation to produce his daily quota of prose, Bech has abandoned whatever sense of artistry he once cherished; casting off "finicky Flaubert and Kafka" as spiritual patrons, he now aligns himself with "those great native slapdashers Melville and Faulkner." Unfortunately, Bech's book, the product of mere persistence and the hope of "Easy Money" (the new working title that helps break the block), lacks the philosophical depth and resonance of these authors' works.

While Bech chooses not to write directly about the publishing industry because he detests such "involution," Updike has no such qualms, and takes full advantage of the opportunity to satirize its current state of affairs. Bech's publisher, Vellum Press, has even fewer reservations about the novel than he does. Bought and sold like a disposable commodity, Vellum is more concerned with design and marketing strategies than with a book's contents. Vellum lacks the rigor characteristic of the earlier era, when Bech recalls how a tough editor challenged his prose and acted as a watchdog of style, craft, and propriety. Instead, Bech's new work is ushered relatively unchanged through production and becomes the focus of an advertising blitz whose slogan ironically serves as the title for Updike's volume. Bech's book may be favorably reviewed by major critics such as Alfred Kazin and Gore Vidal (from whom Updike playfully inserts words of ambiguous praise), but he cannot dismiss the suspicion that his work consists wholly of "idle dreams, hatched while captive in Sing Sing."

Bech thus achieves new identity as a literary lion and becomes a millionaire, yet in completing the novel he grows away from Bea, who at one point blames his sex-filled work for her daughter's loss of virginity. Bech sees his success as one more hook of bourgeois life, especially when Bea's desire to refurbish the house reveals her expectation that he will write another book. His novel has, he realizes, only further enmeshed him in a prison of his own making and put "checkpoints at his escape." Only his former mistress Norma delivers the honest rebuke he feels he deserves, calling his novel slapdash, sentimental, and cozy and berating him for consenting to be a "sow's ear turned into a silk purse." When the sparks generated from their argument lead Bech and Norma into the bedroom, Bech joins the crowd of adulterous Updike characters and begins to unravel his marriage. Marriage and publication have broken long-standing barriers Bech has erected around his privacy, but he has relinquished more than he is willing to continue doing. The misgivings about his accomplishment are further confirmed in the concluding story.

"White on White," returns Bech to Manhattan, where he senses that his compromises have tainted him further than he had imagined. In the wake of his separation, Bech harks back to the past, grasping at the "merest lint of stray thread of old personal connection." One such thread is an invitation to a publication party for a photographer, whose recent book, *White on White*, provides the party's theme. The pervasive white motif—in dress, decor, and even music—reminds Bech of Whitsuntide, and the scene—the apartment of a rich television game show producer who has recently ventured into televised female mud wrestling—is an appropriately ironic setting for launching an avant-garde art book. The photographer's intent to explore "how little contrast you could have and still have a photograph," suggests an artistic precision that Bech has long since discarded, and the whiteness of his photographs contrasts with the first story's blank white pages, upon which Bech, the paralyzed artist, cannot sign his name.

The other authors present provide a contrast to Bech: Vernon Klegg, the alcoholic minimalist, composes his "few hundred beautifully minimal words—nouns, verbs, nouns" during brief dry periods; despite Bech's (and Updike's) misgivings about minimalism, Bech admires the essentially American hollowness captured in Klegg's flat descriptions of spiritually bankrupt trailer park inhabitants. The other successful writers both possess qualities for which Updike has been praised, although they veer off in other directions: the female historical novelist evokes the poverty of her Pennsylvania childhood; "urbane comedies of sexual entanglement and moral confusion" with a religious dimension are the domain of the male novelist. Envious of these writers' prolific output, clarity of purpose, and craftsmanship, Bech realizes that they have all worked their way out of the "dreary quotidian" up to this high place—reminiscent of the literary heaven he enters at the other volume's conclusion.

Yet beneath the party's veneer of whiteness, he suspects, lies a murky underside. In a state of perceptiveness signalled by Updike's characteristic language of epiphany (but perhaps ironically undercut by the fact that Bech has just taken his fourth drink), Bech pronounces the scene he witnesses "Treyf," Yiddish for "unclean"; perhaps he also passes this judgment upon himself, for his participation in and yearning for such rituals. As the book closes, he awaits his rescue from the party by Lorna, one of the female mud wrestlers, whose chocolate-brown leotard beneath a white nightie reinforces the aura of muddy uncleanliness with which he has become sullied. As a performance artist, Lorna is perhaps closest to Bech the celebrity; in addition, she is the last of a chain of women in the book, perhaps the television world's realization of Bech's fictional heroine Lenore. Bech is indeed back, but his return to print is an ambiguous triumph, difficult to savor in its evident impurity.

The recent publication of "Bech in Czech" in the *New Yorker* may signal the likelihood of a third Bech volume in the future. Like some of the characters in Updike's 1987 collection *Trust Me*, Bech has crossed into his sixties and continues to seek solace in travel. Returning to Eastern Europe, where *Bech: A Book* began, he discovers his celebrity status in Prague, visits Kafka's grave, bestows his blessing on a mildly expurgated translation of *Brother Pig*, and meets with both the young, American-educated Communist literary establishment and the Czech literary dissidents, whose privately bound, hand-produced works revive his understanding of a book's true value. Tired and still plagued by self-doubt, he is no longer disturbed by "romantic vertigo," and seems most comfortable safely within the walls of the Ambassador's residence.

Yet Bech cannot ignore Communist oppression, the historical weight of the Holocaust, and a persistent fear that he has become as boring to the Creator as he is to himself. At the story's conclusion, the dormant anxiety that previously peaked in "Bech Panics" returns; in fact, Updike recycles some of the same phrases from the earlier story when he characterizes the panic as "pasty and stiff," although Bech experiences more raw fear of extinction, of having played out his tenure as a character in the human drama. Certainly, Bech's creator would not leave him thus, but will discover other strategies to overcome whatever weariness he might feel with him. Cynthia Ozick has suggested that Updike's next volume might be called "Bech Bound" and feature his protagonist rediscovering his Jewish heritage. While a hint of such an encounter occurs at Kafka's grave in "Bech in Czech," it appears that Bech will continue to be on the move, in various directions. Whether Bech is baptized, banned, bewildered, or bankrupt in the next volume, Updike's alter-ego should never bore his public.

The Search for Faded Radiance:
Museums and Women

The *New Yorker*'s listing of the city's "Goings On About Town" contains a section devoted to "Museums and Libraries"; Updike, long associated with the magazine, adopts a modified version of the column title for his 1972 collection, *Museums and Women*, which chronicles the "goings on" in the lives of middle-aged suburbanites making the passage into the seventies. Appropriately, women rather than libraries are paired with museums, since both embody the receding mysteries for which the characters search as they pass through a "muddled transitional condition"—a phrase used to describe the Dark Ages in "The Invention of the Horse Collar."

Updike's fifth volume of short fiction is likewise a transitional work, containing pieces that span the dozen years previous, organized into three separate galleries: a group of 14 tales; 10 "Other Modes," miscellaneous sketches that range from a meditation on language to illustrated comic fables; and 5 stories featuring the Maples. Critical reception would perhaps have been less mixed had Updike not chosen to include the sketches, although a few which echo the themes of the other stories could have been easily intermingled. Like the exhibits in the provincial museum of the title story, these contents seemed "disturbingly various" to certain critics, who dismiss this phase of Updike's work as lapsing into mere display, and lacking the vigor and originality of his earlier fiction.[36]

Yet it is Updike's characters—not his work—that have lost the energy to fuel the push through the doors of memory or the ability to devise plausible harmonies amid maturity's discord. Their emotional peaks have levelled out, and fatigue is more frequent; numerous characters mention how "tired" they are from struggling to maintain the status quo and to perform domestic and social obligations. While a premature autumn seems to have descended, most still strain for some connection—with remnants of the past, with a spouse or lover, with the community—but their reach is not as far. As the headnote from Ecclesiastes indicates, what they find most easily accessible is "happiness," the volume's other frequently repeated word. While they "eat and drink and take pleasure in [their] toil," Updike's character's often discover such satisfactions to be fleeting, and their happiness degenerates merely to avoidance of pain. They thus settle for a diminished version of past bliss, faint glimmers of a dying light that are merely captured for preservation in a museum of the past rather than interwoven into the texture of their disappointing present.

Inevitably, in both art and marriage, the glimmer of newness becomes tarnished and familiar, but loss seems to be a less urgent issue in *Museums and Women*. In essence, the characters have become, as the narrator of "When Everyone Was Pregnant" states, "survival conscious," less intent on gripping the past as "the decades slide seaward." The growing disparity between former hopes and their diminished realizations still nags, especially in marriage, and the husbands are often not content with being "merely happy." The pressures of duty and estrangement from the past often leave them in a bounded present, searching amid the other suburban castaways for some faded radiance. Fear of death and loss does not seem a prominent force, though it lurks in the background, especially in the last few Maples stories, where absence and being outlasted are stressed.

In general, as one critic observes, the volume is marked by "a winding down of human aspiration."[37] An air of eroded hopes, the anticipation of perpetual disenchantment, and a melancholy awareness that one may have to settle for less are pervasive. Epiphanic moments are less prevalent, as the imaginations of these characters seem less potent; still, these dormant, often bewildered spirits never succumb totally to resignation. Yet like the narrator of "The Day of the Dying Rabbit" (one of the few artist figures in the volume), most attempt to capture as much of the past as they can, however underexposed it may turn out to be. Fear of continued loss and gratitude for past satisfactions blend with their growing sense of limitation. Persistence becomes essential as fatigue encroaches; though spiritually enervated and conscious of further diminishment, they refuse to accept loss passively.

The title story opens the volume with a recapitulation of the course from adolescence to maturity, marital discontent, and beyond, into the phase where Updike's protagonists acquiesce more readily to the contraction of possibility. "Museums and Women" is narrated by William Young, the protagonist of "A Sense of Shelter," who now seeks "radiance, antiquity, mystery and duty" in museums and women instead of Olinger High's provisional shelter. The contradictory pull of these four qualities generates the story's conflict; radiance and mystery hold the strongest allure, but duty finally exerts the strongest influence, as William becomes unable to continue the affair that brings him to "the limits of unsearchability." In his backward glance, William fashions a comprehensive artistic record of his past reminiscent of the "fictive music" of the previous volume, but his tone at the story's conclusion is that of a witness once removed, an outsider facing a future of quickened disenchantment.

For William's narrative, Updike revives the montage form of the final stories in *Pigeon Feathers*: by focusing wholly on the experiential and metaphoric alliance of museums and women, he creates a focused series of lyrical mediations that constitute a museum gallery hung with pictures of William's past. In splicing together seven interrelated memories, "Museums and Women" achieves a remarkable balance between the lyric and narrative impulses: it derives its primary coherence from the rich network of metaphoric connections, yet the incidents are arranged so as to trace William's pursuit of the "unsearchable" from elementary school to just beyond the end of his first affair. As one reviewer observes, Updike displays an "ability to develop a metaphor while telescoping the passage of time, thus flouting the conventional wisdom that a short story should deal with a single event" (Prescott, 112).

The story's structure resembles the archways that figure so prominently in the architecture of its museums; the women featured in its seven incidents, William notes, "were broken arcs of one curve." His trips to the provincial Pennsylvania museum with his mother and the courtship of his future wife in the corridors of Boston galleries comprise the arch's ascending segment, while the marble nude he discovers in a faraway museum forms the essential "thin keystone" that must be inserted at the story's midpoint to support the structure. The other half of the parabola follows the path of infidelity: a mild erotic attraction to an acquaintance at a New York modern art exhibition initially suggests possibilities later realized in his first affair, which achieves fullness in a converted mansion and ends in the same Boston gallery where he and his wife once studied a headless Attic sphinx.

Each museum's spatial geometry and the exhibits William recalls from within are allied with a particular phase in his evolving sensibilities. The provincial museum, entered through "paradisiacal grounds" with tagged trees, evokes an Edenic garden. Ostensibly educational expeditions, his dutiful visits there with his mother comprise a time of relative innocence and nurtured expectations. Among its eclectic contents,

William is drawn to a group of small nude statuettes whose miniature scale, realism, and vivid translation of emotion into "dimension and permanence" stir his nascent artistic sensibilities. Recognizing their depiction of people caught in "tarnished fate," William wants to "touch and comfort" them, a desire that persists outside of museums; the bare toes of his future wife as she stands on the college museum's stone steps also seem to call out for his "touch and comfort."

While William and his mother wander separately through the museum, visiting museums with his future wife is part pursuit; his courtship is partially conducted while practicing the techniques of aesthetic analysis they learn in their art classes. William is more verbal, but she—a fine arts major—is the "gatekeeper of the temple," whose capture will give him access to its mysteries. She reminds him of "a room full of vases: you enter and find your sense of yourself abruptly sharpened by a vague, tranquil expectancy in the air." The college museum's implicit promise is similarly embodied in the female openness of its "radiantly hollow" courtyard, containing statues of the seasons that implicitly signal mutability. In contrast, the headless Attic sphinx they study in Boston foreshadows the broken life ahead, but also serves as a fitting emblem for the separation of the head and heart that leads William into an affair and finally enables him to terminate it.

The ideality of the "imaginary woman," a nude marble statue he discovers in an upstairs alcove of a distant museum filled with masculine artifacts, is a harbinger of the essence William will eventually seek in other women when married familiarity breeds predictability. Sequestered in a remote corner, this polished marble nude reclines on a mattress, embodying the sensuality and repose that have become the objects of William's search. Her inaccessible aesthetic perfection awakens a sense of "dread and a premonition of loss" in him, but nonetheless offers the possibility of a temporary escape from the "bounded present" toward a "final unsearchability that leads us to hope, and return." This image embodies the apex of William's aspiration—the keystone that supports both the narrative attempt to structure his past and the continued desire that guides him in the present.

In his next phase, an unexpected surge of desire occurs on the spiral stairs of a modern gallery, where William and his companion are spatially locked in an architectural "wizard's spell." Their actions are innocent enough, as she merely grabs his arm when she stumbles and then clings to him for the rest of their tour. The gallery's abstract art—"menacing magnifications of textural accidents"—and the "siren chasm" of the stairway provide an atmosphere that portends the dangerous allure of William's quest for the radiant ideal when he abandons the traditional path and begins his extramarital explorations.

The home-like converted mansion that William and his mistress visit after lovemaking presents an unattainable ideal of a domestic life amid aesthetic splendor. William likens their sojourn to "a bridge whose either end is dissolved in mist—its suspension miraculous, its purpose remembered by the murmuring stream in the invisible ravine below."[38] Such removal from the stream of daily life is momentary, but characterized by a rare fullness and accessibility; both she and the museum become "perfectly open and mutually transparent" during this sojourn. In contrast, his final attempt to revive their affair takes place in a museum office after his mistress—more of an interior decorator than an art student—shows him the furniture she catalogues. Fixated on their own pain, both are "blind to all beauty" in the gallery, although William does notice the Attic sphinx, a reminder of his former visit with the wife he chooses to retain.

His concluding epiphany appropriately occurs outside the museum as he glances back and realizes that "nothing about museums is as splendid as their entrances—the sudden vault, the shapely cornices." Not surprisingly, the same applies to his experience with the women in his life, as the architectural imagery evoking the female form suggests. The mysterious treasures both contain will inexorably attract him, but the radiance for which he searches will be faded and perpetually behind him. Duty likewise beckons strongly, but William reconciles himself to the cycle of disenchantment awaiting those who persistently seek to fathom the "limits of unsearchability."

"The Hillies" presents a slice of the sixties in a historical sketch of Tarbox that recalls "The Indian" in tone and position in the volume. Narrated by a member of the town's status quo, the story chronicles the genesis of and community response to this "less exotic" breed of hippies, whose name springs from their occupation of an undeveloped slope between the town's hilltop green and downtown. Since the hillies are the citizen's own children, a dispassionate sociological study is difficult; indeed, the problem they pose ultimately reveals as much about the more conventional citizens as it does the stratified counterculture of passive rebels. In the resulting polarization, the hillies, like the town's original settlers, prepare for an onslaught—in this case by the fearful generation that no longer understands them.

Like the lawyer in Melville's "Bartleby the Scrivener," the narrator is baffled by the passivity of their withdrawal and their shunning of such socially accepted behaviors as work. Little evidence suggests that they are serious pacifists; like Bartelby, their main vocation seems to be "preferring not to," although they indulge in beer, pot, and pills—vices which Melville's forlorn scrivener would no doubt shun. In their rejection of the work ethic and materialism, the narrator perceives the hillies as a threat to "the foundations of our lives, the identities our industry and acquisitiveness have heaped up beneath our flag's blessing." They thus become the focus of Tarbox's dormant energies, and provide a litmus test of the residents' tolerance and political sympathies. Yet as the narrator realizes, the hillies originated in homes that can no longer assimilate them; while they seem to have learned their parents' lessons about the pursuits of happiness, their directionless pursuit illustrates how such values are subject to the same erosion by time and circumstance as personal relationships.

The title of "The Day of the Dying Rabbit" may recall the plight of Rabbit Angstrom, yet this rabbit is neither trapped nor able to run; clinging to life, it becomes a focal point for the recounting of this day from the narrator's family vacation. A photographer who has been married 15 years and fathered six children, he fixes his gaze on the recent past, before the "merely happy days" of the present. His retrospection, which captures domestic tension and a family in flux, refrains from the nostalgic mode of the Olinger stories. His lens of memory is not the beautiful "selfless" lens used by the photographers of the Hindu valley landscape he admires in *Life*, but his story shares with a photograph the inherent selectivity of its frame and the subtle distortions of the lens: "The camera does lie all the time. It has to," he remarks, granting the subjectivity behind his picture.

The narrator asks the reader to accept that the day he depicts is more than "merely happy," despite the obvious deterioration of intimacy between himself and his wife, Margaret. He is devoted to, though at times bewildered by, his children; when they crowd around the rabbit brought in by a stray cat, the barrier they form is symbolic of the obstacles they present. Despite his inability to deal effectively with his son Jimmy's brooding and his adolescent daughter's frequent swearing or entry into womanhood, his children provide him glimpses of the eternal in everyday life, especially when the dawning understanding in their faces reveals "passageways for angels, sometimes whole clouds of them" (*MW*, 27–28). Jimmy's sudden comprehension of the word "casket" in a humorous context provides one such redeeming moment, spurring his father's pride that he "got the picture." The photographic language is echoed more soberly in a later passage, when Jimmy understands that the rabbit will not survive the day.

As an artist, the narrator is overly fond of photographic similes: he compares pupil size to an f-stop, equates screams with flash bulbs, and—most successfully—notes how children are like fine-grained film in their "susceptibility" to events. By contrast, his own memories seem "underexposed" to him; what he remembers from the beach party, for instance, is a series of quick impressions—"glances, inklings, angels." Nonetheless, his story is an attempt to revive his own susceptibility and transmute his memories into affirmations. He thus tends to overdramatize, characterizing their party at the beach, for instance, in near-apocalyptic terms: "We sat in a ring, survivors, around the fire, the heart of a collapsing star, fed anew by paper plates"—although the irony of the last detail brings the rhetoric down to earth. Upset with Jimmy's reaction to the rabbit's death, Margaret accuses her husband of deliberate melodrama, yet he recalls that "nothing could fleck the happiness widening within me, to catch the dying light" (*MW*, 36). As he faces a diminished present, he strives to coax this "dying light" of emotion from memory.

The rabbit's last flickers of life suggest to him a picture of "Eternal solicitude brooding above us, holding a match, and burning its fingers." Diana Culbertson argues that the conclusion depicts the discovery of "a present and future salvation in the face of the world's contradictory evidence,"[39] but its ironic undertones ultimately produce a more modest affirmation. When the single star the father locates winks out as they paddle in the kayak, he perceives the phosphorescence of the pond's teeming life and feels "afloat on a firmament warmer than the heavens." Not only is this light generated in the natural world rather than the heavenly one, but, ironically, in his moment of glory, the narrator steers the kayak into a bank, bringing himself back to reality in the moment before the tangle of voices from the other boat—the chaos of family life—overtakes them after this short reprieve. The "gallantry" he retrospectively bestows upon these events seems disproportionate, unless the term is more widely defined to encompasses any struggle against "things that would snag." In the end, the story itself becomes his reprieve, a bit of gallantry in which the narrator is "trying to get, what may be ungettable" through multiple takes of significant moments, all the while conscious that his focus on the bygone past will continue to fall short of the eyes' "elastic tolerance."

"The Deacon" features a somewhat older protagonist: Miles, an electrical engineer over 50 who, after a job transfer to New England, reaffirms his identity as one devoted to halting his church's physical and social deterioration. While alone one evening in the empty church—the only one who makes a meeting during a winter storm—he comes to understand why he is more at home there than anywhere else and rediscovers a possessive "pride in this ancient thing that will not quite die." In "I Will Not Let Thee Go, Except Thou Bless Me," Tom Brideson, a computer software expert who has been transferred to Houston after 10 years in New England, seeks the blessing of his former mistress, Maggie, before he moves and relinquishes her forever. Unlike Tristan and the other separated lovers in *The Music School*, who drift "away, away from the realm of compromise and muddle," Tom has continued to live in the same suburb as Maggie and move in the same social circles. Despite such proximity and his reconciliation with his wife, Lou, Tom has maintained an idealized vision of Maggie, whose wide-sleeved white dress at the farewell party reinforces her angelic image. Similarly, he has difficulty parting with his accumulated possessions, "each one a moment, a memory, impossible to keep, impossible to discard." For Tom, "departure rehearses death," and instead of leaving this phase of life wiser because he had witnessed his generation's growth and survival, he merely feels fatigued, unlike the Olinger protagonists, who struggle more vigorously to cling to past memories.

Like Jacob, to whom the story's title alludes, Tom contends with his angel, refusing to release Maggie after they dance until she grants him some sign of an amicable parting. While Jacob is rechristened after his struggle with Yahweh's angel, Tom merely seeks "something inoffensive" that might somehow right the "nagging misalignment" he perceives between them. Jacob receives his new identity after his thigh is disjointed; Tom only become further disjointed after Maggie's response. Instead of Maggie's blessing, he receives a blunt confirmation of his worst fears of fading identity when she spurns him and proclaims that he is "nothing" to her. Tom nonetheless chooses to interpret Maggie's warm farewell kiss to Lou as an oblique blessing. Whether the kiss is meant to convey sympathy from one wronged woman to another, to disrupt Tom's departure further with irony, or to signal the end of something, Maggie's unexpected gesture springs from a weariness similar to Tom's. These veterans of marital strife should be experiencing life's fullness, yet their generation has resignedly settled for less than the security of its predecessors (the "warriors" from World War II) and the liberation of its successors (the "rebels" of the sixties). Unlike Jacob, who moves to a new land bringing the best of Laban's goods, Brideson, unable to escape a sense of his own ghostliness, gropes for whatever oblique consolations he can bring with him to what he fears will be a new suburban desert.

"The Witnesses" is the first story in the volume that steps back to the fifties—"high noon of the Eisenhower era"—for a sketch of the generation that served as torch bearers for the postwar society, carrying its values intact into the turbulence of the sixties. The narrator, whose marriage appears secure, recalls Fred Prouty, who suffered through two divorces before dying of cancer. Fred's death spurs the memory of their last two visits: Fred's apparently "tactless" exhibition of his mistress before his first divorce was settled and a chance encounter in an airport after Fred's second divorce, which prompts a reassessment of Fred's social ostracism. The vestiges of connection are severed when Fred commits a social faux pas in using his "respectable friends" to validate his relationship, although the narrator later realizes that they have been called upon to witness the ephemeral happiness of a life "cracked and mended." Ultimately, the focus of the story is not Fred's affair but the reactions of his witnesses, who are unable to understand Fred's desperate attempts to imprint a record of the moment on another consciousness, hoping for its survival.

The protagonist of "Solitaire" is clearly the local boy from "Pigeon Feathers" and the other Olinger stories, as the details about his parents divulge. Updike returns to the abstract-personal mode in this story, using the card game's progress as counterpoint to the protagonist's inner debate until the conclusion, when it suddenly becomes the means of resolving his deliberations. Solitaire harks back to his childhood, when his mother would play it in a similar situation—alone while her spouse attended community meetings. In retrospect, he realizes how she was also locked in her own confusion and burdened with the question of divorce. The irony of this parallel is not lost on him; his relationship has turned out little better than the one whose tensions he sought to escape by early marriage. For both mother and son, solitaire represents a "final retreat" beyond which madness lies. As a youth, he fears the desperation behind his mother's scenario of the gambler risking it all; as an adult, he hopes that the game will create a blankness of mind, so that some epiphany, a "saving decision," will arrive to fill the emptiness. The game thus becomes a metaphor not only for essential human solitariness, but of the methods by which we attempt to sort out the problems life has dealt.

The issue—withheld until mid-story—is not that his wife leaves him alone while attending meetings, but that a confessed affair lies on the table between them. Early in their marriage, in order to overcome his lingering uncertainties about parenthood and the direction his life will take, he resolved to follow a "straight line . . . to the night of his death." Although setting out not to make the same mistakes as his parents, he too ends up preserving his marriage for the sake of convention. The obstacles encountered in the game metaphorically begin to reflect the predicament that has developed: "A king uncovered, but nowhere to put him," he muses when he recalls that revealing his affair to his wife and her knowledge of it to his mistress only compounds the problem.

The children intended to make his escape from marriage irrevocable become a "finite" consideration when he is forced to weigh the insoluble dilemma posed by the two women, whom he juxtaposes like two suits of cards as he compares their features and habits. The power of conventional morality, the weight and dearness of his possessions, and the self-conception derived from marriage all dictate that he abandon his mistress and resume the straight course; his mistress seems to offer only transient happiness and eventual bereavement. Since a rational weighing of these variables proves impossible, when his game seems similarly blocked by buried cards, he decides to let the two remaining ones decide the impasse. While his wife's card is a "strong 10," he becomes appalled by the implications of his action and tears his mistress's card in half, even though it is the missing ace that would solve the impasse of his blocked game and, in life, allow a cathartic relief from marriage's confines. Neither result, he wisely realizes, will remedy his essential solitariness.

In "The Orphaned Swimming Pool," the forces kept under control in the game of solitaire burst forth with the dissolved marriage bonds of Ted and Linda Turner, a suburban couple whose separation is metaphorically paralleled by the state of the pool that once made their house a neighborhood center. Constructed of a fragile plastic liner, the pool endures beyond the two summers of happiness, while the Turner's marriage dries up before the symbolic summer drought that occurs during their separation. Orphaned in their separation, the pool becomes "desolate and haunted, like a stagnant jungle spring; it looked poisonous and ashamed." Yet it springs back to life when a neighbor takes charge of its upkeep in Ted's absence. Gradually, it becomes the neighborhood watering hole, freely abused by the neighbors as well as a humorous array of visitors who drop in from parts unknown.

This "public carnival," rumored to be the site of evening trysts, depicts the community's unconcern with the Turner's problems. Ironically, when Ted returns to the house for a night with his mistress, the crowds trap the couple, attempting to preserve some discretion, inside for the day. As summer ends and the pump breaks, the crowds give way to "small deluded toads" who live in its stagnant water. The "heavenly blue" pool liner no longer holds intimations of eternity; for Linda, who realizes on her return that she cannot live in the house, "it held bottomless loss, it was one huge blue tear"—an emblem of her sorrow and solitariness. After she sells the house, the new owners drain and seal the pool so that it is like a "chained dog"; ostensibly, they are concerned with their toddler's safety, but the implication is that this couple will keep a tighter rein on their marriage.

In "When Everyone Was Pregnant," a securities broker fond of alluding to Proust resurrects details from the fifties as he travels on a train from work. While he has read that the 1950s are making a comeback, he has no illusions that *his* fifties will return; the ache for the past and the sense of loving immersion in it that prevades earlier meditative stories such as "In Football Season" are absent. Though the fifties are closer in time than the Olinger era, the narrator's recall is not quite as sharp; the fragmentary style reveals that he must capture the details as they strike him rather than craft an intricate metaphor-laden lyric. Whether his hand shakes from the train's motion through time and space or from the emotions that accompany the memories of an era of relative innocence, his hurried jottings reconstitute a time when the world was viewed with "two lenses since discarded: fear and gratitude." Those whose young adulthood occurred in the fifties, however, still retain vestiges of these sensibilities, even though other tints have since been added. He claims that he "never get[s] bored with how the train slices straight," but a sense of mild nostalgia creeps into this attempt to counter the way that time "cuts sleepwalking through everything."

For the narrator, the fifties were a fertile and guiltless era during which comfort and paternity replaced poverty and chastity; consumption and procreation, not ecological consciousness and population control dominated the decade. While he remembers that many of the words spoken at parties were insignificant, he recognizes that "the breath we took to speak them was life." The atom bomb cast its shadow, but the threat of the bomb's flash is replaced by the Kodak flash—along with an obsession to capture on film the happiness alluded to in the volume's epigraph. The thrice-repeated refrain—"Sickening sensation of love"—

suggests the narrator's retrospective suspicion that the happiness of the fifties was finally cloying. His repeated infidelities with women from their social circle, while perhaps initially an escape, also become part of the surfeit. His life impulse has survived the decade, but in metamorphosed form now that their friends have aged, divorced, and dispersed. "Fifteen shared years have made us wary, survival conscious," he proclaims near the conclusion, worried that his life has not amounted to anything. He still puzzles over whether ripeness lies ahead of or behind them as the decades recede, and fears that these accumulated memories are "Notes not come to anything."

The title of "I Am Dying, Egypt, Dying," which echoes Antony's words to Cleopatra in Act IV of Shakespeare's play, introduces the story's strongly ironic dimension. Clem, a rich, handsome, unmarried American tourist from Buffalo, is hardly the ardent conqueror seduced by Egypt; he seems oblivious to the subtle overtures of a green-eyed Egyptian woman and, for most of the Nile River cruise, remains impervious to Ingrid, the bikinied Swede who finally takes the initiative, only to have the fatigued Clem fall asleep as she sits on the edge of the bed. Only 34, Clem seems convinced that his demise is well underway; he had become a tourist in life, a perfect but hollow shell: "The world was his but slid right through him." Spiritually enervated, he cruises through a warring land during the 1967 Arab-Israeli conflict with an array of 20 characters of varied nationalities. Their ship is named the *Osiris*, yet it holds no regeneration for him, especially not in the sense alluded to in the Egyptian myth that relates how Osiris is resurrected "by a hawk alighting on his phallus." Clem's sustained world-weariness, however, seems to lack sufficient cause; a woman he once loved jilted him for a Harvard man, but this incident hardly seems sufficiently tragic to induce his condition.

Clem's insomnia seems to be his humanizing flaw, but it indicates that he is not living as intently as he might during the day. Just as he is encased in a "gleaming placenta of suntan oil" on deck, Clem spends most of the trip mentally insulated from his surroundings, shying away from potentially disturbing situations; aboard ship, he travels in a "gliding parenthesis," twice removed from the shore. The surrounding desert, arid and empty, provides the closest equivalent of his inner condition, although he attempts to make a virtue of this "lightness"—a symbolic freedom from the burdens of commitment and sympathy that is metaphorically equated with dying. Amid the sandbags in the war-readied Cairo museum, he encounters an emblem of his condition: King

Tut's sarcophagus, with its "whisper of death, of flight, of floating." The Egyptian vision of death, however, is different from his premature death-in-life. Whenever he articulates his fatigue, Clem declares "I'm dead," a phrase whose idiomatic origin derives from a Western opposition; the ancient Egyptian language, his guide informs him, lacks such a distinction between death and life. The present progressive tense of the story title, however, suggests that Clem is "dying," an unfinished process that, like the incompleteness of the tombs, does not "close in life behind."

Clem, who—as the guide states about the Russians—is "not convinced that the world really matters," seeks insulation from alien experiences; in his nightmare, hieroglyphs and cartouches symbolically become stamps threatening to indent themselves upon him. Egypt's beggars and merchants likewise menace him; he only purchases the caftan because he is convinced it will be a stunning costume—one which, appropriately, will cover him fully. Clem finally experiences a surge of emotion, however, when Ingrid spends the night with the young German; at first he feels relieved—a "freedom from litter" as he uncharitably puts it—but, as he listens to the Russians next door methodically making love, his jealousy is provoked. Despite this temporary "thaw," fatigue prevents the consummation of his sexual advances.

As the cruise ends, Clem retrospectively pronounces that "he had been happy," but such happiness seems even paler than the "merely happy" state the narrator seeks to preserve in "The Day of the Dying Rabbit." If the desert is a metaphor for Clem's inner emptiness, the plume of water at the Aswan, where the landscape is a "merciless gray that had never entertained a hope of life," signals a sexual and emotional vitality he lacks: "though accustomed to reflect love, he could not originate light within himself; he was as blind as the silvered side of a mirror to the possibility that he, too, might impose a disproportionate glory upon the form of another" (*MW*, 140). Clem's "dying" could have generated a rebirth, but in continuing to define happiness as "freedom from litter," he risks dissipation from the ensuing lightness, with his life behind him like the "heaped rubble" of the Aswan, and his past gaping like the "abyss of the trip."

One explanation for Clem's superficial characterization is that the story, as the book jacket blurb states, "allegorizes our foreign policy." The allegorical dimension, however, at times seems at odds with the portrait of Clem's hollowness. His well-meaning egocentrism is certainly representative of foreign perceptions of the United States, but he hardly

101

embodies the "menacing American energy" mentioned by one of the other tourists. His indecision in purchasing souvenirs nicely depicts American tendencies in economic aid: he wants to help, but suffering repulses him and he fears he will make the wrong choice. Finally, desperate to spend some money after the token purchase of a cheap scarab, he tosses a portion away on an impulsive purchase destined to feed his own vanity. The Russians appear not to be well-liked, but they are never fully realized enough to be the force in the story that they have been in recent world politics. Whether Clem's inability to consummate his affair with Ingrid is a commentary on U.S.-Scandinavian relations is not quite as clear.

Few commentators have recognized the merits of "The Carol Sing," in which the narrator's reflection on the Tarbox Christmas tradition dramatizes the attempts to come to terms with change and death. The recent suicide of Mr. Burley, one of Tarbox's more distinguished citizens, forces the narrator—who speaks in the first-person plural as the voice of the town—to question their own reasons and strategies for survival in a diminished present. The story is reminiscent of E. A. Robinson's "Richard Cory," with the baffled town confronted with the suicide of a leading citizen envied for his education, vigor, and spirit. Educated and expected to transcend Tarbox, Burley returned to settle there after college, even though his family hosiery business closed down before he could head it; instead, he spent his time inventing environmentally safe products in a private laboratory. Though admired, Burley attracted some malice, even a bit of the narrator's own: he calls Burley fat, fussy, arrogant, and betrays his distaste for Burley's habit of slapping the accompanist's arthritic hands when she slows down the tempo of the carols. Limited to the narrator's knowledge of events, the reader is forced to abandon a search for the reason for Burley's preholiday suicide and focus on the narrator's efforts to cope with the changes wrought by the absence of Burley's muscular voice at the annual carol sing.

Recent changes in Tarbox are subtly worked into description of the remaining singers: the hardware store has become a dropout's hangout; an atomic power plant encroaches on the marsh birds; the Vietnam War has caused one young man to enroll in divinity school, while another returns from the service and becomes a flower child. In the counterpoint provided by the snippets of carols that punctuate the narrator's reflections, Christ's birth promises hope in the winter season, when the surrounding world, as one carol's refrain states, is "bare/and blank and dark with want and care." Yet Burley's absence belies the promises of renewal and reveals a thinness in the voices that attempt to celebrate and reaffirm communal ties. The "new blood" Tarbox needs is present in the form of the young couple, yet the woman with "long thighs glossy as pond ice" appears vital but cold, and her husband, with his "mumble of a mouth" in no way compensates for Burley.

The memory of his bass voice booming out the refrain of "Good King Wenceslas," exhorting others to tread boldly in his footsteps, assumes ironic overtones in reference to the puzzled survivors who continue living in the winter world that he could no longer endure. The carol sing will continue, but with less vigor and a subdued air of desperation, masking "something failed, something hollow." Unlike the more successful and ambitious music of *The Music School*, the music here is less inspired, and more habitual: "If you listened to the words," the narrator reflects, the carols "would break your heart. Silence, darkness, Jesus, angels. Better, I suppose, to sing than to listen." While Schweigen is pierced by the music at his daughter's school, the narrator here sings submissively, numbing himself to the carols' emotional highs and lows. Whatever the cause, Burley's irritated outburst at the arthritic and indifferent accompanist shows his inability to tolerate flagging tempo and enthusiasm. Vulnerable to disillusion, he perhaps listened too intently to the words of spiritual promise he sang, and finally became unable to tolerate the absence of their fulfillment. While Burley's suicide clashes with the seasonal message of rebirth and nags at the town's consciousness, they merely continue to sing, unsure of why; not expecting unalloyed happiness, they find solace in tradition despite evident change.

Since Updike later decided that "Plumbing" belonged with the Maples stories in *Too Far to Go*, it will be discussed in that context, although the narrator's meditation on the comparative durability of human life and new plumbing serves as a fitting conclusion to the main group of stories. The "Other Modes" that intervene between "Plumbing" and the chronologically arranged cluster of Maples stories fill out the volume, but vary in quality. Updike's considerable stylistic talents receive exercise as he ventures further beyond the traditional narrative, although the weight of his well-chosen words threatens to collapse the slighter subjects. For the most part, the "modes" are clever and whimsical, allowing Updike to emerge as a social commentator and fabulist; most in some way echo the volume's prevalent thematic concerns. For example, the two sporting sketches, "The Slump" and "The Pro," develop an analogy between the inability to connect solidly and fluidly with the ball and the diminished happiness of middle age. A number of similar pieces were subsequently included in the "Persons and Places" section that opens *Hugging the Shore*, indicating that perhaps Updike has found a more congenial home for his fugitive prose piece.

In "The Sea's Green Sameness," the most ambitious and successful piece in the group, Updike adopts the pose of authorial self-consciousness that has become the trademark of John Barth and other experimental writers. With his intrusive voice, the writer beside the sea makes the pretense of pulling aside the fictive curtain separating author and reader, creating an essay-like document that resembles the abstract-personal mode of "Leaves" and the other meditations in *The Music School*. Like Emerson, the narrator explores the tension between dualities such as Art and Nature, the Me and the Not-Me. His ostensible subject, the sea, frustrates his attempts to penetrate its surface by its sameness, yielding only subtle distinctions in color; in contrast, meaning unfolds progressively and more easily in written art. Most of the sketch is thus devoted to the artist's dilemmas concerning the rationale behind and techniques of making meaning.

Updike uses "The Sea's Green Sameness" partially to address a personal artistic question: whether a writer should rely on adjectives or trust nouns to be evocative: "I have had only fair luck with people's imaginations; hence tend to trust adjectives," his persona declares. Many commentators admonish Updike for descriptive excesses, yet given language's subjective nature, his concerns seem justified: even adjectives share the fallibility of all words, deriving "intrinsic power" only from some shadowy source. A more universal problem, however, is the artist's need for an "excuse" to justify breaking the silence between ego and external object and bridging the gap; humankind's succession of reasons (none obsolete in the modern age) is varied: the narrative appetite, money, beauty, realism, the search for meaning, and the quest for effect perfected by Joyce and Proust. Updike's purposeful omission of a definitive answer illustrates that the writer's task is not to offer truth—notably absent from his list.

Science, as well as literary modernism, has augmented the writer's difficulty, explaining and diminishing nature's wonder. In an echo of Prufrock's vision of himself as "a pair of ragged claws/ Scuttling across the floors of silent seas," the narrator compares himself to "one of those large crabs . . . scrabbling across a beach, stiffly waving their tentacles at a distended, dim, and oblate sun." Yet Updike's persona may not be as ineffectual as he believes. His quirky experiment concerning altering one's angle of vision does yield a revelation: lying prone, with chin in the sand and one eye closed, he perceives the sea one-dimensionally, as an impenetrable wall. In temporarily defamiliarizing the surrounding environment, he thus grasps its essential quality. He does not accept this wall as absolute, however, but rather maintains a faith that something exists on the other side, encouraging him that repeated attempts to translate its essence would not be fruitless.

Like many of the volume's characters, Updike's persona is tired: "all my stratagems are exhausted. I am near death," he calmly states. Yet this sketch was written in 1960, which perhaps accounts for the sustained belief in art's redeeming power absent from many of the collection's preceding stories. While the reader may be frustrated that the sketch has not really delved into the sea's green sameness and that the writer concludes with his own bafflement, its real point turns out to be the necessity of continuing to write amid diminished expectations: "I do not expect the waves to obey my wand, or support my weight. . . . All I expect is that once into my blindly spun web of words the thing itself will break; make an entry and account of itself." Updike's commentary on the piece reinforces this adjustment of artistic expectations: "narratives should not be *primarily* packages for psychological insights, though they can contain them, like raisins in buns" (*PUP*, 518). While "The Sea's Green Sameness" may be doughier than some of the fiction, it still fulfills Updike's requisite qualities for providing artistic satisfaction, which derives less from "incidental wisdom," than from the realization of the desire "to keep an organized mass of images moving forward," to produce "an instinct for action and pattern," and "To hold through your voice, another soul in thrall" (*PUP*, 518).

The remaining "Other Modes" are cameo portraits and whimsical sketches. "The Slump" is narrated by a baseball player whose sense of wonder and visual acuity have both diminished; an aging athlete who swings in Rabbit's shadow, he seeks a cure for his spiritual torpor in Kierkegaard as well as in the batting cage. In "The Pro," whose narrator is taking his 412th golf lesson, the green unexpectedly becomes a psychiatrist's couch, as the pro works through the narrator's golf anxieties and dreams. The following pair of monologues—"One of My Generation" and "God Speaks"—both reveal how "The world is mocked—belittled, perforated—by the success of our contemporaries in it," as the narrator of the latter declares. In "Under the Microscope," the first of four illustrated stories that appear to be influenced by Donald Barthelme, the volvox which held cosmic significance for Peter Caldwell in *The Centaur* is reduced to an hors d'oeuvre. Updike adjusts his focus to the microscopic, using the unashamed cannibalism of micro-organisms as the basis for a parody of the antagonisms beneath the surface politeness of human gatherings. "During the Jurassic" is another satiric party sketch which uses mildly humanized textbook descriptions of dinosaurs to heighten the grotesqueness of human social interactions. The emotions and ambitions expressed are as genuine as those in "I Will Not Go, Lest Thou Bless Me," but the host's lust, awakened by a female diplodocus, and her husband's ambition to abandon his business and enter seminary to find himself, strike the reader as delightfully absurd when acted out on this scale. The dry encyclopedic tone of portions of "The Baluchitherium," a fanciful interview with the world's largest land mammal, is redeemed somewhat by the blend of comedy and moral lesson on gracefully accepting evolutionary doom. The costs of progress are likewise the concern of "The Invention of the Horse Collar," an adaptation of the Cain and Abel story set in the Dark Ages. Finally, "Jesus on the Honshu," fleshes out a supposed newspaper report of a legend concerning Christ's survival among the Japanese.

While of some interest as evidence of Updike's humor and his talents in adapting other material, these experiments on the fringes of fiction lead back to a heightened appreciation of what Updike does best: portraying the nuances of the ongoing emotional and spiritual crises that accompany maturity and marriage. *Museums and Women* restores the reader to this domain in the final section of stories concerning Joan and Richard Maple, who reemerge as Updike's preferred representatives of wedded tribulations. In these five stories, the sway of eros increasingly strains their relationship, but does not break the bonds that keep them trapped in the circularity of an enduring marriage. Their marriage has become what Tristan avoids in *The Music School*'s "Four Sides of One Story" through his escape: the "paradoxical ethical situation" of being "repeatedly wounded by someone *because he or she is beloved*." Locked in a dance of mutual need and wounding, they seem to have strayed dramatically from the goal of simple happiness evoked in the headnote. Updike provides a measure of this distance when he incorporates these stories into *Too Far to Go*.

Mapping Marital Fault Lines:
Too Far to Go

Updike's married, separated, and divorced protagonists, critics complain, seem mere masks for the same educated, chafed middle-class sensibility, but when Updike began to employ Joan and Richard Maple as repeated characters in the mid-1960s, he did so not to answer his critics but rather to converge upon and cluster a particular set of experiences concerning the inherent fault lines of marriage. Although he originally may have had no plans to gather these stories together, Updike nonetheless had created a series linked in readers' minds. In 1970, when only a few of the eight extant Maples stories had been collected (and half of the total had not yet been written), Alice and Kenneth Hamilton observed that Updike was in the process of devising a strategy for overcoming the intrinsic difficulties of treating marriage within the short story's confines: "As a 'thing' to be reported, married love does not fit easily into short story form. Each marriage, after all, is a developing experience in the context of a particular society caught up in the stream of history. . . . Updike has attempted to provide historical perspective by making his married couples, in general, age along with their creator. . . . However, he has also found a strategy for making the short story record marriage-history. This involves linking stories, divided in time of writing, through the expedient of having them depict successive incidents in the history of one specific marriage."[40]

Updike subsequently acknowledged the evolving coherence and integrity of the Maples stories by grouping five then-uncollected tales in the final section of *Museums and Women*: "Marching Through Boston," "The Taste of Metal," "Your Lover Just Called," "Eros Rampant," and "Sublimating." Along with "Plumbing," which appears elsewhere in that collection, this cluster forms the core of *Too Far to Go*, whose stories ultimately span five collections and over 20 years of Updike's career. As Jane Barnes remarks, "None of them suffers from the stylistic excesses that mark other stories—as if the Maple series were the best stories from any given stage of Updike's developing perception."[41] Symmetrical and tightly crafted, most contain recurrent motifs and an ironic conclusion; with some variations in form, they focus on moments of present tension while allowing glimpses of a shared past. Perhaps the reason behind their success is a quality about his couple that Updike notes in his foreword: "they talk, more easily than any other characters the author has acted as agent for."[42] Thus, a stylistic as well as a substantive unity distinguishes this remarkably coherent chronicle of a representative marital history.

This definitive gathering of the Maples stories, however, might not have been part of the Updike canon had producer Robert Geller not decided to adapt the Maples stories for a television drama.[43] When Updike's publisher requested a television tie-in edition, however, the author (well aware that literary adaptations often wander far afield[44]) eagerly accepted the chance to put the Maples in a book of their own. The result, which Anatole Broyard characterizes as "another order of experience" from the television version,[45] is a short story sequence resembling *Olinger Stories* and the Bech books. Like Bech, the Maples are somewhat static, blocked in their quest to end their marital distress by either reconciling their differences or terminating their relationship. Just as *Olinger Stories* simultaneously memorializes an attachment to a place and depicts the local boy's separation from it, the Maples stories enact a similar ceremony of farewell, celebrating the end of a marriage with a series of snapshots that capture significant moments during its gradual dissolution.

While primarily an arrangement of the Maples stories published in other collections, *Too Far to Go* goes beyond inspired editing. Updike included seven previously uncollected stories (two of which subsequently appeared in *Problems*), as well as two stories—"Wife-Wooing" and "Plumbing"—that he concluded "from internal evidence appear to take place in Richard Maple's mind" (*TFTG*, 10).[46] The cluster from *Museums and Women* is broken up somewhat by intervening stories; only the first three remain together. Overall, evidence of changes in the Maples and their children indicates uninterrupted chronological progress from the mid-1950s to the mid-1970s, and the collection as a whole is well-balanced: the first four stories, which conclude with the reluctant decision to separate in "Twin Beds in Rome," are offset by the final quartet, in which this resolve is finally acted on. Updike's hand, however, is most evident in the placement of the uncollected and "newly discovered" Maples stories, creating juxtapositions (such as the reflective "Plumbing" with the chaotic "Eros Rampant") that add another dimension to the work. In addition, certain repeated motifs—

some of which may be coincidental, others which clearly are not—cut across the grain to provide coherence: Richard's illnesses, the characters Mack and Eleanor Dennis, the focus on the couple's homes, images of voids, and even allusions to Hänsel and Gretel recur in different stories. Finally, Albert Wilhelm's study of the volume's first story, "Snowing in Greenwich Village," clearly demonstrates that Updike has revised its conclusion so that Richard appears "slightly less juvenile in his behavior and less innocent in his moral perspective."[47] Such efforts clearly mark the finished product as more than a hasty assembly of old stories cashing in on the television drama.

The genesis of these stories in the marital crises experienced by Updike and his first wife, Mary, also lends the volume unity and realism. Certain autobiographical parallels between the Maples and Updikes are easily inventoried: both couples are married for over 20 years, have four children, follow a similar pattern in their relocation, oscillate between infidelity and reconciliation, and finally obtain one of the first "no-fault" divorces in Massachusetts. However thin the veil between fiction and life, *Too Far to Go* is not a public airing of dirty laundry; rather, Updike uses the contours of his own life to create a study of the evolution of a prototypical marriage subtly affected by the sociopolitical changes sweeping the modern era. The marriage, in fact, becomes the book's real protagonist, since its partners essentially become subsumed by it. While Joan and Richard are clearly sketched as separate characters, they struggle to maintain their identities as marriage compresses them into a single individual. "Their eyes," the narrator of "Sublimating" observes, "had married and merged to three," so that they see not only into each other but also through a common lens. Generally, Updike seems to be more comfortable working through Richard's consciousness, revealing how the marriage binds him, but the narration switches as needed to a more objective view of the relationship.

The opening story, "Snowing in Greenwich Village," depicts Richard as easy prey to adulterous temptations, and as early as the volume's third story, "Giving Blood," the Maples seem on the verge of splitting; in "Twin Beds" they achieve temporary release from the forces holding them together, but Richard's pronouncement that they've "come too far" in their marriage and "have only a little way more to go" turns out to be mistaken by about 10 years and 13 stories. In reality, neither seems to be able to go physically or emotionally far enough away from the other to separate, despite their adulteries; furthermore, neither seems to be able to make concessions that would move the couple closer to lasting reconciliation. Like the trees evocative of small-town life for which they are named, the Maples maintain what Updike characterizes as "an arboreal innocence," and their marriage continues to provide a shelter of "cooling leafiness"—at least during portions of the seasonal cycle. Although they progress inexorably toward divorce, their actions, which Updike compares to "a duet . . . repeated over and over, ever more harshly transposed," form a cycle finally broken only by legal action.

Their marriage evolves through phases: beginning with early doubts, temptations, and overtures toward separation; next moving into increasing frustration, demystification, and adultery; then bogging down in a series of arguments and stalemates; and finally culminating in a legal separation that renovates their vision of their marriage's enduring value. As Updike asserts in the foreword, "Though the Maples stories trace the decline and fall of a marriage, they also illumine a history in many ways happy, of growing children and a million mundane moments shared. That a marriage ends is less than ideal; but all things end under heaven, and if temporality is held to be invalidating, then nothing real succeeds" (*TFTG*, 9–10). Unlike the more protected realm of youth that the maple tree evokes, the security of marriage does not shower unexpected gifts, but rather teaches that "all blessings are mixed," whether they be children, lovers, new homes—or even no-fault divorce laws. Still, as in his earlier work, Updike continues to insist on the need to believe that human endeavor—no matter how ambivalent—begets something persistent.

"Marching Through Boston," first in the section from *Museums and Women* and fifth in the Maples volume, picks up quite naturally where "Twin Beds in Rome" left off; in fact, the juxtaposition with the other Maple stories creates a number of echoes that lend the book coherence. Last seen walking through Rome nursing Richard's "precious and fragile" pain, the Maples have preserved the marriage they resolved to end—although they have not nursed it back to health. In "Marching Through Boston," the tourist's stroll of the previous story becomes a more purposeful civil rights march that Richard endures even though he is once again ill, this time with a fever. He still attempts to use his ailments to command attention and manipulate Joan, who has become more earnestly independent through her civil rights activism; while concerned with her week-long cold in "Snowing in Greenwich Village" and apologetic about his stomach problems in Rome, in this story Richard more openly flaunts his malady and revels in his own pain. The motif of separation receives further reiteration: previously consigned to perpendicular tables in "Giving Blood" and the twin beds in Rome, the Maples are divided once again when the marchers assemble in rows. Situated between an African with tribal scars and her former analyst, Joan seems surrounded by "her id and superego"; Richard, meanwhile, relishes being next to an uncomfortably cold 16-year-old girl attending only because she hopes it will help her in writing a term paper.

As in the other Maples stories, the viewpoint is limited to Richard's consciousness; even so, he comes across as much less sympathetic; the jealousy he feels about Joan's happiness at the end of "Twin Beds in Rome" has acquired a new bitterness. His skepticism about the civil rights movement may be a corrective to Joan's zealous liberal commitment, yet his eagerness to debunk the cause, as well as the concluding parody of black dialect, stems from jealousy of Joan's quest for self-realization and annoyance that their accustomed "rhythm of apathy and renewal" has been disturbed rather than from genuine opposition. Joan flourishes in her altruism, while Richard subsides into self-centeredness. His promise to march with her, whatever its original motives, becomes an opportunity to prove himself a martyr. His combination of lust, medication, and fever makes him "strangely exalted and excited, as if destined to give birth"; by the time the Maples arrive home, however, Richard gives birth instead to a childish "voice crying for attention from the depths of oppression." His protest against Joan's insensitivity, begun on the drive home in a quarrel reminiscent of the one in "Giving Blood," becomes extreme when his parody of the black leaders' rhetorical style degenerates into crude mimicry of a slave. This attempt to dramatize his "oppression" deliberately alienates Joan, who dismisses his problem as a "tiny cold" and ignores his feverish and pathetic babbling in order to return to her fight against real oppression.

In "The Taste of Metal," Richard's recent dental work sets the context for a lesson in diminishment. Driving home from a party in his new Corvair with their recently separated friend Eleanor Dennis, the inebriated Richard reflects on how he is "resiliently cushioned: Eleanor was beside him, Joan behind him, God above him, the road beneath him," yet he gives no thought to what lies ahead of him. Inevitably, the car slides on the icy roads, into the telephone pole, and while Joan goes for the police, Richard remains in the car with Eleanor. After he sobers slightly, the taste of metal from his dental work extends his earlier reflections on how he is "slightly less than himself" into a consciousness of the irreparable losses that time will claim: his new car, his original teeth, Eleanor's high kicks. In the face of such diminishments, Richard succumbs to the adulterous yearnings that first flared in "Snowing in Greenwich Village"; as Greiner has noted, the police car's blue light, illuminating the guilty lovers' groping at the story's conclusion, provides a marked contrast to the police on horseback at whom Joan marveled in more innocent days (190). While Rebecca Cune's apartment was "hot as hell" during Richard's first winter temptation, the mangled Corvair is chilly until he turns on the heater and turns up his passion for Eleanor. Richard ignores this blatant warning of the consequences of reckless behavior, seeking to banish the taste of metal with a taste of adultery.

"Your Lover Just Called," balances Richard's embrace of Eleanor with Joan's affectionate display toward her ex-husband. Joan again comes across as the more sympathetic of the two, while Richard, given his record of infidelity, overplays the role of the wronged husband. At this impasse in their marriage, both Maples suffer from an escalating paranoia that makes what may be a simple wrong number into an excuse for mutual accusation. "Eros Rampant" subsequently provides another dimension to the possible validity of Richard's accusations, however, when readers learn that Joan also has indulged in extramarital affairs. Overall, the reader finishes "Your Lover Just Called" unable to pass judgment on whether the suspicions of either spouse are justified; while the caller could have dialed a wrong number, the narrator reinforces the title's premise in the concluding sentence when he states "the lover hung up." Whichever Maple is correct, their marriage has become blighted by their mutual doubts and defensiveness, even though this story concludes with a tenuous truce after Richard's once-again unsuccessful sexual overtures.

Inserted between this story and "Eros Rampant," "Waiting Up" confirms Richard's infidelity and presents its repercussions on others' lives, although on her return from her mission as the intermediary who must smooth out the situation, Joan reports that the aggrieved neighbors are "full of goodness and love." "Eros Rampant," which begins with a verbal echo—"The Maples' house is full of love"—immediately modifies any notion of Joan as the innocent victim when her infidelity is revealed. Ironically, the house of a couple perpetually on the verge of separating fairly brims over with love in many different forms, but the title foreshadows the potentially chaotic effects of unrestrained erotic attraction on the Maples' domestic order. Updike's lengthy catalogues of each family member's cherished items demonstrate the range (and limitations of) their loves. While Joan—as an object of erotic desire— tops Richard's list (which also includes Penelope Vogel, the office secretary, and "the memories of six or so other women"), he is notably absent from hers, which begins with her psychiatrist and ends with the children, whose love surrounds her and excludes him from her warmth. In this house so full of love, the mutual attraction of the two key players is the essential missing ingredient. Their behavior has come to resemble that of Esther and Esau, their two cats: Joan, like the recently spayed Esther, "merely accepts and understands him. She seems scornful of his merely dutiful attentions"; Richard, like Esau, "now must venture from the house in quest of the bliss that had once been purely domestic" (*TFTG*, 125).

Richard, however, is a pitiful tomcat whose planned seduction of Penelope never gets off the ground. Rebounding from an affair with an Antiguan, she expresses wariness of married men who are "too wrapped up back home" and a preference for black men. When Joan suddenly confronts him with her affairs that evening, he again finds himself rebuffed by her allusion to the incident: "you look pale to me too." Although he calls her a "whore," he perversely enjoys the stature of his new status as cuckold and feels a secret excitement in knowing she is attractive to other men. Even though it momentarily returns them to the "elemental constituents" of their marriage, bringing these affairs out in the open does little to close the gap between them. With this command of metaphor, Updike suddenly transforms their bedroom into an aquarium, and the Maples become "dark fish in ink, their outlines barely visible, known to each other only as eddies of warmth, as mysterious animate chasms in the surface of space." With these familiar strangers, even the shock of Joan's revelation fails to clarify their vision.

While Richard seeks titillation in exacting details from Joan, his dream, in which she exults in her promiscuity and demonstrates her flexibility with strange new yoga postures, reveals his true anxiety. After he awakens, the bed seems "the lip of a vortex," only Richard does not fear the godless universe that haunts David Kern in "Pigeon Feathers" but the depths of Joan's character, "an abyss of secretness, perfidy, and acceptingness." Down in the familiar kitchen (the site of the dream), he finds comfort in the children's drawings, visible evidence of loving domesticity. Yet absent from the short list that echoes an earlier inventory of their contents are the previously mentioned drawings of dogs, indiscriminate in their love, and families, whose continued existence amid the turbulent forces of eros seems ever more precarious.

Although the most violent scene in the collection is embedded in its center, "Plumbing"'s meditative mood provides a dramatic shift in tone.

Just as the Maples' marriage has persisted but developed problems, so the plumbing of their new house has survived into another age; it too needs work, a victim of decay's eventuality. The plumber, like the artist who reveals daily life's intrinsic beauties, makes Richard (who becomes the narrator in the context of the volume) aware of the art involved in the antique plumbing: "He knows my plumbing: I merely own it." Richard holds a similar attitude of simple proprietorship toward his marriage, a subterranean maze of personal history taken for granted. In buying a new house the Maples move into another phase of their relationship, but the accretions of over a dozen years of shared experience symbolically remain in the nearly clogged pipes that need replacement.

Memories, of course, are more than sludge, but the metaphoric connection between the house's history and his own sends Richard sifting through the sediment of his past, hoping to counter the suspicion raised by the discovery of the deteriorated pipes: "We think we are what we think and see when in truth we are upright bags of tripe" (*TFTG*, 145). The precariousness of existence is further illustrated by the ease with which the movers erase their presence from the old house: "Nature is tougher than ecologists admit. Our house forgot us in a day." Yet memories, however ghostlike they appear, seem to build like the mineral deposits in the conduits below, forming "myth upon myth" that becomes "stamped deep, like dinosaur footprints"; even the indelible stains on the carpet can preserve a key to the past.

Images of spring's renewal and memories of carefree Easters during Richard's childhood and the couple's early days balance the foreboding images of pipes clogged like arteries, threatening to "burn out the pump." More so than the volume's other stories, however, "Plumbing" dwells on the persistent intimations of mortality. Both the antique plumbing and the Maples' marriage, however carefully crafted, inevitably spring leaks. Yet, as the plumber innocently remarks, pipes can be replaced "to outlast your time here"; his ambiguity about the time frame creates a quiver of mortality in Richard, who emerges from the basement to a vision of the "temporary timeless clouds" that provide further reinforcement that we are surrounded by change as well as outlasted. Again, Updike concludes his story with an echoed variation of an earlier phrase: initially, the plumber muses on "the eternal presences of corrosion and flow," but by the story's conclusion, after their full impact has struck Richard's consciousness, these presences have become "unspeakable" rather than eternal.

"The Red Herring Theory" portrays the Maples—led by Richard—

spinning elaborate webs of deception that only serve to alienate them further from each other's affections. While the party guests after whom they clean up may be messy, the Maples' extramarital entanglements with them have made their own lives just as untidy. As they engage in an oddly dispassionate analysis of strategies to divert suspicion of adultery, Joan, perched in a director's chair, clearly holds the upper hand in this game of verbal obfuscation; a guilty Richard prolongs the conversation, attempting to throw her off the track of his current affair with Ruth by claiming to pursue women in whom he currently has no interest. Joan's harder edge is juxtaposed with Richard's nostalgia: he fondly recalls the scene with the police on horses from "Snowing in Greenwich Village" and rues their move from the New York apartment, as if staying there would have maintained that innocence. Richard's resolution to sleep with his "red-herring" illustrates how far the Maples have proceeded on the road to estrangement.

"Sublimating" begins as an experiment in renewal with potentially comic overtones but quickly becomes another skirmish in the Maples' ongoing war of wills. Ostensibly, their abstinence is undertaken as a self-prescribed "cure" for an ailing marriage whose only "sore point"—at least according to their diagnosis—is sex; their efforts to stay apart, however, may be an unwitting rehearsal for their subsequent separation. An undercurrent of discontent strengthens as they prolong this game of self-denial, which turns out to be more treacherous than the psychological one-upmanship of "The Red-Herring Theory": sublimation ultimately culminates in the emergence of Richard's suppressed violence and Joan's inability to suppress his fear of death.

Initially, Richard marvels at his receptivity to beauty, rediscovering sensuality and youthful joy in the vegetable aisle when he purchases a cabbage, whose pleasing spheric heft becomes sexually suggestive. At first, Richard uses this cabbage as an exercise in self-discipline: his anticipation of eating its spicy heart is a rehearsal of deferred pleasure. Later, it reminds him not only of Joan's skill at presenting her affairs so neatly packaged but also—cut open—of the female brain's convolutions. Joan too begins the experiment resolutely, sublimating her energies into domestic routines and discovering sensual wonder in the workings of a car wash. Yet by the second week, Richard's sexual frustration emerges in his merciless pruning of the yew trees that he claims deny him entrance to his front door; just as his rapacious pruning may kill the rare trees, so may his experiment in celibacy damage the remnant of the Maples' marriage. By the fourth week, Richard becomes increasingly alienated from his family and suppresses his desire to punch Joan in the face only because he fears breaking one of a dwindled set of treasured honeymoon glasses. The only benefits of this celibacy appear to be an improvement in Richard's golf game, a clean car, and the accomplishment of an enormous amount of yard work.

Despite Joan's subtle overture to end their celibacy, Richard resists, enjoying for once the power of refusal. She attempts to find compensation in her heightened sensitivity to nature, but it also increases her consciousness of her mortality; when ignoring the call of eros, the voice of thanatos clamors louder. For Richard, a month's abstinence has convinced him that "transient satisfactions of the living flesh were a flawed and feeble prelude"—a mere "backswing" for a flight that leads beyond the withdrawal of sex to a self-satisfied withdrawal of himself. The concluding image of the Maples lying parallel in bed, praising the similar "cleansing" that unleashed the Crusades and pronouncing their experiment a success is highly ironic; both continue to hold out, but neither sincerely believes that sublimating has remedied their problems.

"Nakedness," which takes place three years later, makes a discernible shift in the couple's interpersonal dynamics: relieved of the responsibilities for their scattered teenagers for the summer, they find themselves "too exposed" and unsure of how to relate to each other. Although the story's narrative time stretches over a single day, Updike employs two symmetrical scenes—one on the beach, the other in the bedroom—to bracket a free-ranging central catalogue of Richard's reflections on nakedness. Provoked by the nude couple's "invasion" of the family beach, it ranges from allusions to nudity featured in art, literature, and the media to the memory of an incident during his affair with a woman who slept beside a mirror. When the adulterous couple once thought they had been caught in the act, he guiltily hid himself, while she, like a "trespasser from Eden," strolled through her house brazenly nude. Richard's recent memory of being naked at the nearby pond, where "sex dropped from him and he seemed indeed the divinely shaped center of a bowl-shaped Creation, shows that he can momentarily transcend nudity's erotic dimension"; the moment ends abruptly, however, when he discovers ticks crawling up his legs.

Similarly, the precarious freedom of the nude invasions in both the opening and concluding scenes dissipates abruptly. The nudists' trespass invites a repercussion from the police officer, who disperses other nude sunbathers from the adjacent beach; Joan, sympathetically liberal, sees this eviction as recapitulating the banishment of Adam and Eve.

That evening, Joan and Richard seemingly reverse the process as they disrobe, yet while they stand together in a "new nakedness," their condition is clearly post-Edenic. Too aware of nakedness as a prelude to lovemaking, they cannot emulate the unaffected nudity of the couple on the beach, whose sexuality is defused by their even tans and the public setting. Still, Joan's sexual refusal brings them closer to that state, so that Richard feels "thrilled, invaded," assaulted with the defamiliarized— yet not deeroticized—body of the same women whose elusive raptures he sings in "Wife-Wooing."

"Separating" poignantly chronicles the Maples' painful task of informing their children about their decision to embark on a trial separation. After Richard accedes to Joan's plan to tell each of the children separately, however, his grief overwhelms him at his daughter Judith's welcome-home dinner; the incessant tears streaming down his face force Joan to reveal the truth prematurely, eliciting reactions that range from the eldest daughter's cool rationality to the youngest son's bizarre cigarette and napkin eating. The task of breaking the news to their eldest son, Dickie, remains Richard's—a final "knife-like wall" that he cannot sidestep; the ironic location of this disclosure, which takes place between a church and the house of a former mistress, is not lost on him. Although Dickie initially appears unshaken by the news, his masculine facade breaks down in the story's conclusion, when he kisses his father passionately on the lips and asks the simple but crucial question: "*Why*. It was a whistle of wind in a crack, a knife thrust, a window thrown open on emptiness. The white face was gone, the darkness was featureless. Richard had forgotten why" (*TFTG*, 211). After all the pain and well-rehearsed answers, Richard can no longer account for the fading of love and the resolve to discontinue an enduring relationship.

Earlier in the story, Richard makes last-minute repairs on their house—sublimating his nervous energy in a final gesture of loving concern for the security of the family he must leave. "Obsessed with battening down the house against his absence," he becomes "a Houdini making things snug before his escape," yet as he replaces an old lock, signs of the futility of his preparations suddenly become evident. These small reminders of entropy can be successfully repressed as he works, but Dickie's question forces a confrontation with the inevitable emptiness that yawns on the other side of the last obstacle Richard must surmount. Although Richard's manliness during this crisis is never explicitly questioned, there are a number of role reversals in the story; not only is it Richard who is unable to control his tears, but when he and his youngest son return to the table, he notes that where Joan is sitting has become the head, foreshadowing the state of affairs that will ensue when the couple ultimately manages to separate.

"Gesturing" finds the Maples three months later, trying to enforce their unsuccessful trial separation, only to discover that as they progress further toward the finality of divorce, the lovers for whom they are ostensibly sacrificing their marriage are less real than their shared history. While Joan professes a willingness to give up her lover, Richard is wary of exacting such a sacrifice, especially since her current affair now gives him tacit license to continue his own. Certain actions in "Gesturing" recapitulate events from the collection's earlier stories: Richard's delight at being newly established in his bachelor apartment in Boston is reminiscent of the couple's pleasure in "Snowing in Greenwich Village" when they move into their first apartment; in addition, when they go out to dinner, the couple feels illicit, just as they did during the impromptu pancake breakfast that concludes "Giving Blood." In this case, however, Joan reveals secrets about her lover over a meal that ends not in Richard's diatribe and the renewal of an ongoing quarrel but in a muted recognition of the endurance of gestures that will ultimately transcend any separation decree.

Updike's skill in weaving a network of motifs into the fabric of events is particularly evident in "Gesturing." As the story progresses, Richard becomes more attuned to the arresting gestures that make up the texture of daily life, ranging from Joan's nonverbal flourishes to the more physically enduring wedding vows etched on the apartment window glass through which he studies Boston's Hancock Building. This ill-fated structure, itself a grand gesture of architectural vision, becomes Richard's new "companion and witness" and the story's central symbol: "The skyscraper, for years suspended in a famous state of incompletion, was a beautiful disaster, famous because it was a disaster (glass kept falling from it) and disastrous because it was beautiful" (*TFTG*, 216). The ragged skyscraper attempts to embody an ideal and (with its mirrored surfaces) harmonize contradictory elements; like the Maples' marriage, unstable pieces of the facade keep slipping off, revealing ugly substructures such as jealousy, hypocrisy, cruelty, and selfishness beneath the smooth surface.

Close up, the building loses the grandeur that Richard can still endow it with from a distance: "so lovely in air, [it] had tangled mucky roots," like the clogged pipes in "Plumbing" or the vine in "Twin Beds in Rome"—other metaphors for the Maples' marriage. Similarly, while together, the Maples are all too aware of the mundane elements of domestic life; as they recede from direct daily contact, their marriage assumes greater luster. Thus, Joan, "giddy among the spinning mirrors of her betrayals" can sit at dinner and anatomize her lover's foibles (much to her husband's discomfort), trusting Richard fully despite his betrayals. Like the etched wedding vows, Joan's gestures will endure, he realizes, part of the haphazard assembly of memories that will outlive their relationship.

The title of "Divorcing: A Fragment" calls attention to the fact that it "cried off completion," as Updike remarks in the foreword. The only piece that never gains an independent existence beyond *Too Far to Go*, it lacks the symmetry and tightness of the other stories; within the story sequence, it serves as an interlude between the Maples' physical separation and final divorce. Vignette-like in texture, "Divorcing" consists of a single scene in which Richard must comfort a depressed, suicidal Joan and simultaneously preserve the momentum of their separation, even though he doubts the "tired mottoes" he spouts to preserve their "numb marching forward." The wording coincidentally recalls the "marching" through Rome and Boston in previous stories, but Richard, decidedly kinder and healthier here, is more resolved to see the divorce through. While Joan's strength of character has been ascending since the second story, in "Divorcing," Richard, guilty about the health and happiness he has achieved on his own, must finally take the lead and demand the final "letting go" that has eluded them for so long. Although lacking the reach back into the past and structural symmetry that characterize many of the companion Maples stories, "Divorcing: A Fragment" weighs enough to be a story—especially given the manner in which Updike has been responsible for altering our conception of the short story's scope.

Ironically more appropriate to the introduction of a new couple at the close of a wedding ceremony, the final story's title, "Here Come the Maples," derives from the language of the affidavit required for the Maples' no-fault divorce. The no-fault concept, designed to reduce unnecessary charges and to speed up the process, is particularly appropriate to the Maples' situation, since it suggests the impossibility of assigning blame to either party. The story consists of three main sections: Richard's trip to City Hall to procure a copy of the marriage license, his visit to the doctor for a psychosomatic flare-up of arthritis, and the divorce "ceremony." Richard's journeys in preparation for their divorce become retreats into memory, punctuated by his reading of a scientific article on the forces of nature that provides oblique commentary on the forces that hold couples together and push them apart. The collection's last story uncovers the earliest layer of their marital history, as Richard gains new access to "forgotten doors opening on the corridor of shared addresses" which the previous stories have chronicled. On the eve of permanent commitment to separate addresses, Richard encounters an image of domestic "fidelity and solidarity and stability" on the notary's desk, yet amid the flood of conjugal memories, he guiltily fulfills the tasks needed to undo their marriage.

The retrieval of these memories is more sporadic than the more sustained plunges that mark Updike's earlier ventures into memories of childhood and adolescence. Richard's spotty recollections lack the characteristic shimmering detail of the Olinger stories; instead, they are likened to "legible patches on a damp gray blotter" and a "box of slides"—images which could readily be used to describe the volume as a whole. The remembered snippets move back in time, touching on their early married days at a summer camp, their wedding and honeymoon (during which they play croquet naked in the quest to create enduring memories), and their courtship in college. In a redux of the fairy tale motif that appears previously in "Giving Blood," Richard remembers them obtaining their wedding license, like "Hänsel and Gretel in his mind's eye," running "up the long flight of stairs into a gingerbread-brown archway." The same image recurs in the courtroom, before the decree is granted: "He had set her free, free from fault. She was to him as Gretel to Hänsel, a kindred creature moving beside him down a path while birds behind them ate the bread crumbs" (*TFTG*, 253). This new innocence, however, occurs too late, and only as a function of their divorce. No indicators of the path back exist; it is indeed "too far to go," since they can now move only forward, accompanied by lawyers. In the end, the Maples enact a ritual that neatly mirrors the wedding ceremony, complete with Joan declaring "I do" in answer to the judge's final question and Richard bestowing the kiss he forgot at the close of their wedding ceremony. Thus the Maples come full circle, with a gesture that provides closure to both the story itself and to the volume as a whole in a civilized and ambiguous end to a marriage.

Updike sets up an equation between the forces of nature and those that affect a relationship and leaves it purposely undeveloped: the correspondences set up (ranked in order of increasing strength) are gravity and love; the weak force and habit; electromagnetism and time; and the strong force and boredom. The latter two forces, Richard notes, become the great levelers of continued relationships, although the article he reads notes that the strong force "gets weaker as the quarks are pushed closer together"—much the same way physical attraction works with the Maples. Even as they undo their marriage, the weaker forces of love and habit exert a pull; in the courtroom, Joan is "the only animate object . . . that did not repel him." Like the enduring gestures in a previous story, these forces maintain ties even as other forces compel them toward legal separation.

Similarly, the Maples stories, each generically discrete, are held together by "weak" forces: the creative gravity that brought Updike back to this particular couple and the fictional habits that produced repeated motifs, sustained ambiguity, and stories rather than chapters. Updike also manages to overcome the leveling effect of the stronger forces. Narrative time becomes a framework for organizing the stories into a coherent history, and, concentrated in a single volume, the Maples stories in no way breed boredom; instead, they engage the reader in the active development of character and theme, so that even as the Maples finally separate, the strands of their story are woven together.

The Geometry of Guilt: *Problems*

From his reading in Kierkegaard, Updike states, he "received the sensation of human life being intrinsically difficult and intrinsically flawed, a sensation that there are more problems in life than solutions" (Reilly, 153). In his other 1979 collection, *Problems*, Updike concentrates on the adversities of middle-age, a "kind of idling time," he remarks, "when things are cooking but nothing comes to a boil."[48] For his middle-aged characters, disengaged from security by the collapse of relationships, trouble increasingly obscures youth's acute perception of mystery. Like Ferguson in "The Egg Race," who readily accepts his past as paradise but sustains no desire to dwell there, they are oriented more toward present sorrows than past bliss. As they separate and seek new attachments, they engage in an ongoing struggle with guilt. Former ties no longer bind, but still complicate any attempt at a fresh start. Such adversity, Updike maintains, "in immunological doses has its uses; more than that crushes" (*HS*, 840). Confronted with the continued dissolution of stability, his characters discover no easy solutions to foster imaginative reengagement with the world and are often consigned to be witnesses rather than actors.

Divorce carries a profound burden of guilt for these troubled protagonists, and the emotional wreckage strewn in the wake of separations fills the landscape of middle age with what the title of one story calls "guilt-gems." *Problems* conducts sustained archeology into the world that the narrator of "The Egg Race" so eloquently describes:

> The stratum of middle age has its insignia, its clues, its distinguishing emotional artifacts: the glaze of unreality, for instance, that intervenes even in moments of what formerly would have been rapture. The middle distance blurs, and the floor appears to tilt, as if in unsteady takeoff toward some hopelessly remote point. New glasses help. The axis of astigmatism is rotating, the world is turning, the soul finds itself locked in a house with smeary windows. Contrariwise, the mail, once so pregnant with mysteries and stimulations, can now be read without opening the envelopes. . . . Into the wastebasket it can go unopened, cleanly posted to the void.[49]

Diminished rapture, spiritual disorientation, and mystery's remoteness all increase as death seems closer than youth and the past seems less accessible. Like the unopened mail, Updike's characters often feel "cleanly posted to the void," yet only explorations of the painful geometry of guilt help surmount melancholy. Whatever epiphanies they now experience are tinged with guilt or irony, driving home with a poignant sting the lesson that suffering may ennoble but does not purge; thrust back into the midst of new domestic tribulations, they must discover how to avoid succumbing to tragic resignation. Their souls may grow calluses, but such hard-earned protection may be part of the problem— not the solution—if the cost is lost sensitivity to the sad beauties inherent in life's waning. They may discover, as Farnham does in "Atlantises," that actuality is "a second–rate club" in which membership "is secured through a mix of mediocre credentials and fortuitous qualifications, while a host of preferable possibilities vainly clamor outside for admission" (*P*, 255).

Updike's author's note replaces the usual epigraph and—using language that evokes the cover illustration depicting the geometry of marital difficulty—obliquely alerts us to his personal hardships during the "curve of sad time" *Problems* subtends.[50] The note begins by punningly drawing attention to the interim between collections—"Seven years since my last short-story collection? There must have been problems"—and concludes by dedicating the volume to his four children. Persistently in the background of Updike's earlier short fiction, children assume the foreground in many of these stories, as the gulf between them and their separating parents widens and sometimes erupts with suppressed anguish. Although Updike's wry apology seems to allude to artistic difficulties, he appears to have had few formal or stylistic problems with the short story during the period of his separation and divorce; in fact, Greiner confidently declares that "*Problems* will eventually be judged as one of the major collections of American short stories published in the twentieth century."[51] Updike's continued experiments with the sketch and the "abstract personal" mode appear in the first third of the collection; in addition, he continues to refine the montage technique. Nor has he abandoned his vintage excursions into memory or more traditional stories with crisply nuanced dialogue. Sustained lyric flights have become less frequent, and his style has become leaner and less adjectival, but metaphors and similes still unexpectedly transform the texture of everyday objects and events.

"Commercial" opens the collection with a metafictional tale that juxtaposes an analysis of a silent television commercial for gas heating and an episode from the life of the man who views the commercial. Both incidents are explicated in the same fashion, using capital letters to emphasize the key images and ideas of the evolving dramas. The narrator, who adopts the first-person plural, serves as a roving camera eye as well as a commentator dramatizing his attempts to connect the two scenes and to unravel their theme and purpose. He exults that "There is so much to see," even in a piece of commercial nostalgia featuring stereotypical characters such as an impish boy and a tolerant grandmother. He is fascinated by the commercial's unsupplied details, its artistic contrivance, the recurrent motifs, and the mystery of what product is being sold. The commercial's warm ambiance contrasts with the cold pervading the subsequent bedroom scene. Although described in the same deadpan fashion, this second incident is obviously not a commercial: its hero lives in a less idealized home and performs a television taboo (urination); furthermore, the in-depth excursion into his thoughts and the "cameo mug shots" of the philosophers lend the second narrative a more abstract and less pictorial texture. A tension absent from the natural gas advertisement underlies the man's battle against insomnia, which finally concludes with a reluctant capitulation to using ear plugs.

Updike's technique suggests that the line between the fiction and reality is more blurred than readers might at first imagine. By maintaining the same analytical technique, the narrator creates parallel narrative mysteries, yet the more problematic domestic scene does not yield the same neat message as the commercial, and the story concludes with a sense that the narrator poses the wrong question when he asks what is being advertised. The correct response—"nothing"—gets readers no closer to the real problem, which concerns his sleeping wife, his unfulfilled lust, and his longings for ideal beauty amid the mundane. Such irresolution is Updike's intriguing way of setting up the questions that will constitute this volume's central concern.

A series of brief vignettes spliced together using a cinematic quick cut method, "Believers" resembles "Museums and Women" in structure but lacks its dense imagistic coherence and tone of yearning. The eight chronologically ordered scenes are loosely connected by their focus on Credo, a self-proclaimed believer with a somewhat ironic allegorical name who seems to give more thought to the present than the eternal. Although at one point he reads St. Augustine, Credo does not grapple with spiritual turbulence; instead, he serves on a church committee overseeing the move to a new church. Although he favors selling the church's historic furniture, he senses that these hefty remnants from past "giants of faith" signal the gulf between the past and present.

Escaping the old church's oppressiveness may be liberating, but it also creates disappointment: the new building not only possesses construction flaws but also appears to be affected by the earth's shifting—a symbol to Credo of his own sliding faith. Caught between the erosion of past certainties and the inferior refabrications of faith, Credo returns Augustine's emotionally searing work to the shelf, although it later provides him with quotations that fuel his ardor as he seduces a woman whose dedication to Lenten sacrifices challenges and arouses him. In quest of spiritual succor, he discovers signs of providence in adultery, in his serendipitous relief from pain, and in an interval of brightness as he emerges from the subway underground. Yet Credo must finally entertain the possibility that faith does not mark him as special, that believers and nonbelievers share divine attention equally in a life that, as the Venerable Bede's simile portrays it, is like a sparrow's brief flight through a bright mead hall.

"The Gun Shop," a more conventional narrative depicting the tensions between three generations of males, recalls Updike's earlier Pennsylvania stories, but the primary focus shifts from the young boy's initiation to the father's dilemmas. Ben, a Boston lawyer, has traded rural life on the family farm for a legal career in the city; this choice, he fears, has deprived his son Murray of "the taste of the world" experienced in his own childhood, substituting instead expensive amusements such as golf, sailing, and skiing. On a Thanksgiving visit to the farm, his son's welcome interest in his old gun is frustrated when it fails to fire; in the ensuing visit to the gun shop, both father and son are initiated into a world where the "metallic smell of murder lurked" and craftmanship is supremely prized.

Dutch, the gruff gunsmith who serves as a surrogate father figure, is an atypical Updike hero, yet he clearly embodies recognizable artistic virtues: not only does he possess a sharp eye and the talent for transforming his materials with precision, but in shaping metal, "he could descend into the hard heart of things." While the literal problem on which Dutch works is a sheared firing pin, Ben's father Murray directs attention to the story's central problem when he remarks that Dutch would have been a more effectual model for Ben than he was. Both Ben and his father sense their sons' dissatisfactions but suppress guilt about their parenting: the elder Murray rues the embarrassment his humor has caused Ben and his inability to instill him with an appreciation for manual skills; Ben regrets the gently ironic manner of handling crises he has developed and feels that his caution has deprived his son of an adventurous childhood. Ben envies his father's easy manner of relating to his namesake, to whom he is more temperamentally allied in the cyclical affinity that develops with freedom from father-son conflicts.

Although the experience in the gun shop produces a temporary alliance between all three generations, Ben has obviously been less at home in Dutch's "cave," as his awkward behavior there and his subsequent worry over exposing his son to another customer's violent stories indicate. His father's success in handling young Murray's outbursts does not alter Ben's outlook, and the ambiguous tensions between fathers and sons remain in a delicate equilibrium at the story's conclusion. Fathers, the elder Murray affirms, exist to be worn out, as both his weariness and the shooting competition between Ben and his son illustrate. When young Murray outshoots him, Ben, proudly proclaims, "You're killing me," thus affirming his displacement with pleasure rather than panic about this show of continuity and succession.

"Nevada," another of the six stories focused on fathers and children, is the first concerned with the aftermath of divorce. Culp, a stoically suffering petroleum engineer, hopes to "extract some scenic benefit from domestic ruin" as he drives through the desert, taking his daughters home so that his ex-wife Sarah can honeymoon in Hawaii on the heels of her quickie divorce and remarriage. The desert's vacancy and towns such as Lovelock remind him of his family's impending breakup; his intimations of the void, however, are temporarily vanquished through sexual consolation with the change girl. "Son," set in "the tiring year of 1973," consists of a series of vignettes spanning four generations of conflicts between fathers and sons. The narrator's juxtaposed images of his son, his boyhood self, his father, and his grandfather are linked thematically in their portrayals of youthful defiance. The son's active resistance is much more pronounced than his great grandfather's suppressed anxiety about being unsuited for the ministry, yet such youthful resistance, so seemingly divisive at the time, ultimately provides continuity across the generations. Like his son, the narrator recalls that he too spent much time retreating in his room; his writing is analogous to his son's electric guitar playing. Ultimately, his scrutiny of the past, while uncovering a pattern similar to the repeated notes of the Romanza his son plays at the conclusion, culminates in a more overt awareness that sons inevitably spend their youth as reluctant visitors, perpetually seeking escape. In the companion story, "Daughter, Last Glimpses of," a father whose daughter has left to live with a harpsichord maker has reached a stage where "the soul grows calluses" that numb him to each day's remarkable newness. Despite this seemingly resigned conclusion, his engagement of memory to assemble his collage of "last glimpses" represents an attempt to pierce these calluses and to recover bits of lost joy.

"Transaction" veers successfully from the realm of the typical Updike tale of domestic tension, although the protagonist, an astronomer attending a convention, alludes briefly to marital problems and a mistress at home. This account of his encounter with a prostitute stands out in its sexual explicitness and gritty realism, a tone particularly appropriate to the incident, in which the usual warmth of passion is repressed when sex becomes an economic rather than a human transaction. While similarly explicit scenes exist in some of Updike's novels, the short story form proves well-suited for depicting the one-night stand.

The action occurs during the Christmas season; the exact year and the full name of the city are withheld, as if the narrator is protecting the identity of "Ed," who gives the prostitute a false name. Initially shielded behind packages for his family, Ed defensively continues his evasions throughout the encounter with Ann, a former librarian nearly young enough to be his daughter. While she later thumbs through Blake's *Auguries of Innocence*, Ed's gift for his wife, Ann is anything but innocent, although she does embody both realms Blake celebrates: sweet delight and endless night. Whatever visions of sexual abandon he may initially have harbored, Ed, "a stranger to the etiquette of prostitution," is quickly disillusioned by his impotence and awkwardness. Naked except for her boots, Ann does not provide the easy gratification of an unwrapped Christmas package; she is more like "a column faced with mirrors," guarding her inner life just as he does. Despite the unspoken prohibitions Ed senses, Ann remains an unpredictable commodity with whom he vies for control of the interlude; as the male and the customer, he wants to dominate, but his impotence subverts the authority he desires.

The characters' ostensible "problem" is to overcome Ed's impotence and achieve sexual consummation, but the story has a more compelling concern with what happens when sex becomes an "interlocked abasement," reduced from a spontaneous passionate act to the level of financial negotiation. As he becomes more anxious about getting his money's worth, Ed suppresses his inclination to be intimate, yet the more the encounter is reduced to a bald transaction, the less Ed's chances for any type of success become. Without "the empathy for the other sex that Eros in his blindness bestows," their actions become mechanical, despite small attempts to humanize the encounter. Ultimately, Ed acquires more than he bargains on in the process; after Ann's departure, he realizes that "What she had given him, delicately, was death. She had made sex finite." The dried husk of the condom lying on the dresser near the presents becomes an ironic reminder of this gift: his new consciousness of the void that sex had previously obscured. Updike's most candid fictional venture thus reinforces the collection's pervasive sense of an increasingly demystified world.

Updike is one of the few writers who could so closely juxtapose an explicit story of a sexual transaction with "Augustine's Concubine," a quasireligious account that also concerns the sorrows of the flesh.[52] Alternating quotations from the *Confessions* with scenes between Augustine and his nameless concubine, Updike depicts an anachronistic relationship with a strikingly modern flavor (as he did in "Four Sides of One Story"). Augustine finds his lust for this mistress quickly turning into jealous attachment, and his successful attempt to end her dutiful adherence to her husband leads to a familiar paradox: once she becomes his exclusively, he draws back from the domestic arrangement he originally sought and uses social convention to terminate this illicit relationship and retreat into a renunciation of physical love. Yet rather than being punished, as he envisions, the concubine also "tastes the dry joy of lightness, of renunciation"; in her celibate placidity, she becomes saintly in her own right. The ironic conclusion, which notes Western culture's subsequent thousand year "endeavor to hate the flesh, because of her," does not endorse misogyny arising from a renunciation of physical love; rather it heightens Updike's sympathetic portrait of the anonymous concubine, whose maddening endurance and insularity achieve an unchronicled personal triumph.

Sapers, "The Man Who Loved Extinct Mammals," retreats from the complications of the present by reading about large prehistoric mammals generally scoffed at as evolutionary aberrations. His meditations on these neglected fossil creatures are interrupted by successive phone calls from his ex-wife, his mistress, and his mother, whose problems he deals with sympathetically and patiently, despite growing feelings of ineffectuality. His fondness for extinct mammals derives from his identification with their relative neglect, their contingency, and their failure to move in what one paleontologist considers "essential directions." Sapers (whose name derives from the root for "wisdom") seems content to be an anomaly, dying out of the active role of husband and father, while temporarily attached to a younger, insecure mistress, whom he equates with *Eohippus*, the proto-horse that resembles "a furtive little desire that evolves from the shadows of the heart into a great, clattering, unmanageable actuality" (*P*, 145).

Updike, who obviously enjoys incorporating this wide and various reading into his fiction, has previously toyed with paleontology in the whimsical sketches in *Museums and Women*; in this story, however, its extended metaphoric connections to character and situation create significant thematic implications. The mammals into whose history Sapers delves provide him with a "shapeless, shameless, fearful archetype" that reflects the pattern and direction of his life—an absurdly sublime yet somewhat self-indulgent drift toward extinction. The extinct mammals are counterpointed by his family's dying dog, which he advises his distraught daughter to let die naturally; as Sapers wrestles with the knowledge that he too is destined to be a vanished species, he struggles to keep his daughter insulated from the premonitions of loss from which the "myriad, irrelevant, deplorable facts" about extinct mammals cannot insulate him.

In "Problems," the characters engaged in the familiar drama of yearning and betrayal are portrayed as abstract variables in a series of mathematical teasers. Six interrelated word problems form a composite portrait of the difficulties separation and its ensuing guilt and strain create as "A" attempts to rebuild his life. Updike adapts the mathematical genre, but undercuts its form: there are no simple correct answers to the problems of A's life, since the numerous variables that affect human behavior—such as "Tristan's Law" that attraction exists in inverse proportion to psychic distance—wreak havoc on simple numerical calculations.

Those which can be performed show the absurdity of such an analysis of matters of the heart. The apparent answer to the second problem concerning the financial strain of A's divorce (which one suspects even before doing the calculations) is that A cannot continue a moment longer, burdened as he is by taxes, alimony, and bills for his children's schooling—unless he finds another source of income. Adding up the fractions that constitute these expenses yields the entirety of A's income ($92,400), thus making it impossible for him to afford his visits either to the psychiatrist or to the laundromat. The distance between these puzzlers and traditional math problems emerges in Updike's language; no traditional word problem would ask one to calculate which woman is "more profoundly" betrayed; even when Updike pretends that human affairs might possess the exactness of a formula (e.g., the ironic "helpful hint" in problem #4 that assigns a value of 3/7 to the "somewhat" in Tristan's Law), other variables defeat mathematical precision.

Updike's conceit, however, illustrates one way in which the human mind attempts to make sense of personal problems, while revealing the virtues and inadequacies of the approach. The geometric figure described in problem one (and sketched on the cover) not only delineates the characters' relationship, but also incorporates the image of the circular driveway that plays a significant part in A's memories and financial problems. Indeed, the physical distance between A and his new love B is greater than that between A and his ex-wife C, yet the straight line AB is impossible to travel except in his mind. While the final "problem" introduces fortuitous solutions to all of the preceding ones, neither the scholarship money, the plummeting price of peastone, nor the psychiatrist's relocation above the laundromat can finally resolve the real problems of discontent and guilt that make the psychiatrist a necessary adjunct to the difficulties of separation.

The next story, "Domestic Life in America," is almost a concrete illustration of the principles outlined so abstractly in the preceding story. One review mistakenly refers to the story as "Divorce in America"[53]—a slip which betrays how inexorably these two realms have become allied in *Problems*. Fraser, whose name seems chosen for its reference to the Christmas trees that figure as central images, aptly illustrates Tristan's Law that psychic distance augments desire: the house he has just legally relinquished to his estranged wife Jean now seems a "lovely place," although it continues to be a responsibility. Guilt and his children draw him back, yet "even guilt gets boring," he admits. Both here and at his mistress Greta's apartment, Fraser feels out of place; his dutiful visits home possess the lost continuity of an occasionally read comic strip, and his teenaged children seem indifferent to his presence. The old house is nonetheless a "warm chaos" whose pull he attempts to avoid, while Greta's apartment is full of tension arising from her bitterness over her estranged husband's lack of financial support and her young son's constant craving for his father. The main pleasure Fraser has surrendered with his old house—the dock from which he could dive naked into the channel—is replaced (through Updike's art of metaphoric transformation) by his evenings in Greta's bed, where she becomes the "sustaining element" whose "silken resistance . . . buoyed him above its own black depth" (*P*, 165–66).

The Yeats quotation Fraser cites in the brief game with his ex-wife suggests his underlying worry that "mere anarchy" will be the result of the marital center's failure to hold; however, his decentered condition yields a bewildered drift between mirror-image domestic spheres, both of which he struggles to hold together. The symmetry of the two families is most evident in their Christmas trees: Greta's store-bought tree is fat and full, with a variety of elaborate ornaments that embody her family tradition, while Fraser's son cuts a typically lean tree full of gaps, for which most of the cheap, carelessly stored ornaments are broken. In neither of these homes does Fraser feel like he belongs, so he makes the return trip to the Spartan domesticity of his bachelor apartment in Boston that evening. Between parallel tracks that imagistically evoke these two homes, he sees a hopeful vision that relieves his holiday melancholy: consoling fires lit against the cold, "each fire burning alone, apparently untended yet part of a design of care, or perpetuation" (*P*, 173). In this state of mind, even the alternating numbers on the electric sign—10:01 and 10°—seem a miraculous revelation. The symmetrical numbers of the time reiterate how the two families mirror each other, while the temperature may suggest Fraser's eventual remarriage and return to a similar domestic arrangement; more important than the symbolic equivalents assigned to the numbers, however, is the suggestion of repeated alternation between corresponding states.

"Love Song, for a Moog Synthesizer" is one of the collections more underrated pieces, perhaps because its characters, Tod and Pumpkin, seem to be much shallower versions of the Maples. They appear again in "The Fairy Godfathers," relieved of the "guilt–gems" that their analysts tk;1have expertly extracted and bereft of old friends and former obligations; as a result, the couple has nothing left to stand between hollowness and terror when they finally dismiss their psychiatric fairy godfathers. In "Love Song," however, Updike traces the contours of their relationship from the initial excitement of illicit infatuation to the onset of routine with remarriage, noting the changing winds of lust, anger, and indifference that affect them in the process. Less saccharine than its companion story, "Love Song" is interesting because of its 12-part form. Updike's choice of the moog synthesizer—which can replicate the sounds of a dozen instruments simultaneously—signals this love song's modernity and accentuates the diverse emotions that simultaneously draw Tod to Pumpkin and repel him.

Tod, in fact, begins the story yearning for some synthesis of the disparate parts of this fragmented new relationship and hoping that time can reconcile what he cannot, just as it has done with the wrinkles on Pumpkin's face, creating a web that interconnects her formerly discrete facial features. By the end of this love song, Tod momentarily achieves a coherent vision of Pumpkin as his wife and she becomes "of a piece, his," yet the narrator's simile ironically undercuts this epiphany: comparing Pumpkin's presence to "the earth's beneath his feet" suggests that she maybe a mere adjunct, there to be walked on. Tod's egocentrism causes some of his difficulties, and he wants "nothing to be his fault" in their relationship; still, he recognizes his tendency to rush into love before his heart, that "problem-learner—had time to collect quirks and spiritual snapshots, to survey those faults and ledges of the not-quite-expected where affection can silt and accumulate" (*P*, 175). Given the fatality of such uncontrollable attachments, enduring affection can hardly be expected as a result. Pumpkin and Tod, the woman who repeats herself and the man who can't stand to do so, seem destined to assume different rhythms in their lives, and to remain perpetually out of sync.

Updike's ongoing struggle with a skin disease lends added pathos to "From the Journal of a Leper," a better story than its few commentators have allowed.[54] Its main theme concerns the relationship between art and alienation; as Updike remarks in his memoirs, "Psoriasis keeps you thinking. Strategies of concealment ramify, and self-examination is endless" (*SC*, 45). The potter's leprous skin not only leads to self-imposed isolation but also spurs him to create delicate, smooth pottery, seeking in art to create the perfection his condition prevents in life. His disease, a "torture skin deep," leaves him mockingly healthy in all other respects; spiritually, however, it has caused deep humiliation. Remission becomes the near-equivalent of divine forgiveness, yet leprosy has defined his being for so long that when a cure becomes available, he initially clings to the familiar condition—just as the Maples, their separation facilitated by the passage of no-fault divorce, cling to each other. Once his skin clears, however, he feels whole, even though the metamorphosis has cost him his devout girlfriend Carlotta and the business of the gallery operator who formerly bought all his work. As if in compensation for his now-creamy skin, his new designs become marked by granulation and stains, a reflection of his former condition. Liberated from being "a toy in the gilded cage of my disease," the potter loses the "fanatic" intensity that created his prized pieces and becomes correspondingly more interested in the city's stimulation and "contagion of bliss."

Updike's motifs in this story are in some ways like a potter's signature patterns: pottery, of course, is the dominant motif, with the waitress's skin likened to kaolin, and the light treatment compared to being baked in a kiln; imagery linking geometric figures (prisms, parallelepids) with light also recurs. In addition, glass and mirrors become allied with geometry as Updike skillfully works the infamous window shedding of Boston's Hancock building into the story as a parallel to his narrator's shedding scaly skin. Its "vulnerable perfection" stands as an emblem of human fragility, and the building's renewed window dropping at a key point in the story (when he resumes treatments) converges with the cracking of two recent pots to suggest susceptibility to unforseen loss. Ultimately, the Hancock building, which the former leper comes to care more for than for humanity, proves to be a distorted mirror, just as his own art becomes grotesque with his attempt to recapture his lost pain. Like his protagonist, Updike recalls wondering after his cure: "was not my sly strength, my insistent specialness, somehow linked to my psoriasis?" (*SC*, 74–75). Ultimately, this "Journal," which symbolically begins on Halloween and ends with a new year underway, uses the metaphor of skin disease to explore the characteristic ambivalence toward the seeming cures of middle-age problems.

"The Faint" presents a tightly woven tale of inversion in which Freddy Python, an egotistical real estate developer proud of having slithered through the grasp of a chain of women whom he has dated since the breakup of his first marriage, is unwittingly snared by a show of female frailty. Most of the volume's themes, however, converge in the final trio of stories, which rank among Updike's finest excursions into memory and clearly delineate the distances travelled from earlier phases. Ferguson, the protagonist of "The Egg Race," is an archaeologist, but he cannot use the past as a buffer against encroaching time, unlike the archaeologist-narrator of "Harv Is Plowing Now." He is all too aware that, in middle age, the best a "digger" such as himself can do is "to bring what was hidden back to light" for study and appreciation. As he stands at the bedside of a dying colleague, unable to "lift [him] up from the bed as if he were a shard," Ferguson realizes that whatever his skill at exhuming artifacts, archaeology cannot overcome death. This colleague criticizes him for focusing so intently on a single shard in his recent work and thus displacing other historical data. In this story, however, he uses the metaphor of the egg race as the key to an imaginative excavation that pieces together assorted shards of memory.

A layered series of journeys comprises the story's loosely structured first half; the conclusion climaxes in Ferguson's return to Hayesville, the "lost city" of his youth, for his twenty-fifth high school reunion. As Ferguson's thoughts shift from musings on the egg race to recollections of a dream about travelling with his father to his memories of visiting colleges with his son, Updike creates smooth transitions from one incident to the next with verbal echoes. Ferguson's postreunion exploration of Hayesville concludes with an epiphany concerning the origins of his present condition, which he suspects derive from the same caution that made him "too intent on finishing with his egg intact to move very fast" during his youth. Standing on the playground where the egg races took place, he realizes in retrospect that its earth willingly absorbed the race's careless waste and rues his caution, since his youthful perception of the game's tragedy has engendered a conservative attitude that has intensified with age. The story concludes with his nostalgic drift into memories of childhood safety; ironically, Ferguson eats eggs while he recalls this pleasurable morning of staying home, sick from school, with no responsibility beyond the gentle cradling of his egg-like self. His reminiscence, however, hints that he has not truly travelled far: he has unearthed potentially tragic bits of past ruins, but withdraws from their implications.

Ferris, the recently divorced narrator of "Guilt-Gems" is a "traveller in the land of guilt," amassing memories of perceived lapses as a father, husband, and son, much as Ferguson unearths the fragmentary shards of his past. Ferris, however, is more concerned with polishing each of these moments to a brilliant sheen and relishing the feelings of culpability they bring; thus, as Daniel Murtaugh remarks, adapting a line from Wallace Stevens's "Sunday Morning," "Guilt is the mother of beauty."[55] The first in the string of incidents that comprises the story occurs during the last phases of Ferris's marriage and the final one transpires after his divorce; yet Updike's story is less concerned with the forward thrust of narrative than with understanding the paradoxical nature of the shimmering, piercing moments that have "volunteered for compression" from the "gaseous clouds of being awaiting a condensation and preservation—faces, lights that glimmer out, somehow not seized, save in this gesture of remorse" (*P*, 251). Guilt thus becomes one way to hang on to those from whom separation threatens to sever him. Ferris feels only minor qualms concerning his ex-wife; when it comes to his children, however, guilt is a long-standing habit derived from parental responsibility and exacerbated by divorce.

Ferris is a connoisseur of the degrees and varieties of guilt. Nurturing such moments of regret and self-chastisement is his safeguard against capitulating to a "blanket permission for all derelictions in the world." In the first and more poignant incident (a thinly fictionalized version of the struggle with asthma Updike has documented in his memoirs[56]), Ferris is finally unable to deprive his children of the pets that have been discovered to worsen his asthma. When a compromise—keeping the cats in the cellar—proves unworkable, Ferris ruefully departs, burdened with the image of the youngest son desperately throwing the cats downstairs, hoping that by doing so his asthmatic father will remain. Not until the second vignette, when he attempts to explain his departure to his eldest son, does Updike explicitly reveal that Ferris's inability to breathe is more than a literal problem; he is stifled by a marriage that no longer provides him enough breathing room. The guilt–gems concerning his daughters, both focused on sports, reveal "an urgent futile need to *undo*." Ultimately, such guilt arises from an inability to live up to his romantic self-expectations, and he fails to realize that smoothing out inevitable grits and bumps of existence may in many cases deprive his children of learning experiences.

The anxiety Ferris causes his elderly mother is the source of the final guilt–gem, which suggests that some of his inescapable guilt may be misplaced. On the last leg of a long trip home from England, she drives alone, symbolically becoming Ferris's "forward scout in the wilderness of time" while he takes a shuttle flight home to Boston. The final paradox, however, is that even as the odd beauty of these moments fades, Ferris augments the cycle of guilt with the consciousness that in beautifying and elevating these moments he is oversimplifying his past. These glittering, guilty-making memories are qualitatively different from the unexpected gifts of Olinger; dredged up in Ferris's "midnight brain," they represent the legacy of learning to live and find order in the wilderness of time that he now faces alone.

The final story, "Atlantises," recasts the metaphor of the archaeological dig amid the buried past into an imaginative dive into the waters of time's deluge. For the Farnhams, remarried refugees from the vanished continent of Atlantis, their inaccessible past becomes idealized: Atlantis, with its marshy landscape and perpetual parties, is another incarnation of Tarbox—a phase of life to which this story symbolically bids farewell. Its community accord, however, masks an inherent instability and vulnerability to the tides that gradually overrun the island, just as Farnham's fondly remembered stirrings of desire ultimately engulfed his first marriage. Updike intersperses the account of the Farnhams with snippets from Plato's *Critias* concerning the splendor and harmony of Atlantis, yet the mention of human sacrifices suggests that it is a less than ideal realm, based on substantial human costs. By juxtaposing the two Atlantises, Updike thus distorts the story's otherwise realistic texture, effectively conflating the fabled Atlantis with the Farnhams' lost continent so that their past assumes mythic dimensions.

Now displaced from the sea (in "a state people confused with Ohio"—most likely Iowa), the Farnhams are exiled inland amid "alien corn," repressing memories in quotidian life. Mrs. Farnham's initial immersion in the "Living" section of the newspaper rather than in life's mysteries typifies their current lack of stimulation, yet like Ruth attempting to glean in alien fields, they must eke out an existence in a new land rather than yearn for their homeland. Mr. Farnham's opening remark, however, is a "slip of misplaced nostalgia" in which he momentarily assumes his second wife to be his first. He seems more prone to drift into memories of past loves on Atlantis, where "every woman was a priestess," than his wife does, yet her later nostalgia is an ominous indication of the potential danger of an idealized past swamping the present when the latter fails to measure up.

The final movement of the story is eastward, back toward Atlantis, travelling toward the "mazy coast" to their daughter's wedding in Connecticut. As Mr. Farnham wonders whether he should go to Mystic, the appearance of a tall tower provokes his wife's recollection of a frogman she once knew who conducted training for emergency submarine escape there. Instructing divers how to avoid embolism from too quick an ascent, the frogman teaches the literal equivalent of a smooth passage from the submerged depths of memory to the surface of the present—a relevant lesson for most of the collection's characters. He thus serves as a model of the self-controlled passage through mid-life transitions and the basis for the volume's metaphoric coda: Mr. Farnham's prayer for news from the inundated past via an intermediary who can "Keep us in touch." In *Problems*, Updike has become such an intermediary, schooling readers in the problematic transitions back to actuality rather than diving deeply into the sea of nostalgia.

The Anatomy of Betrayal: *Trust Me*

Updike reasserts himself as Joyce's successor in refining the epiphanic short story in *Trust Me*, his tenth collection. Full of poignant, expertly crafted tales and interspersed with controlled flashes of his distinctive prose, it may be his best and most consistent effort thus far. With the volume's title, Updike solicits the reader's trust that his stories will provide an aesthetically pleasurable and personally meaningful experience—prerequisites for any fiction's success. As he states in "The Artist and His Audience," "Both sides of the creative event demand trust: on the output side, we must hope that some sort of audience is there, or will be there. On the input, we must sit down in the expectation that the material will speak through us, that certain unforeseeable happiness of pattern and realization will emerge out of blankness as we write."[57] In his latest volume, Updike continues to show that he can be relied on to provide all the necessary ingredients for intellectually illuminating and emotionally and aesthetically satisfying tales.

Compared to his previous collections, some of which were composed entirely of *New Yorker* stories, *Trust Me* contains more stories from diverse fictive homes.[58] Furthermore, Updike continues to experiment, surprising the reader with atypical settings (the Central American "Ideal Village"), protagonists (the factory worker of "Poker Night"), and narrative strategies (montage stories spanning an entire marriage). A renewed interest in dramatic interaction has emerged in these stories, while the meditative mode and the stylistic flights are muted, though not absent. As one reviewer observed, the proportion of prose to event in *Trust Me* is more balanced.[59] While Updike's earlier writing has been criticized as overly stylized, the highly adjectival style has been replaced by a slightly leaner one that accentuates his poetic precision and makes it even more evident that his command of the language exceeds that of most of his contemporaries. In addition, his Proustian love of detail has been harnessed to serve the ends of the story more efficiently; rarely do these details form an "overparticularized clot in the flow of prose" that Updike recognizes as disrupting the smooth progress of narrative.[60]

Although the volume's title is taken from the lead story, the thematic concern with trust resonates throughout the entire book. While Updike's previous collection focuses on "problems," this one emphasizes realistic, often provisional trust as the earned resolution of the problems inherent in relationships. "Trust me" can be the plea of the confidence man, the ploy of the sexual opportunist, the last ditch appeal of the friend who continually betrays—or merely the reassurance of loved ones who mistakenly believe in their ability to provide happiness and security. Still, despite recognition that such appeals may spring from false confidence or the intent to dupe, his characters long to believe in others, particularly in an era in which public trust has been eroded by political scandals such as Watergate and interpersonal trust is threatened by sexual diseases, rising infidelity, and rampant self-interest. While the stories touch on contemporary social concerns, such as euthanasia, cancer, the increase in single young women, the growing emphasis on pragmatic careers, and class consciousness, Updike is not writing for the evening news; his stories still dwell on familiar themes—sex, marriage, suburban life, and death—and take place for the most part in his accustomed New England suburban locale.

As in other Updike collections, the moral crises faced by the various characters are similar. For the most part, the characters are older and increasingly conscious of death, aging, and illness. Having nearly passed through the territory of "middle-aged restlessness" and established new relationships after failed first marriages, they are somewhat less desperate, though not immune to visitations of dread. Plagued by broken promises, infidelity, earthquakes, illnesses, crises of self-worth, fading memories, illusions of ideal mates, class climbing, and even lost wallets, the characters have the uneasy foundations of their trust shaken and struggle to regain some semblance of belief in themselves, others, and the frail social structures that they have come to take for granted. This thematic concern with trust serves as a counterpoint to Updike's latest novel, *Roger's Version*, which explores crises of religious faith.

Trust is faith on a human scale, and within the smaller compass of the short story, Updike can manageably examine the basic issues: the human need for interpersonal trust, its uncertain fulfillment, and its inevitable betrayals. Rarely, as the stories show, can we afford to believe blindly in a world that continually disappoints us; such investments of confidence involve unavoidable limitations and compromises. Those in whom we yearn to believe are only human, prone to lapses in judgment and whims of desire; those social bonds and routines on which we unconsciously rely—marriage, family, community, memory—are unfortunately subject to time's erosion. Amid the inescapable ironies of betrayal, Updike combines a detached sympathy for his characters' plights with honest exposure of their shortcomings. If his protagonists often do not confront the hard questions of existence head on, most are at least aware of the price they must pay for security and of the terror that the particulars of daily life imperfectly mask.

The volume's thematic coherence extends even to its dust jacket (designed by the author), which features Picart's depiction of *The Fall of Icarus*. While Daedalus has instructed his son to use the wings fashioned for his escape prudently, Icarus betrays his trust, succumbing to the temptation to soar close to the sun. It might also be argued that Icarus trusts these wings beyond their inherent limitations, just as children often trust their parents beyond their capacities for protection. Whatever the case, the painting focuses on Icarus, poised in midair before his fall, shedding feathers from his wings; in the background, Daedalus glides on, steering a middle course, unwittingly assuming that his son follows. Thus, Updike has provided an appropriate mythological parallel before we even open to the first story, since these issues—broken trust, family bonds, the fragile nature of promises, and our inevitable falls—are central to the stories within.

The lead story, "Trust Me," is vintage Updike: a richly textured, tightly woven, and gently concluded version of the montage, it provides a succinct record of one man's ongoing skirmishes with trust. In four juxtaposed segments, each of which reenacts a drama of trust and betrayal, Harold swiftly advances from childhood, through marriage and divorce, and into the uneasy territory beyond: the rocky beginnings of a new relationship. The first scene serves as a touchstone for those that follow, as his future relationships follow the pattern established in childhood, binding the past and present into a coherent but exasperating whole. In this early memory, Harold's father, "eerily stable" while treading water, coaxes his son to jump into the pool[61]; unfortunately, he misses catching him and Harold momentarily sinks in "the darkening element," water filling his lungs as he gasps for air, before his father pulls him to safety. Despite the mishap, he retains trust in his father; however, the aftermath of the plunge—his mother angrily slapping his father—echoes in the "acoustics of memory" and breeds a distrust of his mother's "swift sure-handed anger." His father, apparently stable but treading water to avoid sinking, typifies the human condition, and by asking Harold to trust him when he cannot guarantee safety, he unwittingly teaches the hazards of extending and cultivating assurance.

With Harold and his first wife the situation is inverted: her acute fear of flying, reinforced by news of recent air disasters, contrasts with his easy acceptance of being airborne. When a near accident occurs after takeoff from Rome, however, his shaken confidence forces him to reexamine its basis: "He had often felt through one of these scratched oval windows, something falsely reassuring in the elaborate order of the rivets pinning the aluminum sheets together. *Trust Me*, the metallic code spelled out; in his heart, Harold, like his wife, had refused, and this refusal in him formed a hollow space terror could always flood" (*TM*, 6). Trust serves as mankind's riveted defense against this hollow space: an existential dread of the world's inevitable dissolution and of human isolation and extinction. Faith that planes will not fly apart on takeoff, or that parents will act as safety nets when children fall, allows daily life to proceed smoothly; yet despite constant attempts to repress doubt, Harold discovers, the tension between absolute trust and fear of its fragility is inevitable.

Between those who demand trust and those who extend it, Harold concludes, the "crucial space . . . of indifference is where we breathe." In his relationships, he becomes both the victim and perpetrator of this necessary indifference. During a ski trip with his girlfriend Priscilla (after his marital breakup), he assumes a paternal role, and, like his father, manipulates an innocent's confidence when he urges her to attempt a more advanced trail. To Harold, her refusal is a transformed version of his mother's slap, and the emotional backlash of this breach of faith shakes the newly erected foundations of their relationship. As they plod down the mountain, the natural world reshapes itself around a key image in his memory, as the surrounding woods wear "a magical strangeness, the ironical calm of airplane rivets."

Symmetrically, the story concludes with Harold once again the victim, this time of his son's casual indifference. In his more fragile position—after a divorce, involved in a floundering relationship, and pursuing his children's affection—the effect on his psyche is more shattering. After eating a hashish brownie that his son assures him is harmless, Harold fumbles through the normally routine trip home in a somewhat giddy, self-conscious euphoria. Updike's comic depiction of Harold's heightened consciousness during this subway journey home is interlaced with language that recalls his childhood plunge into the pool: emerging from the subway, "he was in air again. . . . Something in his throat burned" (*TM*, 11). Instead of public embarrassment, however, he receives a private rebuke from Priscilla, shaking his confidence in the "protective, trustworthy" half of his brain that has just guided him home automatically. The sound of her hanging up the phone evokes the memory of his mother's slap; he perceives that he is still replaying his childhood scenario, with different actors in the other roles: "his father had become his son and his mother was his girlfriend. This much remained true: it had not been his fault, and in surviving he was somehow blamed" (*TM*, 12).

Harold's epiphany, with all its Freudian implications, mingles consciousness of his inescapable repetition of the past's patterns with a perplexed sadness that, no matter how hard he tries to be trusting and trustworthy, his efforts will be consistently undercut and he will suffer unjustly. Still, Harold's attempt to sidestep blame for the betrayals he has authored qualifies sympathy for his plight. While a lesser artist might be content with this ending, Updike takes the story one step further. Finding the dollar bill rejected by the subway gate, Harold "turned to its back side, examined the mystical eye above the truncated pyramid, and read, over and over, the slogan printed over the ONE" (*TM*, 12). The single bill recalls his own singleness and recent rejection; its slogan, "In God We Trust," is not so much a reminder or affirmation of religious faith as it is tangible evidence that trust, despite its failings, remains the currency with which human affairs are conducted.

The volume's next two stories involve protagonists who discover some sense of connectedness during phases of transition that force confrontation with painful memories. Although they remain hurt and confused, the result in both cases is reawakened trust in themselves. "Killing" ventures into a woman's consciousness to explore a daughter's decision to forego life-support machines for her terminally ill father and to oversee his protracted death. Recently separated, Anne plunges selflessly into this role as her father's caretaker, seeking to repay him in kind with her bedside vigils for his uncharacteristic sensitivity to her adolescent insomnia. Anne's role temporarily lends her life purpose, but the burden of guilt and confusion does not lift until after his death, when an episode with her estranged husband Martin symbolically clarifies her situation. After various sexual overtures fail, Anne's unsuccessful attempts to arouse him yield a surprisingly clear link between Eros and Thanatos: Martin's limp penis unexpectedly becomes an imaginative substitute for the withered hand of her father that she was unable to hold when he died. This recognition not only compensates for the missed moment but also illustrates the impossibility of reviving her dead marriage and liberates her from regret.

In "Still of Some Use," chosen for *Best American Short Stories 1981*,

Foster struggles against the fear that divorce has ended his usefulness to his family. While Updike's talent for capturing realistic particulars is evident in the catalogue of the era's popular games, the game metaphor subtly augments the story's dialogue and action. As the family weeds through the accumulated paraphernalia in their old home's attic, the forgotten, incomplete games Foster discovers remind him poignantly of missed opportunity. He is forced to admit, however, that his yearnings for travelling along the familiar pathways of either these games or his former marriage should be discarded as excess emotional baggage, just as the games themselves are tossed into the pickup truck below—boxes bursting, pieces scattering on impact. Encountering these mementos of happier times has likewise cracked open his memory, exposing the sorrow and guilt that might otherwise have remained stored away. Standing by his ex-wife's boyfriend, Foster uncomfortably feels that he occupies "the wrong square"; sensing his youngest son's kindred melancholy, however, he volunteers to accompany him to the dump, thus moving beyond self-pity and feelings of insignificance to a renewed faith that he is still of some use.

In "The City," another prize-winning tale, a more profound renewal occurs for Carson, a 60-year-old sales representative for a computer firm who reprograms himself during a medical crisis that requires hospitalization in an unknown city. Like his protagonist, Updike, who "was spared appendicitis until [he] was fifty and could make an epiphanic story out of it" (*SC*, 152), finds that even illness can yield something extraordinary. The story opens with a symbolic airplane descent, provoking Carson's observation that many stewardesses, like himself, are "on second careers, victims of middle-aged restlessness—the children grown, the long descent begun" (*TM*, 34). His ex-wife remarried, his son travelling in Mexico, and his estranged daughter living in a feminist commune, Carson has accepted his "essential solitude" and refashioned his life, but has recently grown weary of its routine. On this business trip, persistent stomach problems disrupt his normal routine, and lead to his rediscovery of the "brilliantly real, moist and deep-toned" world around him. Sensitivity to the beauty inherent in the commonplace awaits at the end of his ordeal—an unexpected reward, but only possible through suffering.

His experience of the city, then, is ultimately that of the hospital which his pain-riddled vision transforms from the impersonal realm he expects to one in which his surroundings and caretakers possess a romantic, compassionate aura. His most significant memory involves a midnight check by a saintly nurse, her "black and symmetrical face outlined like an eclipsed sun with its corona"; her image illuminates his dark night of the soul with a radiant vision of a woman who resembles his estranged daughter and personifies forgiveness. As Carson heals, he experiences a gradual revival of interest in the world outside; taking comfort in being "invisible and anonymous," he begins to view his surroundings with an intimate eye for detail, discovering subtle differences in the stairwells he climbs and beauty in the surrounding inner-city neighborhoods. As a result of his descent into pain and ritual healing, Carson has experienced an intimate sojourn in a city he has never touched directly and ascends from its airport as a "recovered, risen self."

"The Lovely Troubled Daughters of Our Old Crowd" are single women in their late twenties, detached from society's mainstream and inhabiting the fringes of their New England hometown. Unlike Carson's daughter, their quiet rebellion involves a passive withdrawal from the traditional pattern of marriage that has proved unsuccessful for their separated or divorced parents. On the surface, the story seems a bemused study of a contemporary American social type, but a closer reading reveals that the narrator's mildly ironic and somewhat condescending treatment of the single women's troubles fails to take into account his generation's role in causing the troubled daughters' hesitancy to trust the conventional route to happiness. While his marriage has endured, the narrator's casual mention of his amours among his old crowd provides some evidence of his own marital failings and further disqualifies him as an impartial observer; indeed, his sympathy for the daughters may arise because they evoke wistful memories of their mothers.

"Unstuck," the only story in the volume to treat a young couple, depicts the early stages of a marriage already plagued by routine and sexual problems.[62] The central incident, Mark's attempt to get the car unstuck from the snow so that he can get to work, provides him with a lesson in cooperation and transcending traditional roles that may prove valuable in their stalled sex life. Working cheerlessly alone, oblivious to the new snowstorm's beauty, Mark only succeeds in getting the wheels stuck; when he works together with his wife and trusts her behind the wheel, they are able to free the car and enjoy a brief moment of closeness together in its warmth. Whatever their problems, if the couple can work together (in and out of bed) to improve their relationship, they may also become unstuck, reliving in other ways this momentary triumph and its afterglow.

"A Constellation of Events," a less optimistic vision of marital fidelity, examines—through a female protagonist's consciousness—the process by which a bored wife becomes a mistress. Confronted with the visible icons of her past in the Philadelphia museum where she met her husband, Betty realizes, like many of Updike's characters in this phase of their lives, that "The daring passes into the classic in our very lifetimes, while we age and die" (*TM*, 77). Rather than continue settling into a classic mode, Betty opts to court the daring and initiate an affair. After she reexamines the past over the course of the story, it ultimately assumes a pattern in her mind: "not scattered as is a constellation but continuous, a rainbow, a U-turn." Reduced to four images—snowy fields, dripping eaves, a painting, and a law office—these formerly dizzying incidents gain meaning by compression and assuage—but do not banish—the inevitable guilt and ambiguity of her marital betrayal. If the past reveals an unexpected gift, it is renewed trust that the chosen path is the right one—not the wistful longing for the past that pervades many earlier stories.

The greater ambition of "More Stately Mansions" is evident in its length, its poetic epigraph, and the framed structure, which resembles the chambers of a nautilus shell, its central symbol. The epigraph—the second stanza of Oliver Wendell Holmes's "The Chambered Nautilus"—bemoans the "wreck" of a nautilus shell, its empty chambers broken open, the former life fled. This image provides an appropriate metaphor for the narrator's memories of a past affair, which are evoked by a nautilus slice brought in by one of his students. While he conducts a brief lesson on the shell and its former inhabitant, the reader tours the chambers of his memory as he probes old guilts and longings. Initially, the nautilus provokes rancor toward his former lover, and he takes pains to remind his students of its deadliness: the "predatory hydrostatic magic" it performs with the aid of its beautiful chambers. By the story's conclusion, however, he has softened his initial cynicism enough to draw a more hopeful moral, similar to that which concludes Holmes's poem.

The narrator, Frank, is a biology teacher whose Italian immigrant ancestors helped build and worked in the mills that were once the lifeblood of the New England town where he has remained despite yearnings to escape. Karen Owens, his lover, is a transplanted West coast activist married to the Stanford-educated son of a local mill owner, against whom Frank harbors resentment because of his social class. While Karen and Frank argue politics because of his conservative views about the Vietnam War (sentiments which parallel Updike's own[63]), they conduct a torrid love affair in the Owenses' Victorian house, whose rooms resemble nautilus chambers. While his wife Monica embraces liberal causes in an attempt to strike out on her own, Frank seeks shelter from the era's political and social tumult in sex. Karen's husband, Alan, degenerates into alcoholism and the Owenses eventually divorce, but Monica reclaims Frank—a unique situation in Updike's fiction, dominated as it is by failed marriages. Just as the nautilus outgrows its shell, so Frank and Monica move to their own more stately mansion on Elm Hill, two blocks from the Owens house, where Alan still resides, an alcoholic shell. His death, a week after Frank visits and buys a bottle of liquor for him, evokes Frank's guilty reflection concerning the extent to which his affair with Karen and his final service to Alan resemble the predatory behavior that he originally ascribed to his former lover.

Thus, from the simple evocation of Karen's image and his anger at her predatory ways, Frank reaches a more complex understanding of the shell's symbolic implications: "Maybe it was that bottle I thought of when the student brought in the nautilus shell. Or the shell Karen never got to give me. Or that big house with all its rooms and this naked freckled woman waiting in its chambers" (*TM*, 119–20). In this multifaceted reading of the symbol, Frank has transcended his initial emotional backlash and achieved a more realistic perception that his own guilt about Alan, his frustration at losing Karen, his ambivalence about his own success, and his class resentments are all intertwined. In essence, Frank resembles the "frail tenant" of the Holmes poem, one who has "shaped his growing shell" to accommodate himself to the path his life has followed. In the course of the story, his own "dim dreaming life" has been sliced open like the souvenir shell. The benefits of this painful process are evident in his concluding lesson to the class—"We all have to grow"—the same lesson contained in the final stanza of the poem, the source of the story's title: "Build thee more stately mansions, O my soul / As the swift seasons roll! / Leave thy low-vaulted past! / Let each new temple, nobler than the last, / Shut thee from heaven with a dome more vast, / Till thou at length art free / Leaving thy outgrown shell by life's unresting sea!" Holmes's stately mansions are creations of the soul that transcend the "low vaulted past," as Frank has done, though the unqualified optimism expressed in the poem may never be his. Like many of Updike's mature characters, Frank has become reconciled to the tensions and compromises of existence; his growth culminates in a fuller awareness and acceptance of change's inevitability, so that he is more at home on "life's unresting sea."

The protagonist of "Learn a Trade" also comes to terms somewhat grudgingly with the inevitable, in this case by letting go of his objections to his grown son's artistic pursuits. Fegley, a successful junk sculptor with a six-figure income and low self-esteem, retrospectively perceives some wisdom in his father's injunction to "learn a trade" rather than court the inevitable disappointments that a career in the arts breeds. Despite his efforts to steer his children into more practical vocations that might guarantee them security, they nonetheless eventually strike out in uncertain directions toward "the limbo of artistic endeavor." When he learns that his youngest and most pragmatic son has taken up making mobiles, Fegley becomes dismayed at his own powerlessness and sense of waste, until his ex-wife coaxes him into viewing his son's work; struck by its beauty and pathos, he resolves to trust his son to follow his chosen path, whatever disappointments might ensue. Echoing his father's ambivalent blessing to him—"Keep breaking my heart"—Fegley reluctantly forgoes the vain attempt to be a guardian from sorrow; despite his qualms, he accepts the need to let go, along with the inevitable heartbreak involved in his youngest child's independence.

"The Ideal Village," like Updike's noel *The Coup*, takes a refreshing step outside his usual settings to portray a familiar theme: that the human condition is one of perpetual unrest and dissatisfaction. The narrator's concluding pronouncement—"Man was not meant to abide in paradise"—could certainly be Updike's own voice intruding in the volume's central story, confirming the human unwillingness to trust idyllic happiness as an enduring and satisfying condition. In this isolated jungle clearing, where no piranhas inhabit the river, the villagers appear to have created a Latin American Eden of easy luxuriance that strikes a balance between radical politics and tribal ritual. The outsiders' "cultural intersection" is an amiable one—they feast, swim, experience the community's peace, and bring home souvenirs—but discover they are happy to leave. It is enough that the ideal village exists "out there," relatively untainted by the civilization whose binding edges of the social contract they appear to require.

In contrast to Updike's lyric stories, which usually unearth memories relevant to a present crisis, "The Other" sketches the course of a relationship over a 25-year period. Beginning at Harvard in the fifties, the story precisely captures the sexual mores that guide the courtship of future lawyer Hank Arnold and his Radcliffe girlfriend Priscilla through the "large and not laughable sexual territory [that] existed within the boundaries of virginity" (*TM*, 150). Their intimacy progresses to the point where Priscilla will parade nude for him, but she concludes her brief exhibitions by jumping into bed for a chaste philosophy study session of "Idealism from Plato to Whitehead." More than a bit of throwaway humor, Updike's comic touch introduces the underlying theme of idealism crucial to understanding Hank's later fascination with Priscilla's twin, Susan. Once he learns of Susan, Hank is unable to think about Priscilla without consciousness of her twin's specter. His continued fixation on this "other"—a sexual doppelgänger whose image shadows their relationship—reveals the same lingering discontent with reality that plagues numerous Updike characters. Even after he meets Susan at his wedding, however, she remains endowed with a "superior authenticity" beyond her actual self, representative of the pure but unreachable ideal, while Priscilla remains an all-too-familiar and accessible reality.

As is often the case with twins, the sisters' lives run oddly parallel—at least initially, as their families grow symmetrically on opposite coasts. Yet while the more ethereal Susan symbolically loses weight as her marriage to a San Diego builder begins to fracture, Hank settles into a comfortable routine with Priscilla, who becomes earthier after putting on weight from frequently hosting parties in their social set. Despite Susan's troubles, he distances her so that she remains "so magical a stranger"; even when she attempts to discuss her marital discord with him, he blocks out sympathy for her troubles by projecting the image of his mistress onto her face as she speaks. Only when his own weakened marriage crumbles can he finally discard the veil of ideality with which he has enshrouded his wife's twin. Strangely, Susan ceases to be her twin's "secret sharer" when, at his urging, she reenacts Priscilla's courtship ritual of "parading." In this case, however, the couple is not guided by the absolute moral standards of the fifties but by the disease-conscious prudence of the eighties. Hank's glimpse of her body, emaciated by grief, leads to an epiphany of blissful realism: "Plato was wrong; what is is absolute. Ideas pale." Thus Susan becomes just another woman, not the ghostly, idealized "other," and he moves beyond the obsessive psychosexual Platonism that doomed his marriage from the start.

"Slippage" uses the metaphor of an earth tremor to illustrate how easily the secure trusts on which daily life is based can shift, just as the earth does along its fault lines. The quake causes no physical damage, but produces emotional and spiritual aftershocks for Morrison, a 60-year-old history professor for whom the event becomes a symbol of the chasm between his present life and his unrealized ambitions. Feelings of nausea and cosmic insignificance arise from his perception that he has not made a major scholarly breakthrough in his study of Austria-Hungary, an empire whose "inertia and fragmentation," seem an appropriate analogy of his personal history. As his musings continue, one despair slides into another: he bemoans his waning interest in sex, his diminished stature in his children's eyes, the loose bicuspid that anchors his bridge—all palpable signs of his decline. Later, he witnesses the ultimate result of the process in which he is engaged, when he meets a woman at a party whose seemingly radiant energy derives from her own recent "slippage" over the edge of insanity. Thus, when he believes he feels an aftershock that evening, Morrison dismisses the event as a product of his imagination, resolving that his runaway obsession with slippage must give way to provisional trust in life's stability.

In "Poker Night," a rare Updike blue-collar protagonist recounts a substantial emotional tremor in his life: learning that he has cancer. Like Morrison, the narrator of "Poker Night" attempts to control his sense of dread; in an engaging vernacular, he sketches the oscillations between self-assurance that "nothing too bad was going to happen to me, ever" and an increased consciousness of death. Attending his regular poker game after he receives the doctor's news is his way of testing himself; by carrying on his routine, he courageously refuses to succumb to despair. His style of playing poker, in fact, is characteristic of the way he will face cancer: to "fold" in despair while there is still a chance to live would be "a sin against God or Nature or whatever"—even worse than delusions about miracle cures. Nonetheless, his confidence is not absolute: studying his cards, he envisions his own fragility: they "looked incredibly thin: a kind of silver foil beaten to just enough thickness to hide the numb reality that was under everything" (*TM*, 187). This foil represents belief in social rights, in others, in appearances, in the continued miracle of life—a trust which the shaken narrator must now struggle to retain. When his wife learns of the disease, the narrator resorts to one final poker metaphor to understand her plight: handed this "terrible edge" (as his potential survivor), she remains uncertain of how to "play her cards," yet unlike so many of the other marriages in Updike's stories, this one appears stable, despite the temporary distancing caused by his news.

"Made in Heaven," another of Updike's sweeping chronicles, traces the courtship, marriage, and separation by death of Brad and Jeanette Schaeffer, using the progression of Presidents as a backdrop to mark time's passage.[64] The only story in the volume specifically concerned with religious faith, "Made in Heaven" links Brad's religious observance with his masculine desire to possess and control. Initially attracted to Jeanette because of her "shy uncertain reverence" and overriding concern for salvation, he gradually usurps her role as a reverent worshipper and recasts it to suit his more secular needs, leaving her with no tangible connection to her former faith. In his unthinking exuberance, he is "invading a fragile feminine space" when he begins to accompany Jeanette to church during their courtship; throughout the story, reiterated images of violated space signal that Brad's actions resemble a type of spiritual rape. While he is initially extremely cynical about religion, part of Jeanette's attractiveness is the unique certitude of her piety, which he embraces as part of the package he desires. Although he steers her to a Methodist church closer to his apartment during their courtship, not until he perceives his own human smallness beneath "the black firmament of spattered stars" in the mid-Pacific does Brad become a believer.

After their marriage, he continues to control their religious life, which becomes an extension of his business life when he joins a nearby Episcopalian church attended by clients and associates. He believes that his committee work, ushering, and Sunday school teaching elevate him above the "mere worshippers," and envisions Jeanette's faith will remain, "like water sealed in a cistern, unchangingly pure." Almost vampirically nourished by his image of her faith, Brad fails to realize that he is draining the cistern dry. To him, his marriage seems made in heaven, but this trust is only an illusion, fostered in part by his wife's withdrawal. He does not learn of her lost faith until she is in her seventies, near death, because he continually fails to notice signs of her struggle to preserve it against his intrusion.

At home, she establishes an upstairs retreat, a "room of her own" for preserving some remnants of the privacy he has invaded by usurping her commitment to churchgoing. At one point, her protests assume a more feminist tone: "Are you sure it's me you love or just some idea you have of me? . . . Did it ever occur to you . . . that you love me because it suits you? That for you it's an exercise in male power?" (*TM*, 197); Brad dismisses her outburst, however, as the product of her reading. Retreat rather than confrontation is more Jeanette's style; when Brad visits her upstairs, he is disturbed by her motionlessness, unaware that he has brought her to this stasis. Not until she is close to dying does she reveal that faith has become "an awful lot of bother"—a confession containing an element of vengeance as well as an honest desire to expose his culpability. After her death, Brad, betrayed by his own illusions, continues to go through the motions of religious observance, attempting by "sheer inert motion" to preserve some remnant of faith to shield him from emptiness.

Updike exhibits his talent for satire in "Getting into the Set," which turns a critical eye on the social pretensions of a young couple, recent arrivals in a class-conscious New England town. For Katie, who craves to become a member of the town's yuppie elite, the shameless damage this unruly crowd does to their meticulously renovated house and family heirlooms is not a tragedy, but rather "an initiation rite." She weeps happily over the destruction, trusting that she has made the right decision; yet in seeking validation from others, she willingly betrays herself, surrendering her identify and sacrificing her possessions as the price of becoming one of these brutal "beautiful people."

Like "Slippage," "The Wallet" depicts a struggle by an older man to regain a firm footing in reality after an erosion of confidence by circumstance. The coincidental loss of his wallet and the delayed arrival of a significant sum of money in the mail cause Fulham, a semiretired stockbroker, to panic as the accustomed order of his world begins to unravel. Out of a very ordinary incident, Updike creates a revealing study in human fragility and the necessity of trust in a world that gives numerous signs to the contrary. Even before he loses his wallet, Fulham is susceptible to bouts of panic, especially at the movie theatre, where his youthful experiences of imaginative transcendence are now replaced by visions of graves and voids. Though exacerbated by the images on the screen, his temporary afflictions of existential dread emerge when the everyday props of belief give way, although Fulham's age and the surrounding culture both tend to augment his apprehension. In a scene that recalls "Pigeon Feathers," in which David Kern eases his dread with the "merciful distraction" of a pinball machine, Fulham plays a video game, which becomes an unexpected reminder of extinction and his own powerlessness.

Fulham's subsequent crisis only confirms fears that he successfully represses outside the theater. Normally just "a friendly adjunct to his person," the missing wallet becomes a metaphor for his identity, the locus of his social and financial selfhood as well as a symbol of his existence in time. Only after Fulham cancels all his credit cards and stops the check does the long-awaited check arrive and the wallet turn up, yet once Fulham's submerged doubts have been awakened, his well-ordered world can never be the same. Despite the lost wallet's recovery, the incident has provided him with an equivalent near-death experience more real than the humiliating loss of his fighter in the video game. Feeling "very grandpaternal, fragile, wise, and ready to die," he has become conscious that at his age losses are not so easily redeemed.

One of Updike's strengths as a short story writer is his ability to take an everyday event and pressure it to reveal an extraordinary insight. "Leaf Season," in contrast, deliberately employs a limited omniscience in a straightforward chronicle of the surface events of a weekend visit to Vermont by five families—older versions of the young suburban couples in Updike's earlier fiction. With its ensemble cast and its portrayal of youth verging on troubled middle age, "Leaf Season" has the flavor of an Updike version of *The Big Chill*. Though the story concerns the passage of time, however, its actors seem curiously static, and the weekend's events without lasting significance. With 10 adults, 17 children, and five pets, the story is finally too crowded, and the narrator's detailed relation of meals, bridge games, and sleeping arrangements further dissipates the story's focus. As a set piece, Linda Tyler's nature lesson to the children contains a poignant image of the changes that the adults are experiencing: the inescapable losses, deteriorations, and seasonal recessions. The imperceptible but inevitable shedding of leaves, she notes, only becomes evident when one can see more light: "Nobody sees it happen, but it does. For suddenly, it seems, the woods are bare" (*TM*, 268). Similarly, their parents will make such a discovery about changes in their lives, unable to recognize, as perhaps the narrator attempts to do here, when and where the losses occurred.

"Beautiful Husbands," like "The Other," explores the psychology of an oblique sexual attraction, in which Spencer Ridgeway finally manages to cast aside the aura of "otherness" that attaches to his second wife. His initial attraction to Dulcie Gunther is related to his admiration of her husband, Kirk. Although it would be easy to categorize this attraction as latent homosexuality, Spencer is drawn more toward the masculine ideal and the "impeccably eighties suburban" image that Kirk embodies than to Kirk himself. The volume's final story, "The Other Woman," also studies the psychology of one of the partners involved in an affair, but shifts focus to the betrayed husband, Ed Marston, who schemes to untangle himself from his marriage of 22 years and "the suburban cat's cradle he had helped weave" after he discovers a homemade valentine from Jason Reynolds sticking out of his wife Carol's lingerie drawer. Ed, an engineer who specializes in stress analysis of tall buildings, calls himself a "connoisseur of stress," and he treats his marriage with the same objectivity he would give to studying a blueprint. After learning of Carol's affair, he coldly calculates how much strain his marriage will endure while he is undoing it. Ed becomes both the architect and a conspirator in a complex, self-serving scheme to free himself from Carol and keep Jason's wife, Pat, ignorant in the process, lest she seek a divorce and spoil his careful plans for comfortably extricating himself from his marriage.

Not surprisingly, Carol becomes more attractive to Ed when viewed through the eyes of another interested male. Still, when she offers to drop her lover and reconcile, Ed refuses to deviate from his plan to replace himself with Jason. To some extent, his scheme resembles the "condominiumization" he advocates for saving old buildings from the wrecker's ball; instead of razing them, he feels, one might preserve them by getting someone else to "buy in," as he hopes Jason will do with his family. During the transitional phase, after Ed has moved out and while Pat remains in her "protected bubble," the two households informally merge, with Ed often making a fourth in their tennis games. Thus Pat is not "the other woman" in the traditional sense of the term; rather than being involved in a sexual triangle with the Marstons, she remains on the periphery of the knowledge that the others share. Since Ed avoids romantic involvement with her, she remains a depersonalized other woman, and not *his* other woman. Only once, while examining her sore foot during a tennis game, does Ed experience a momentary burst of tenderness for this "tiny white piece of womanhood," but such feelings are repressed by Ed as "activated random stress within a situation he had thoroughly analyzed."

The conclusion involves ironic symmetry: after their marriage, Jason and Carol, in a humorous gesture among old co-conspirators, send Ed a homemade valentine. Yet Updike characteristically goes beyond constructing such a simple exit from his tale, concluding instead with Ed's chance meeting with Pat. She has obviously suffered in the process of divorce, but when she greets him with a lingering kiss on the lips, the gesture disturbs him. Since so little of Pat's character has been revealed through Ed's limited consciousness, it is difficult to know whether the kiss represents forgetfulness, forgiveness, a fond marker of the past, or an acknowledgment of that moment on the tennis court. More significant is that Ed favors the explanation that "fit best" with his construction of events. Her kiss might just as well be a Christ-like acknowledgment of his duplicity, but in order to continue his life without guilt, Ed chooses the least stressful reading—one that shows him in the best light. Of all

Updike's protagonists in this collection, Ed perhaps remains blindest to the true nature of trust, betraying himself as well as others.

As Jonathan Yardly has pointed out, "Updike has always, inescapably, dealt with trust; it is after all, the rock upon which domestic life rests or founders."[65] Still, as these recent stories show, trust transcends domestic matters, perpetuating our continued social existence above the abyss that lies beneath. An informed trust—one achieved through numerous betrayals and self-doubts—is the only foundation that provides safe footing, but it constantly shifts with the course of events. While Updike's older characters acknowledge the shadowy presence of their unsettled past and their separation from sources of past bliss, they recognize the necessity of investing faith in the uncertain present as they rebuild their lives. *Trust Me* has an autumnal mood: amid the fallen leaves of life's bygone summer, Updike's characters attempt to create their own precarious shelters between themselves and the increasingly visible horizon of death. Like the chambered nautilus in "More Stately Mansions," memories become sealed chambers of the "low-vaulted past," filled with happiness and guilt, upon which they must continue to build with a refurbished sense of trust.

Conclusion

Updike's critics perpetually await the production of a big, important book on a controversial subject, without realizing that the cumulative weight of his short fiction may embody an achievement on par with the one they seek—and in a form that may be more congenial to the author's gifts. Likewise, many of his readers will automatically turn to his award-winning Rabbit tetralogy for a chronicle of the changing cultural landscape and American domestic life over the past four decades, yet the study of Updike's canon of short fiction over the same span of time can yield just as rich a lode of sociological revelation. As one reviewer has recently stated, "At his best [Updike] is, more truly than John Cheever, the Chekhov of American suburbia" (Lurie, 3).

Yet beyond the manners, morals, dress, and cadences of his middle-class suburbanites, Updike captures those more universal dilemmas of loss, separation, and yearning that humanity never resolves. The title of his memoirs—*Self-Consciousness*—highlights his ongoing concern with one of the fundamental questions of existence: "the precious, inexplicable burden of selfhood" (*SC*, 257). His characters are painfully self-conscious human beings, perpetually aware of being cast out of the past into a realm in which time's erosion works at a pace faster than human strategies can unearth and attempt to recover lost territory. Indeed, the archaeological metaphors which Updike occasionally favors may capture the crucial endeavor of much of his short fiction: to obtain insight by digging down through the layers of the past or of quotidian life and discovering meaningful artifacts that deserve rescue from time's flux. Still, this image of excavation takes place in a particular social and spiritual context, and Updike's fiction is pervaded not only by a consciousness of the last few decades' effect on marriage and the family but also by a religiously informed vision of the gap between the actual state of affairs and the desired sense of connection that characters often seek in the realms of eros or memory.

Updike's loosely autobiographical characters have aged with him, and the initial gap between the author and his youthful protagonists has closed somewhat; in a few of Updike's recent stories, he projects himself forward into an older consciousness—much as he did (albeit from a greater distance) in his first novel, *The Poorhouse Fair*. He continues to write of dislocated individuals wistfully longing for the past—persistently dissatisfied and perpetually deciphering new lessons in separation, grief, and death. In Olinger, his characters are poised for flight, yet in a recent story, "A Sandstone Farmhouse," the protagonist, sorting through the memorabilia his mother has clung to until her death, reflects: "He felt guilty, anxious, displaced. He had always wanted to be where the action was, and what action there was, it turned out, had been back there."[66] More than simple nostalgia, these reflections on the past reveal a renewed sense of perishability and fragility that has never been absent from Updike's fiction but which his characters more successfully countered in earlier works.

Taken as a whole, Updike's canon of short fiction presents a composite portrait of a specimen middle-American life, traced through its varying phases: from the sketches of an "innocuous boyhood" filled with dreams of flight; to the subsequent nostalgic excursion into memories of seemingly halcyon days; to the entry into an era of domestic strife exacerbated by changing personal needs and social mores; to separation from past sources of ambivalent bliss and a series of fatiguing reassessments; to a renewed dedication to redeeming a provisional trust with a full consciousness of human failings. The backward glance and retrospective illumination are trademarks of Updike's short fiction. "At all times an old world is collapsing and a new world arising," he states. "We have better eyes for the collapse than the rise, for the old one is the world we know" (*HS*, xix). Yet while his stories consistently possess an elegiac quality, they never succumb to the tone of a lament. His characters' epiphanies, even when tinged with irony, are finally redemptive moments of perception presented with authorial sympathy.

Even if the range of experience presented in Updike's short fiction is as narrow as some critics maintain, Updike has succeeded admirably in illuminating the corner of existence he has chosen to delineate, generating new light among the shadows of everyday experience in a form that may be more naturally suited to his gifts of style and observation than the novel. Moments of crisis and perception, more dependent on the ability to sketch an evocative image than on a facility for plotting, are the center of Updike's short fiction, and emerge more naturally from his verbal gifts. While the traditional epiphanic story may be Updike's forte, he has also been a technical innovator whose experiments with the lyric, the

155

montage, and the sketch exhibit his ability to stretch the flexible genre of the short story.

As William Abrahams notes in his 1976 citation for Updike's Special O. Henry Award for Continuing Achievement: "the majority of short-story writers continue to conduct their explorations within the hardly visible confines of the tradition itself. Few have done so as consistently, or with such rewarding results, as John Updike. . . . His story, 'Separating,' characteristic of him in its maturity, control, stylistic ease, authenticity of emotion, and accuracy of observation, provides the occasion to honor him once again. . . . His unflagging mastery is at once an example and a consolation for addicts of the short story, readers and writers alike."[67] As a writer of short fiction, Updike still looms above his contemporaries and remains a formidable figure in the eyes of a talented younger generation of writers (among them his son David). In a 1978 interview with Stephen Banker, Updike expressed a desire to gather his stories for posterity,[68] yet until he slows his current pace, such a compilation may be quickly dated. In fact, by the time this study reaches print, another new volume of short stories may soon follow. With Rabbit Angstrom supposedly at rest, Updike may devote more attention to his short fiction: Bech may be ready for another series of travels in the rapidly changing international arena, although American domestic corners harbor numerous shadows that remain to be explored.

Notes to Part 1

1. John Updike, *Picked-Up Pieces* (New York: Knopf, 1975), 38; hereafter cited in the text as *PUP*.

2. John Updike, "Foreword," *Olinger Stories* (New York: Vintage, 1964), vii; hereafter cited in the text as *OS*.

3. John Updike, "The Artist and His Audience," *New York Review of Books* 18 July 1985, 16. A portion of this article is reprinted in Part 2.

4. In his introduction to *Best American Short Stories 1984*, ed. John Updike and Shannon Ravenel (Boston: Houghton Mifflin, 1984)—hereafter cited in the text as *BASS*—Updike remarks that one of his criteria for exclusion was the status of the piece as a "thinly disguised memoir" (xv) rather than a fictional creation. A portion of Updike's introduction is reprinted in Part 2.

5. See Robert McCoy, "John Updike's Literary Apprenticeship on *The Harvard Lampoon*," *Modern Fiction Studies* 20 (1974): 7–12, for a thorough discussion of the highlights of Updike's early efforts in short fiction.

6. See, for example, "Fragments of America," *Times Literary Supplement* 27 April 1962, 277, which notes that Updike's stories show the "less happy influences of *The New Yorker*." *Time*'s reviewer, in "Cool, Cool World," *Time* 17 Aug. 1959, 98, praises Updike's eye for detail, but feels the stories lack passion. A. C. Spectorsky, "Spirit under Surgery," *Saturday Review* 22 Aug. 1959, 31, feels, as I do, that these stories resemble those of the *New Yorker* genre, but carry the form to another level.

7. James Joyce, *Dubliners*, ed. Robert Scholes and A. Walton Litz (New York: Viking, 1969), 253.

8. Neither Ace's nor Mark's story, however, is included by Updike in *Olinger Stories* because they have crossed the threshold of adolescence and entered the working world.

9. John Updike, *The Same Door* (New York: Knopf, 1959), 9; hereafter cited in the text as *SD*.

10. Donald Greiner, 74. However, Albert Wilhelm, in "Rebecca Cune: Updike's Wedge between the Maples," *Notes on Modern American Literature* 7 (1983): Item 9, suggests that Rebecca's last name may contain a verbal echo of the Latin *cuneus*, or wedge.

11. John Updike, *Trust Me* (New York: Knopf, 1987), 136; hereafter cited in the text as *TM*.

12. Updike recounts the composition of "The Happiest I've Been" in "The Artist and His Audience," *New York Review of Books* 18 July 1985, 14–18, a portion of which is reprinted in Part 2.

13. R. B. Larsen's article, "John Updike: The Story as Lyrical Meditation," *Thoth* 13.1 (1972): 33–39 contains an excellent discussion of Updike's lyric mode.

14. John Updike, *Telephone Poles* (New York: Knopf, 1963), 60.

15. Albert J. Griffith, "Updike's Artist's Dilemma: 'Should Wizard Hit Mommy?'" *Modern Fiction Studies* 20 (1974): 115.

16. Alice and Kenneth Hamilton, *The Elements of John Updike* (Grand Rapids, MI: William B. Eerdmans, 1970), 104.

17. Critical opinion of this story generally has not been favorable. Charles Samuels, in *John Updike* (Minneapolis: U of Minnesota P, 1969), 14, remarks that both this story and its companion piece "Packed Dirt" show "their author's laziness." Robert Detweiler calls it "a catch-all for the reminiscences that Updike has not completely refined into fiction" (Detweiler 60).

18. Peter Meinke, "Yearning for Yesteryear," *Christian Century* 7 Dec. 1966, 1512.

19. Updike expresses a similar idea in his review of Denis de Rougemont: "A woman, loved, momentarily eases the pain of time by localizing nostalgia; the vague and irrecoverable objects of nostalgic longing are assimilated, under the pressure of libidinous desire, into the details of her person" (*AP*, 287).

20. John Updike, *The Music School* (New York: Knopf, 1966), 4; hereafter cited in the text as *MS*.

21. Cited in Greiner, 138, from a publication of "The Indian," with Updike's commentary, in a special edition of the *Blue Cloud Quarterly* (Vol. 17, No. 1).

22. Robert Martin Adams, "Without Risk," *New York Times Book Review* 18 Sept. 1966, 5.

23. Updike has recently published another story, "Tristan and Iseult," *New Yorker* 3 Dec. 1990, 42–43, whose title alludes to the legend, although the characters are a dental hygienist and her patient.

24. Larry E. Taylor, *Pastoral and Anti-Pastoral Patterns in John Updike's Fiction* (Carbondale: Southern Illinois Univ. Press, 1971), 118–21.

25. Rachel Burchard, 157–58, characterizes Stanley's experience as a preparation for the approach of God, similar to the type of readiness described by the theologian Karl Barth, whose works Updike has read and reviewed.

26. Charlie Reilly, "A Conversation with John Updike," *Canto* 3 (1980): 160.

27. The first of these mock interviews is reprinted in *PUP*, 10–13; the more recent one appears in the *New York Times Book Review* 27 Sept. 1981, 1, 34–35.

28. John Updike, *Bech: A Book* (New York: Knopf, 1970), v; hereafter cited in the text as *BB*.

29. John Updike, "The Writer Lectures," *New York Review of Books* 16 June 1988, 23.

30. Cynthia Ozick, on the other hand, remarks that Bech's Jewishness is so stereotypical that Updike seems to be using an "Appropriate Reference Machine" to generate his character. Her reviews of the Bech books are included in *Art and Ardor* (New York: Knopf, 1983), 114–29.

31. For Updike's reflections on Melville's literary silence, see "Melville's Withdrawal," reprinted in *HS*, 80–106.

32. John Updike, "Bech in Czech," *New Yorker* 20 Apr. 1987, 32–49.

33. John Updike, *Bech Is Back* (New York: Knopf, 1982), 10–11; hereafter cited in the text as *BIB*.

34. The tenth section, sandwiched between two vignettes on Africa, is itself a pastiche made up of five short incidents that alternate between Africa and Korea.

35. See Updike's chapter "On Not Being a Dove" in *SC* for his retrospective examination of his problems with adopting an antiwar position during the Vietnam War.

36. Guy Davenport, "Temptations," *National Review* 22 Dec. 1972, 1413, for instance, senses "the air of a retrospective show" and concludes that "These stories have about them a distinct air of the bottom of the barrel."

37. Peter S. Prescott, "Following Through, Sadly," *Newsweek* 23 Oct. 1972, 109.

38. John Updike, *Museums and Women and Other Stories* (New York: Knopf, 1972), 14; hereafter cited in the text as *MW*.

39. Diana Culbertson, "Updike's 'The Day of the Dying Rabbit,'" *Studies in American Fiction* 7 (1979): 98.

40. Alice and Kenneth Hamilton, *The Elements of John Updike* (Grand Rapids, MI: William B. Eerdmans, 1970), 51–52.

41. Jane Barnes, "John Updike: A Literary Spider," *Virginia Quarterly Review* 57 (1981), 87.

42. John Updike, *Too Far to Go* (New York: Fawcett, 1979), 10; hereafter cited in the text as *TFTG*.

43. Geller's film credits include adaptations in the American Short Story series—"The Music School" among them. The title *Too Far to Go* was chosen not by Updike but by Geller; it creates ironic commentary on Richard's response to Joan's speculation about whether they are going "back to the way things were": "No. I don't want to go back to that. I feel we've come too far and have only a little way more to go" (*TFTG*, 61).

44. See John Updike, "Embarrassed," *TV Guide* 6 Dec. 1986, 7–8, on the film version of *Rabbit, Run*.

45. Anatole Broyard, "Falling Into Love," *New York Times* 17 March 1979, 17.

46. The uncollected stories were: "Waiting Up" (*Weekend*); "The Red Herring Theory" (*New York Times Sunday Magazine*, 1 June 1975, 95, and 8 June 1975, 103); "Nakedness" (*Atlantic*, Aug. 1974, 33–36); "Separating" (*New Yorker* 23 June 1975, 36–41); "Gesturing" (*Playboy* 1978); "Divorcing: A Fragment" (first published in *Too Far to Go*); and "Here Come the Maples" (*New Yorker* 11 Oct. 1976, 38–43).

47. Albert E. Wilhelm, "Three Versions of Updike's 'Snowing in Greenwich Village,'" *American Notes and Queries* 22 (Jan.–Feb. 1984): 81.

48. Quoted in Kurt Suplee, "Woman, God, Sorrow & John Updike," *Washington Post* 27 Sept. 1981, F1.

49. John Updike, *Problems and Other Stories* (New York: Knopf, 1979), 237; hereafter cited in the text as *P*.

50. Donald Greiner, "John Updike," in *Broadening Views: 1968–1988*, vol. 6 of *Concise Dictionary of American Literary Biography* (Detroit: Gale, 1989), 291.

51. Sandwiched between "Transaction" and "Augustine's Concubine" is "Separating," a story featuring the Maples which nicely foreshadows the final separation of Augustine and his concubine.

52. Daniel M. Murtaugh, "Guilt Is the Mother of Beauty," *Commonweal* 28 March 1980, 189.

53. Rosemary Dinnage, "Guilt-edged Entanglements," *Times Literary Supplement* 23 May 1980, 575.

54. David Evanier, "Wearing Down," *National Review* 22 Feb. 1980, 232, calls the story "dreadful," and comments that it "seems to be more about the heartbreak of psoriasis"; Robert Towers, "Cuisine Minceur," *New York Review of Books* 8 November 1979, 19, notes that it is one of two which "strain for a quasi-theological dimension."

55. Daniel M. Murtaugh, "Guilt Is the Mother of Beauty," *Commonweal* 28 March 1980, 189.

56. See the chapter "Getting the Words Out" in *SC*, 96–102, *passim*.

57. John Updike, "The Artist and His Audience," *New York Review of Books* 18 July 1985, 17. A fuller excerpt from this essay is included in Part 2.

58. Among the periodicals in which stories from this volume appear are *Atlantic, Playboy, Esquire, Vanity Fair, Yankee*, and the *Ontario Review*.

59. Christopher Lehman-Haupt, "Books of the Times," *New York Times* 20 April 1987, C17.

60. John Updike, "The Illustrative Itch," *New York Review of Books* 10 April 1986, 35. Rpt. as the Foreword to *Doubly Gifted: The Author as Visual Artist*, Kathleen G. Hjerter (New York: Abrams, 1986).

61. Updike's memoirs contain a description of a similar incident from his youth that focuses on the missed catch but does not mention the aftermath; see *SC*, 88.

62. Originally published in 1962, the story has been reworked, so that style is less adjectival, the conflict clearer, and less weight falls on the toned-down ending; Updike has embedded a clue to the earlier time frame by specifying the model of the couple's new car in his revision: "a 1960 Plymouth SonoRamic Commando V-8, with fins."

63. See "On Not Being a Dove" in *SC*, 112–63, *passim*, for Updike's account of his differences with those in his circle over the Vietnam War.

64. See Updike's comments on "Made in Heaven'"s subject, scope, and theme in *New American Short Stories: The Writers Select Their Own Favorites,* Gloria Norris, ed. (New York: New Amercian Library, 1986), 25–26.

65. Jonathan Yardly, "John Updike: For Better, for Worse," *Washington Post Book World* 10 May 1987, 3.

66. John Updike, "A Sandstone Farmhouse," *New Yorker* 11 June 1990, 48.

67. Introduction, *Prize Stories 1976: The O'Henry Awards,* ed. William Abrahams (Garden City, NY: Doubleday, 1976), 13.

68. Stephen Banker, Taped Interview with John Updike (Washington D. C.: Tapes for Readers, 1978).

Part 2

THE WRITER

Introduction

Selecting from the vast body of Updike's prose and criticism for relevant commentary on the art of short fiction is a difficult task. As a regular book reviewer for the *New Yorker*, Updike is a charitable critic who tends to focus very closely on the book at hand rather than use his reviews as platforms to advance a particular literary theory or occasions to launch into discussions of his ideas on the art of fiction. Thus, although his reviews constitute the majority of his published prose, none of them is excerpted here. The best and most recent source of Updike's reflections on his self-conscious development as an artist is his memoirs, *Self-Consciousness*, a series of six related essays that focus on those events and forces that shaped his attitudes and art. The importance of his rural boyhood in Shillington, Pennsylvania, on his artistic evolution is a recurring theme in much of his commentary on his art; the two pieces from his memoirs included here explore his early development and his subsequent spiritual investment in the task of writing.

In some of the excerpts from interviews included here, Updike expresses misgivings about granting them; in fact, he has parodied the endeavor nicely in the pieces in which he submits to interviews with his character Henry Bech. Despite his reluctance, Updike submits to an interview a year, generally reserving the right to edit the final product. I have included significant portions of the earliest extended interview, with Charles Samuels, and of a revealing but less readily accessible interview with Charlie Reilly, which contains remarks on *Bech A Book* as well as on the short story in general.

Concerning the short story in particular, Updike's introduction to *Best American Short Stories 1984* contains his most illuminating commentary on the technique and subjects of contemporary fiction. His relatively neglected essay on Melville from the *New York Review of Books* includes reflections on the creative imagination and on the story "The Happiest I've Been."

Interview with Charles T. Samuels

Updike: When I write, I aim in my mind not toward New York but toward a vague spot a little to the east of Kansas. I think of the books on library shelves, without their jackets, years old, and a countryish teen-aged boy finding them, and having them speak to him. The reviews, the stacks in Brentano's, are just hurdles to get over, to place the books on that shelf. Anyway, in 1957, I was full of a Pennsylvania thing I wanted to say, and Ipswich gave me the space in which to say it, and in which to live modestly, raise my children, and have friends on the basis of what I did in person rather than what I did in print. . . .

Interviewer: Most of your work takes place in a common locale: Olinger. . . . Why do you feel so drawn to this material?

Updike: . . . I am drawn to southeastern Pennsylvania because I know how things happen there, or at least how they used to happen. Once you have in your bones the fundamental feasibilities of a place, you can imagine there freely.

Interviewer: That's not what I mean. What I meant to ask is not why you keep writing about Olinger per se, but why you write so much about what most people take to be your own adolescence and family. . . .

Updike: I suppose there's no avoiding it—my adolescence seemed interesting to me. In a sense my mother and father, considerable actors both, were dramatizing my youth as I was having it so that I arrived as an adult with some burden of material already half formed. There is, true, a submerged thread connecting certain of the fictions, and I guess the submerged thread is the autobiography. . . . When I was little, I used to draw disparate objects on a piece of paper—toasters, baseballs, flowers, whatnot—and connect them with lines. But every story, really, is a fresh start for me, and these little connections—recurrences of names, or the way, say, that Piet Hanema's insomnia takes him back into the same high school that John Nordholm, and David Kern, and Allen Dow sat in—are in there as a kind of running, oblique coherence. Once I've coined a name, by the way, I feel utterly hidden behind that mask and what I remember and what I imagine become indistinguishable. I feel no obligation to the remembered past; what I create on paper must, and for me does, soar free of whatever the facts were. . . .

In other words, I disavow any essential connection between my life and whatever I write. I think it's a morbid and inappropriate area of concern, though natural enough—a lot of morbid concerns are natural. But the work, the words on the paper, must stand apart from our living presences; we sit down at the desk and become nothing but the excuse for these husks we cast off. But apart from the somewhat teasing little connections, there is in these three novels and the short stories of *Pigeon Feathers* a central image of flight or escape or loss, the way we flee from the past, a sense of guilt which I tried to express in the story, the triptych with the long title, "The Blessed Man of Boston, My Grandmother's Thimble, and Fanning Island," wherein the narrator becomes a Polynesian pushing off into a void. The sense that in time as well as space we leave people as if by volition and thereby incur guilt and thereby owe them, the dead, the forsaken, at least the homage of rendering them. The trauma or message that I acquired in Olinger had to do with suppressed pain, with the amount of sacrifice I suppose that middle-class life demands, and by that I guess I mean civilized life. The father, whatever his name, is sacrificing freedom of motion, and the mother is sacrificing in a way—oh, sexual richness, I guess; they're all stuck and when I think back over these stories (and you know, they *are* dear to me and if I had to give anybody one book of me it would be the Vintage *Olinger Stories*), I think especially of that moment in "Flight" when the boy, chafing to escape, fresh from his encounter with Molly Bingaman and a bit more of a man but not enough quite, finds the mother lying there buried in her own peculiar messages from far away, the New Orleans jazz, and then the grandfather's voice comes tumbling down the stairs singing, "There is a happy land far far away." This is the way it was, is. There has never been anything in my life quite as compressed, simultaneously as communicative to me of my own power and worth and of the irremediable grief in just living, in just going on.

I really don't think I'm alone among writers in caring about what they experienced in the first eighteen years of their life. Hemingway cherished the Michigan stories out of proportion, I would think, to their merit. Look at Twain. Look at Joyce. Nothing that happens to us after twenty is as free from self-consciousness because by then we have the vocation to write. Writers' lives break into two halves. At the point where you get your writerly vocation you diminish your receptivity to experience. Being able to write becomes a kind of shield, a way of hiding, a way of too instantly transforming pain into honey—whereas when you're young, you're so impotent you cannot help but strive and observe and feel. . . .

Updike: For every novel, however, that I have published, there has been one unfinished or scrapped. Some short stories—I think offhand of "Lifeguard," "The Taste of Metal," "My Grandmother's Thimble"— use fragments salvaged and reshaped. Most came right the first time— rode on their own melting, as Frost said of his poems. If there is no melting, if the story keeps sticking, better stop and look around. In the execution there has to be a "happiness" that can't be willed or foreordained. It has to sing, click, something. I try instantly to set in motion a certain forward tilt of suspense or curiosity, and at the end of the story or novel to rectify the tilt, to complete the motion. . . .

Interviewer: What about the cultivation of pretense—playing around with it. I mean, what do you think of a writer like Barthleme?

Updike: He was an art director of some sort and, just as Kerouac's work was a kind of action writing to answer action painting, so Barthleme's short stories and the one novelette seem to me to be an attempt to bring over into prose something Pop. I think, you know, on the one hand of Andy Warhol's Campbell's soup cans and on the other of the Chinese baby food that the Seven Dwarfs in *Snow White* are making. Then again you do get a hard-edge writing in a way. In one of his short stories he says that the hard nut-brown word has enough aesthetic satisfaction for anybody but a fool. I also think his stories are important for what they don't say, for the things that don't happen in them, that stand revealed as clichés.

Yes—I think he's interesting, but more interesting as an operator within a cultural scene than as a—oh, as a singer to my spirit. A quaint phrase that possibly betrays me.

Interviewer: What of writers who've influenced you. Salinger? Nabokov?

Updike:
I learned a lot from Salinger's short stories; he did remove the short narrative from the wise-guy, slice-of-life stories of the thirties and forties. Like most innovative artists, he made new room for shapelessness, for life as it is lived. I'm thinking of a story like "Just Before the War with the Eskimos" not "For Esmé," which already shows signs of emotional overkill. Nabokov, I admire but would emulate only his high dedication to the business of making books that are not sloppy, that can be reread. I think his aesthetic models, chess puzzles and protective colorations in Lepidoptera, are rather special.

Interviewer: Henry Green? O'Hara?

Updike: Green's tone, his touch of truth, his air of peddling nothing and knowing everything, I would gladly attain to, if I could. For sheer transparence of eye and ear he seems to me unmatched among living writers. Alas, for a decade he has refused to write, showing I suppose his ultimate allegiance to life itself. Some of O'Hara's short stories also show a very rare transparence, freshness, and unexpectedness. Good works of art direct us back outward to reality again; they illustrate, rather than ask, imitation. . . .

Interviewer: In "The Sea's Green Sameness" you deny that characterization and psychology are primary goals of fiction. What do you think is more important?

Updike: I wrote "The Sea's Green Sameness" years ago and meant, I believe, that narratives should not be *primarily* packages for psychological insights, though they can contain them, like raisins in buns. But the substance is the dough, which feeds the storytelling appetite, the appetite for motion, for suspense, for resolution. The author's deepest pride, as I have experienced it, is not in his incidental wisdom but in his ability to keep an organized mass of images moving forward, to feel life engendering itself under his hands. But no doubt, fiction is also a mode of spying; we read it as we look in windows or listen to gossip, to learn what other people *do*. Insights of all kinds are welcome; but no wisdom will substitute for an instinct for action and pattern, and a perhaps savage wish to hold, through your voice, another soul in thrall. . . .

Basically, though, I describe things not because their muteness mocks our subjectivity but because they seem to be masks for God. And I should add that there is, in fiction, an image-making function, above image-retailing. To create a coarse universal figure like Tarzan is in some ways more of an accomplishment than the novels of Henry James.

Interviewer: As a technician, how unconventional would you say you were?

Updike: As unconventional as I need to be. An absolute freedom exists on the blank page, so let's use it. I have from the start been wary of the fake, the automatic. I tried not to force my sense of life as many-layered and ambiguous, while keeping in mind some sense of transaction, of a bargain struck, between me and the ideal reader. Domestic fierceness within the middle class, sex and death as riddles for the thinking animal, social existence as sacrifice, unexpected pleasures and rewards, corruption as a kind of evolution—these are some of the themes. I have tried to achieve objectivity in the form of narrative. My work is meditation, not pontification, so that interviews like this one feel like a forcing of the growth, a posing. I think of my books not as sermons or directives in a war of ideas but as objects, with different shapes and textures and the mysteriousness of anything that exists. My first thought about art, as a child, was that the artist brings something into the world that didn't exist before, and that he does it without destroying something else. A kind of refutation of the conservation of matter. That still seems to me its central magic, its core of joy.

Interview with Charlie Reilly

Reilly: You've written in so many forms—novels, poems, stories, essays, at least one play. And one of your poems, "Midpoint," seems to range over a variety of poetic forms, like Whitmanesque verses and heroic couplets. Do you consider yourself primarily a novelist?

Updike: More and more I seem to be reduced to that, although I persist in writing short stories. As a matter of fact, now that I have finally gotten out from under *The Coup*, I am assembling my stories of the last seven years. I hate to be judgmental in this regard—in fact, I don't know—but the short story may be what I do best. I certainly feel quite comfortable with it, whereas with the novel I occasionally feel uncertain, almost lacking. The problem, I think, is when you write a novel you become aware of the enormous amount of "stuff" you ought to know. When I have to compare short story writing to writing novels, I think of what happens with a box when you double the linear dimensions. You wind up with something four times the volume—at least I think you do. What I am getting at is, the bigger the work the more you have to put into it. But that's part of the excitement and charm, isn't it: to see if you can fill the box.

The beauty of writing a novel is that you don't have anyone looking over your shoulder; you're not trying to screen it through a magazine editor. Perhaps I flatter myself, but I think my publisher at this point would print anything I sent them that wasn't the work of a deranged mentality. So I guess I do want to work most on my novels. . . .

Reilly: I feel one of the services you perform for us readers is your habit of subtitling your novels. In the case of *Marry Me*, you subtitled it *A Romance*. Now, when I think of a "romance," I think of idealized lovers and Virtue Triumphant. And when I read *Marry Me*, I found myself constantly measuring your work against those ideas. . . .

Updike: The book has a curious history. It was a manuscript that I

Reprinted by permission of Charles E. Reilly.

171

had, for a long time, put aside for a number of reasons—not all of them personal. Some *were* personal, but in addition I just didn't think the book, well, "came off." It lacked the kind of playful, creatorly "something" that the novels I'm proud of, and the novels by others that I enjoy, possess. On the other hand, it did seem too good to lie fallow and the second chapter had appeared in the *New Yorker* some years earlier. So I did bring it out. At any rate, my unease about the book's lack of, let's say, "sociology" led me to give it the subtitle as a way of cutting it off from the other novels. . . .

In the same way, I called *Bech* a "Book" because it's not a novel. It began as a single story which was quite successful and it almost seemed to call out for the type of "redux" I later gave Rabbit. It was a way of unpacking the kinds of experience that only a writer has, but I unpacked it via an alter-ego who wasn't myself. Rather, he was my opposite in many ways, and that made it rather fun. The last couple of stories in *Bech* were written, of course, with a book in mind. They were composed to round out—"fill in" might be a better term—the book as such, but basically *Bech* is a set of short stories, not a novel.

Reilly: Now that you mention it, wasn't the "Journal" at the end of *Bech* adapted from something else?

Updike: Yes it was. The "Journal" was part of a long Russian piece which I had contemplated but which didn't work out. As it turned out, I salvaged the little chapter "Rich in Russia" and the "Journal." It would appear they were all I had to say about the Soviet Union.

Reilly: I gather in the case of *Marry Me* and *Bech* and *Buchanan* you drew a line and decided a particular work could not appropriately be called a "novel." I'm sure you don't have a list of definitions on hand, but do you recognize criteria that make a novel a novel?

Updike: I suppose anything that is a compilation of book-length fictional prose by a single author qualifies, and sometimes I wonder if that isn't all there is to some novels. But I feel there is more to it. I feel that some of the long prose works that, oh, some of my fellow *New Yorker* writers produce from their short stories are novels in name only. Personally, I'm rather pleased when no one can excerpt from a novel of mine and make it stand alone. It shows the work really is a novel and not simply a cluster of pieces. I didn't mean to denigrate *Bech* when I called it a book; in fact, I think it has a number of admirable qualities. And I thoroughly enjoyed writing about Henry Bech. I write so often about middle-brow or low-brow people that it was fun to write about someone—there's no adequate way to phrase this—who permits me to write without holding back, without compensating for the character's mind. But the whole texture of the book was that of short stories, and I couldn't bring myself to call it a novel.

Reilly: Bech has some dismal things to say about the agonies a writer must endure. Is it really that bleak? Do you find yourself tormented by bouts of depression, unfavorable reviews, periods of stagnation?

Updike: Alas, poor Bech. I just published another Bech story in the *New Yorker*, and someone sought me out to inquire whether it's all that bad. Actually, it's a happy kind of unhappiness. I'm very happy being a writer and, despite his protests, I think Bech is too. For one thing, I don't feel that my stories are that depressing—at least the *Bech* ones aren't. I suppose some of my domestic tales could be described as depressing, and surely some of the *Rabbit* episodes are meant to be disturbing. But, no, the *Bech* stories treat a sort of playful misery and they shouldn't be extended to suggest I'm bewailing the lot of the writer. I do know some writers who could be described as being "stalled" the way Bech is—you don't have to know many writers to meet such people. But even though they're stalled in a period of aridity, like Bech they continue to enjoy most of the benefits of being a writer in our society. They seem to be able to generate that certain charisma writers are associated with, and they manage to find people to admire them as artists. It's not so bad. Bech's career, I think, is based to a degree on Salinger's and I guess there is something of Kerouac in him. He's a writer who has stopped writing. But keep in mind that Bech's novels, and the novels of other "stalled" writers, have not been forgotten. His problem is that he has to live with the consciousness that, even though he is famous and making money, he's no longer "doing his thing." I suppose he's kind of a modernist. Perhaps I share his faults after all. Bech is nine or ten years older than I, he wants his work to be absolutely right, and he frequently worries that nothing he does is ever quite good enough. . . .

Reilly: Do you give yourself a break between novels? With *The Coup* in final galleys and the new one still in your head, do you take a long layoff or experience a dry period?

Updike: The break I gave myself this time was to work on some short stories, which I have been trying to get to for a long time, and squeeze in a couple of reviews. But typically I get nervous and unhappy if I don't write something after a little while. I like the sense of putting something on paper. In addition, the day to day "business" of being a writer provides a constant "break" from writing itself. . . . And while I'm waiting for the novel to form in my head, I'm writing some short stories as well.

Reilly: Is a short story a fairly spontaneous endeavor when compared to a novel? Does it more or less spring quickly from the head to the pen?

Updike: Yes. What you need in a novel is for several ideas to come somehow together in an interesting way. But with a short story you need only one spark to begin writing. So it is fairly spontaneous, and I think the better ones I've written have resulted from a fairly direct "delivery" from inspiration to production. Otherwise, you tend to cool on the idea and forget what excited you.

Reilly: Are poems similar in nature? Are they written directly and from an occasion?

Updike: Yes, and then you sit down during what you hope is a moment of peace and try to roll it toward a conclusion. Finding the right conclusion for a poem can be difficult, however. . . . At any rate, when it works, you almost run into the ending the way a ball hits a wall. You know you've found the ending. And when you're not doing it right, you can't find the ending at all. Perhaps it's true of short stories as well, perhaps of all the verbal arts. If you're not doing it correctly, you can't determine when you've ended.

Getting the Words Out

My first books met the criticism that I wrote all too well but had nothing to say: I, who seemed to myself full of things to say, who had all of Shillington to say, Shillington and Pennsylvania and the whole mass of middling, hidden, troubled America to say, and who had seen and heard things in my two childhood homes, as my parents' giant faces revolved and spoke, achieving utterance under some terrible pressure of American disappointment, that would take a lifetime to sort out, particularize, and extol with the proper dark beauty. *In the beauty of the lilies Christ was born across the sea*—this odd and uplifting line from among the many odd lines of "The Battle Hymn of the Republic" seemed to me, as I set out, to summarize what I had to say about America, to offer itself as the title of a continental *magnum opus* of which all my books, no matter how many, would be mere installments, mere starts at the hymning of this great roughly rectangular country severed from Christ by the breadth of the sea.

What I doubted was not the grandeur and plenitude of my topic but my ability to find the words to express it; every day, I groped for the exact terms I knew were there but could not find, pawed through the thesaurus in search of them and through the dictionary in search of their correct spelling. My English language had been early bent by the Germanic locutions of my environment, and, as my prose came to be edited by experts, I had to arbitrate between how I in my head heard a sentence go and how, evidently, it should correctly go. My own style seemed to me a groping and elemental attempt to approximate the complexity of envisioned phenomena and it surprised me to have it called luxuriant and self-indulgent; self-indulgent, surely, is exactly what it wasn't—*other*-indulgent, rather. My models were the styles of Proust and Henry Green as I read them (one in translation): styles of tender exploration that tried to wrap themselves around the things, the tints and voices and perfumes, of the apprehended real. In this entwining and gently relentless effort

Reprinted from *SELF-CONSCIOUSNESS* by John Updike. Copyright © 1989 by John Updike. Reprinted by permission of Alfred A. Knopf Inc.

there is no hiding that the effort is being made in language: all professo-
rial or critical talk of inconspicuous or invisible language struck me as
vapid and quite mistaken, for surely language, printed language, is what
we all know we are reading and writing, just as a person looking at a
painting knows he is not looking out of a window. . . .

The writing enterprise that so engaged [my mother] presented it to
me first as a matter of graphic symbols; the tangible precise indented
forms of those alphabet blocks and the typewriter's smart little leap of
imprintation were part of the general marvel of reproduced imagery, of
comic strips and comic books and books and magazines and motion
pictures. This last looks like the anomalous term in a sequence, the one
that must be circled on the aptitude exam, but in fact, in that pre-
television Thirties world, the world of the movies and the world of the
popular press were so entwined, and the specific world of Walt Disney so
promiscuously generated animated cartoons and cartoon strips and children's books and children's toys, that it all seemed one art. The projector
in effect printed with its beam of light the film upon the screen, and the
stylized activities one saw there were being simultaneously read in a
thousand theatres. A potentially infinite duplication was the essence, an
essence wed for me to the smell of inked paper, dead pulped paper
quickened into life by the stamped image of Dick Tracy or Captain Easy
or Alley Oop; the very crudities and flecked imperfections of the process
and the technical vocabulary of pen line and crosshatching and benday
fascinated me, drew me deeply in, as perhaps a bacteriologist is drawn
into the microscope and a linguist into the teeming niceties of a foreign
grammar. . . .

My subsequent career carries coarse traces of its un-ideal origins in
popular, mechanically propagated culture. The papery self-magni-
fication and immortality of printed reproduction—a mode of self-
assertion that leaves the cowardly perpetrator hidden and out of harm's
way—was central to my artistic impulse; I had no interest in painting or
sculpting, in creating the unique beautiful object, and have never been
able to sustain interest in the rarefied exercise of keeping a journal. I
drew, in black and white, exploring the minor technical mysteries of
lettering nibs and scratchboard, of washes and benday, and then I
drifted, by way of Ogden Nash and Phyllis McGinley and Morris Bishop
and Arthur Guiterman, into light verse, and very slowly—not until
college age, really—into the attempt to fabricate short stories. The idea
of writing a novel came even later and presented itself to me, and still
does, as *making a book;* I have trouble distinguishing between the func-

tions of a publisher and those of a printer. The printer, in my naïve sense of literary enterprise, is the solid fellow, my only real partner, and everyone else a potentially troublesome intermediary between him and myself. My early yearnings merged the notions of print, Heaven, and Manhattan (a map of which looks like a type tray). To be in print was to be saved. And to this moment a day when I have produced nothing printable, when I have not gotten any words out, is a day lost and damned as I feel it.

Perhaps I need not be too apologetic about these lowly beginnings. The great temple of fiction has no well-marked front portal; most devotees arrive through a side door, and not dressed for worship. Fiction, which can be anything, is written by those whose interest has not crystallized short of ontology. Coming so relatively late to the novel, as the end-term of a series of reproducible artifacts any of which I would have been happy to make for a living if I could, I find I feel, after completing thirteen of them, still virginal, still excited and slightly frightened by the form's capacity. My assets as a novelist I take to be the taste for American life acquired in Shillington, a certain indignation and independence also acquired there, a Christian willingness to withhold judgment, and a cartoonist's ability to compose within a prescribed space.

On Being a Self Forever

So writing is my sole remaining vice. It is an addiction, an illusory release, a presumptuous taming of reality, a way of expressing lightly the unbearable. That we age and leave behind this litter of dead, unrecoverable selves is both unbearable and the commonest thing in the world—it happens to everybody. In the morning light one can write breezily, without the slightest acceleration of one's pulse, about what one cannot contemplate in the dark without turning in panic to God. In the dark one *truly* feels that immense sliding, that turning of the vast earth into darkness and eternal cold, taking with it all the furniture and scenery, and the bright distractions and warm touches, of our lives. Even the barest earthly facts are unbearably heavy, weighted as they are with our personal death. Writing, in making the world light—in codifying, distorting, prettifying, verbalizing it—approaches blasphemy. . . .

During . . . adolescence, I reluctantly perceived of the Christian religion I had been born into that almost no one believed it, believed it really—not its ministers, nor its pillars like my father and his father before him. Though signs of belief (churches, public prayers, mottos on coins) existed everywhere, when you moved toward Christianity it disappeared, as fog solidly opaque in the distance thins to transparency when you walk into it. I decided I nevertheless *would* believe. I found a few authors, a very few—Chesterton, Eliot, Unamuno, Kierkegaard, Karl Barth—who helped me believe. Under the shelter (like the wicker chairs on the side porch) that I improvised from their pages I have lived my life. I rarely read them now; my life is mostly lived. God is the God of the living, though His priests and executors, to keep order and to force the world into a convenient mould, will always want to make Him the God of the dead, the God who chastises life and forbids and says No. What I felt, in that basement Sunday school of Grace Lutheran Church in Shillington, was a clumsy attempt to extend a Yes, a blessing, and I accepted that blessing, offering in return only a nickel a week and my art, my poor little art.

Imitation is praise. Description expresses love. I early arrived at these self-justifying inklings. Having accepted that old Shillington blessing, I have felt free to describe life as accurately as I could, with especial attention to human erosions and betrayals. What small faith I have has given me what artistic courage I have. My theory was that God already knows everything and cannot be shocked. And only truth is useful. Only truth can be built upon. From a higher, inhuman point of view, only truth, however harsh, is holy. The fabricated truth of poetry and fiction makes a shelter in which I feel safe, sheltered within interlaced plausibilities in the image of a real world for which I am not to blame. Such writing is in essence pure. Out of soiled and restless life, I have refined my books. They are trim, crisp, clean, especially in the moment when they arrive from the printer in a cardboard box, before the reviewers leave their smudges all over them, and I discover, like a tiny flower that insists on blooming in the expanse of a shining level salt flat, the first typographical error.

Yet fiction, like life, is a dirty business; discretion and good taste play small part in it. Hardly a story appears in print without offending or wounding some living model who sees himself or herself reflected all too accurately and yet not accurately enough—without that deepening, mollifying element of endless pardon we bring to our own self. Parents, wives, children—the nearer and dearer they are, the more mercilessly they are served up. So my art, like my religion, has a shabby side. These memoirs feel shabby. Truth should not be forced; it should simply manifest itself, like a woman who has in her privacy reflected and coolly decided to bestow herself upon a certain man. She will *dawn* upon that man. . . .

Wherever there is a self, it may be, whether on Earth or in the Andromeda Galaxy, the idea of God will arise. Religion, once the self has taken its hook, preaches selflessness. The self is the focus of anxiety; attention to others, self-forgetfulness, and living like the lilies are urged, to relieve the anxiety. Insomnia offers a paradigm: the mind cannot fall asleep as long as it watches itself. At the first observed lurch into nonsensical thought, we snap awake in eager anticipation, greedy to be asleep. Only when the mind moves unwatched and becomes absorbed in images that tug it as it were to one side does self-consciousness dissolve and sleep with its healing, brilliantly detailed fictions pour in upon the jittery spirit. Falling asleep is a study in trust. Likewise, religion tries to put us at ease in this world. Being human cannot be borne alone. We need other presences. We need soft night noises—a mother speaking downstairs, a grandfather rumbling in response, cars swishing past on Philadelphia Avenue and their headlights wheeling about the room. We need the little clicks and sighs of a sustaining otherness. We need the gods. . . .

Religion and nothingness . . . are successive doses of anesthetic, the first temporary and imperfect, in throwaway wrappings of dogma and Christmas tinsel, the second permanent and perfect. An age of anxiety all too suitably takes God as a tranquillizer, just as feudal times took Him as Lord or King, leaving us a language of piety loaded with obsolete obeisances, and other eras took him as a magical incantation, or an insatiable repository of blood sacrifice and self-mutilation, or an imperturbable Watchmaker, or a surge of the Life Force. The self's echo and companion must be not only that. One believes not only to comfort one's self but for empirical and compositional reasons—the ornate proposed supernatural completes the picture and, like the ingredient that tops up and rounds out the recipe, gives reality its true flavor. Similarly, in art one has to add a little extra color, some overanimation, to bring the imitation up to the pitch, the bright roundedness, the repletion, of the actual model.

Of my own case, looked at coldly, it might be said that, having been given a Protestant, Lutheran, rather antinomian Christianity as part of my sociological make-up, I was too timid to discard it. My era was too ideologically feeble to wrest it from me, and Christianity gave me something to write about, and a semblance of a backbone, and a place to go Sunday mornings, when the post offices were closed.

What I have written here strains to be true but nevertheless is not true *enough*. Truth is anecdotes, narrative, the snug opaque quotidian.

The Short Story Today

In a way, I want—perhaps we all want—facts, words I can picture. I want stories to startle and engage me within the first few sentences, and in their middle to widen or deepen or sharpen my knowledge of human activity, and to end by giving me a sensation of completed statement. The ending is where the reader discovers whether he has been reading the same story the writer thought he was writing. Two chains of impression have been running in rough parallel; the ending—"the soft shock at the bottom of the story, the gasp of the dimly unfolding wings of finished symmetry" (to quote another story just barely excluded from this collection, "The Dealer's Yard," by Sharon Sheehe Stark)—confirms or dissolves the imagined partnership. . . .

A narrative is like a room on whose walls a number of false doors have been painted; while within the narrative, we have many apparent choices of exit, but when the author leads us to one particular door, we know it is the right one *because it opens*. . . .

The good ending dismisses us with a touch of ceremony, and throws a backward light of significance over the story just read. It *makes* it, as they say, or unmakes it—a weak beginning is forgettable, but the end of a story bulks in the reader's mind like the giant foot in a foreshortened photograph. . . .

Sexual love and its distress of the social order is the common theme of fiction; the more elusive matter of comradeship, within a family or social circle, is a relatively low-octane fuel that comfortably propels the compact form of the short story. . . .

Time, that immense invisible in our midst, is part of the substance of narrative, as it is of music; from the standpoint of our subjectivity, death is time's ultimate fruit, and perhaps I need not be embarrassed or surprised that so many of these stories deal with death—deaths in the family, more or less close, and deaths as experienced or longed for . . . ;

euthanasia and gerontology figure in the eighties short story as distinctively as live-in lovers, Little League, shopping malls, television, and rickety extended families of stepparents and stepsiblings. . . .

The inner spaces that a good short story lets us enter are the old apartments of religion. People in fiction are not only, as E. M. Forster pointed out in his *Aspects of the Novel*, more sensitive than people one meets; they are more religious. Religion and fiction both aver, with Kirkegaard, that "subjectivity is truth"; each claims importance for the ephemeral sensations of consciousness that material science must regard as accidents, as epiphenomena. Fictional technique and the craft of suspense are affected: without a transcendental ethics, of what significance are our decisions? . . .

One has to love Ms. Ozick for daring a bravura style in an age when many short-story writers are as tight-lipped as cardplayers on a losing streak—in faithful reflection, no doubt, of the *Weltgeist*, the post-Vietnam cool, cautious and anti-inflationary. Experience itself, in an age when so much is reported and exposed, has been cheapened. In the stories of, say, Bobbie Ann Mason and Frederick Barthelme, the people seem to be glancing away from television at the events of their own lives with the same barely amused, channel-changing diffidence. . . .

Our information about each other remains, in the midst of a sophistication glut, wonderfully faulty, and for this reason we read short stories. Each is a glimpse into another country: an occasion for surprise, an excuse for wisdom, and an argument for charity.

The Creative Imagination and "The Happiest I've Been"

The creative imagination wants to please its audience, and it does so by sharing what is most precious to it. . . .

The artist who works in words and anecdotes, images and facts, wants to share with us nothing less than his digested life, his life as he savors it, in the memories and fantasies most precious, however obscurely, to him. Let me illustrate all this with a brief example from my own humble creativity.

In 1958 I was a young man of twenty-six who had recently presumed to set himself up in a small New England town as a free-lance writer. My obligations to my career and my family, as I conceived them, were to sell six short stories a year to *The New Yorker* magazine. I had already written and sold a number based upon my Pennsylvania boyhood and my young married life in New York City; one winter day I happened to remember, with a sudden simultaneous sense of loss and recapture, the New Year's Eve parties my old high school crowd used to have at a certain home, and how even after most of us had gone off to college, we for several years continued the custom, which now served as a kind of reunion. The hero of my story is a college sophomore, already committed to a college girlfriend and to aspirations that will take him forever away from his home town. He tells us of a moment in this hectic gathering of nineteen- and twenty-year-olds. . . .

The story is called "The Happiest I've Been." It was accepted, paid for, and has been reprinted in a few anthologies. As I wrote it, I had a sensation of breaking through, as if through a thin sheet of restraining glass, to material, to truth, previously locked up. I was excited, and when my wife of those years read the first draft, she said, "This is exciting." Now, what was exciting? There is no great violence or external adventure in the story, no extraordinary characters. The concreteness, the actuality, I suggest, is exciting. In 1958 I was at just the right distance from the night in Shillington, Pennsylvania, when 1952 became 1953; I still remembered and cared, yet was enough distant to get a handle on the memories, to manipulate them into fiction.

That is part one of creativity; me, my self-expression. Creativity, as I construe it, is a tripartite phenomenon: there is the artist, keen to express himself and to make an impression. But there also has to be a genre, a preexistent form or type of object to which the prospective artist's first relation was that of consumer, the pleasure of his consumption extending itself into the ambition to be a producer. And attached to that genre and inextricable from its growth is the audience that finds in the contents of this form some cause for consolation, amusement, or enlightenment.

For part two, the genre, there was the American short story, the *New Yorker* short story indeed, of which many had been written in the decade preceding 1958, but none, my happy delusion was, quite in this way about quite this sort of material. Non-southern small towns and teen-agers were both, my impression was, customarily treated with conde-scension, or satirically, in the fiction of the 1950s; the indictments of provincial life by Sinclair Lewis and Ring Lardner were still in the air. My self-appointed mission was to stand up and cry, "No, this is life, to be taken as seriously as any other kind." By this prophetic light tiny details, like the shaved armpit gleaming like a bit of chicken skin or the two triangular punctures in an empty oil can, acquire the intensity of sym-bolism. The blurred sexuality of this playful moment is ominous, for it is carrying the participants away from their childhoods, into the dizzying mystery of time.

As to the third part of the creative process, the audience beyond the genre, there was the *New Yorker* reader as I imagined him, needing a wholesome middle-American change from his then customary diet of Westchester adultery stories and reminiscences of luxurious Indian or Polish childhoods. I believed, that is, that there was a body of my fellow Americans to whom these modest doings in Pennsylvania would be news.

Such was the state of my imagination as I wrote this story; actually, many stories not unlike it appear in the magazine now, and perhaps always have: but in my possibly deluded sense of things the material was fresh, fresh to me and fresh to the world, and authentic. By authentic I mean actual and concrete. For the creative imagination, in my sense of it, is wholly parasitic upon the real world, what used to be called Creation. Creative excitement, and a sense of useful work, have invariably and only come to me when I felt I was transferring, with a lively accuracy, some piece of experienced reality to the printed page. . . . The will toward concreteness, the fervor to do justice to the real, compels style and form into being. No style or form exists in the abstract; whatever may be true in painting or music, there is no such thing as abstract writing. Words even when shattered into nonsense struggle to communicate meanings to us; and behind the most extreme modernist experiments with the language of fiction—Joyce's *Finnegans Wake*; the late writing of Gertrude Stein; the automatic writing of Dada—some perception about the nature of reality seeks embodiment.

The creative imagination, then, has a double "interface": on the "output" side, with some kind of responsive audience, and on the "input" side, with reality itself. If either connection breaks down, the electricity ceases to flow. Both sides of the creative event demand trust: on the output side, we must hope that some sort of audience is there, or will be there. On the input, we must sit down in the expectation that the material will speak through us, that certain unforseeable happinesses of pattern and realization will emerge out of blankness as we write.

Part 3

THE CRITICS

Introduction

Much of the academic criticism on Updike's fiction concentrates on the novels; for instance, the articles indexed in the most recent MLA bibliography (1990), except for one entry on style, exclusively concern the novels. Nonetheless, a healthy body of criticism focuses on the short fiction, and each new collection is greeted by a chorus of reviews (often mixed), leaving no shortage of material from which to select a representative sampling. Although many of those who review Updike's work in periodicals have extremely articulate voices, the following selections favor the growing body of academic criticism. Those who seek a sense of the spectrum of reviewers' opinions on individual volumes are urged to read Donald Greiner's fine summaries of the critical responses that begin each chapter in *The Other John Updike* and Macnaughton's comprehensive introduction to his essay collection.

The selections for Part 3 provide critical commentary that spans Updike's career; they generally follow the order of publication of works with which they are concerned. I deliberately have attempted not to include pieces that are readily accessible in the anthologies by David Thorburn and Howard Eiland, William Macnaughton, and Harold Bloom. Space limitations unfortunately dictate that some fine articles be excluded; for every essay or excerpt included, an equally fine piece has been omitted. Different critical perspectives are represented, ranging from structuralist to traditional New Criticism. I also have attempted not to include more than one article on the same short story.

John Gerlach examines one of Updike's early works from the critical perspective of one concerned with closure—an approach that meshes with Updike's own concerns with the short story's conclusion (see the Introduction to *Best American Short Stories 1984* contained in Part 2). Sanford Schwartz's retrospective comments on the "local boy" of the Olinger stories, along with Eileen Baldeshwiler's and R. B. Larsen's remarks on the lyric story, provide some insight into two of Updike's early fictional concerns.

Raman Selden's chapter on "Should Wizard Hit Mommy?" is one of the first direct applications of narrative theory to Updike's short stories.[1]

Albert Wilhelm is represented by his study of the thematic continuity that helps unite *Too Far to Go* as a short story sequence. Erica Jong (whose first novel, *Fear of Flying*, was very favorably received by Updike in the *New Yorker*) compares *Too Far to Go* with his novel *The Coup*, favoring Updike's short story art. The conclusion of Jane Barnes's long article on Updike's more recent fiction places the divorced protagonist of *Problems* in the context of the male protagonist (or center of consciousness) who has dominated his short fiction, and should be juxtaposed with Schwartz's analysis of the Olinger protagonist.

Note

1. See also Albert J. Griffith, "Updike's Artist's Dilemma: 'Should Wizard Hit Mommy?'" *Modern Fiction Studies* 20 (1974), 111–15, for a complementary discussion of the same story.

John Gerlach

Structurally open stories often derive from the pattern Hemingway popularized, the compressed form. Imitations are abundant—Irwin Shaw's "The Girls in Their Summer Dresses" (1947) in many ways resembles "Hills Like White Elephants," and so does John Updike's "Ace in the Hole" (1955)—and crises faced by young couples seem particularly adaptable to this approach. But Shaw, by closing with the revelation that the husband, Michael, can see his wife only as a sex object, adds the sort of "wow" that Hemingway disdained, and it closes off the story. Until the end the reader was likely to take Michael's side against his querulous wife, but the ending abruptly undercuts our sympathy and implies that, as in "Hills," argumentative positions will irreconcilably harden. Action continues, but by saving a snap for the end, making the reader invert his reading of the story, Shaw enforces completion.

Updike's "Ace in the Hole" can be read as a closed story, but certain elements do open it. In some respects Updike's practice seems conventional; he works with the same end-directedness that characterizes many writers, trying, in his words, "instantly to set in motion a certain forward tilt of suspense or curiosity, and at the end of the story or novel to rectify the tilt, to complete the motion."[1] The change in vocabulary, with the emphasis on the slightness of "tilt," and the barely noticeable correction that "rectify" implies, show how muted these objectives have become.

"Ace in the Hole" begins with the same slow development of the problem level, the same slow exposition that moves from simple to more complex levels of suspense, that characterizes the compressed form. The reader's charge at this point is first to assemble the terms of the conflict. The opening paragraph proposes only a simple problem: "The moment his car touched the boulevard heading home, Ace flicked on the radio. He needed the radio, especially today. In the seconds before

Reprinted by permission of The University of Alabama Press from *Toward the End: Closure and Structure in the American Short Story* by John Gerlach, © 1985 The University of Alabama Press.

the tubes warmed up, he said aloud, doing it just to hear a human voice, 'Jesus. She'll pop her lid.' "[2] While provoking the reader to seek answers to these questions—who is "she," why will she pop her lid?—Updike completes the exposition. The first woman Ace meets, his mother, is evidently not "she," because when his mother finds out that he has lost his job, she responds, "Good for you" (p. 16). The "she" in question turns out to be Ace's wife, Evey. At first, the issue of his having lost his job is dismissed—she has already heard about it, but she flares up and threatens to leave him. She's "fed up" and "ready as Christ to let [him] run" (p. 24). The issue of the job was only a smaller one in the context of her greater dissatisfaction with him.

While working to identify the central problem the reader is also likely to attend to minor questions such as Ace's age. Ace seems at first very young, perhaps still in high school, a drag-racing kid, listening to the radio, flipping his cigarette out the window. Yet when another driver pulls up next to his car, he feels himself old, separated by a "little gap of years," some distance from the kids who are "young and mean and shy" (p. 15). There is a disparity between what he thinks of himself and what his actions suggest about him. He thinks of himself as Ace, but his mother calls him Freddy.

A more significant puzzle for the reader is the complexity of Ace as a character. Despite his obvious immaturity he shows signs of wisdom: he ignores his mother's encouragement to break up his marriage, and although he acted foolishly in the incident (involving parking cars) that got him fired, he is neither proud nor defensive. He regrets leaving his past—his nickname comes from his former status as a high school basketball player—but his hesitation in reading the article his mother has mentioned shows a capacity to move beyond his former self. The slow development of the problem permits the reader to invest interest in character study, and it is this particularity, this interest in social realism, that in part differentiates Updike's approach from Hemingway's.

As the story nears its end, the intensity unobtrusively increases. Ace first raises the stakes, giving the theme of the risk of the marriage a new context. The baby interrupts Evey's angry speech about Ace's "hot-shot stunts" (p. 24) by putting an ashtray on her head, an interruption which Evey, by noting sarcastically that the baby is "cute as her daddy," brings us back to the theme of her anger. Ace then makes a demonstration of his own from the baby, using her grasp of the rattle to illustrate her genetic talent as a potential basketball player, a talent he argues is wasted because she is a girl. What they need is another child. His effort is audacious, for at the point of her readiness to leave, he is angling for another offspring, Fred junior.

The ultimate scene brings into play both the progressive and regressive elements in Ace's character. The scene is announced as terminal by two markers. The first is when Ace turns on the radio (the phrase "before the tubes warmed up" [p. 25] is an exact repetition of a phrase in the third sentence of the opening), which indicates that in a moment of crisis he meets the need by performing this ritual. The second marker is a nirvana theme, used ironically. As he begins to dance with Evey to the music of the radio, "he seemed to be great again, and all the other kids were around them, in a ring, clapping time" (p. 26): he has conjured up the past as a salve to self-esteem, as a way to see himself great again.

The ironic note of the ending stresses his regression: "The music ate through his skin and mixed with the nerves and small veins," and in a druglike state Ace imagines he has won the argument, escaping the strictures of the present. Ace is a boy who will never grow up, a boy who has conceived the unfortunate idea of holding together an impossible marriage solely to replicate himself and has compelled his wife into stunned acquiescence in his dreamy, regressive dance.

But a substratum of the text suggests that Ace's progression cannot be ignored. Unlike the males of the Shaw or Hemingway stories, he wants to sustain a marriage, not to evade or destroy it. His transition to adult life has been difficult, and in the ending he retreats to images of the past. But in this story, unlike the others, the wife is part of the scene he constructs. She has been "seized" to participate in the dance, but what follows does not resemble rape—he fits his hand "into the natural place on Evey's back and she shuffled stiffly into his lead." He spins her out "carefully," and then "her hair brushed his lips as she minced in, then swung away, to the end of his arm; he could feel her toes dig into the carpet." She may know she is being taken in, allowing Ace to shift the topic, to seduce her and to score one more time. But acquiescence here need not mean capitulation ever after. In contrast, "Hills Like White Elephants" does not resolve the quarrel, but thematically the story predicts disaster and separation. The train is coming, closing the scene. The scene in Updike's story is still moving; the dance goes on. Ace's regression at the end may be temporary, and his ability to survive may outweigh the pull backward. He is not, as his mother would like him to be, eager to return to his past as if his present does not exist. His wife's silence, if not shared dreaming, may at least indicate a willingness to stay. The dance is an ambiguous ending, for it can be read both as a close and an opening.

Even the title suggests ambiguity—Ace is on the spot, in the hole. Ace may be aiming for another hole, a bedroom hoop. But an ace in the hole is a good card to have, and it can build a winning hand.

Most readers, I suspect, will not want to suspend the ending and will prefer to emphasize Ace's regression. But elements of openness can be ignored only at the cost of the richness of the story. "Ace in the Hole" is typical of the suspension we have come to favor in the short story. The reader will provide a close based on what he or she takes to be the dominant tone, but the suspension is necessary for the final effect. Anything thoroughly closed might not seem modern, might appear to portray life dishonestly.

Notes

1. "The Art of Fiction, XLIII: John Updike," *Paris Review* 12, no. 45 (1968):96.

2. John Updike, *The Same Door* (New York: Knopf, 1972), p. 14.

Sanford Schwartz

There is an extra, intangible dimension in all his work, though it may be seen most purely in his short stories. Talking about R. K. Narayan, he says, "a short story, like the flare of a match, brings human faces out of darkness, and reveals depths beyond statistics." Updike's stories, both the naturalistic ones and the sermonlike monologues, have that flare. Where they take us, though, is into the darkness. In Updike's finest moments, we feel the way we do when, in the country, especially in the fall and winter, after being indoors all evening, we go outside and the night sky is unexpectedly clear, starry, and endless—and we see both the beauty of the moment and, in a good way, the smallness of our concerns.

Reading a good amount of Updike's fiction produces the feeling that he is less a storyteller by temperament than a journal keeper. It is a person's illuminating or dispiriting moments that he most wants to re-create, and many of his best stories have the confessional, blurting-out drive of a powerful journal entry. He resembles some journal keepers, too, in that he seems to continually describe and analyze those moments because, doing it, he can put off settling some other, larger issue—an issue he knows he will never settle. Updike always asks the right questions, in his reviews as much as in his fiction; yet, perhaps because he feels he cannot bring certain problems to a head, or doesn't want to, he comes up with answers too quickly. . . .

The real point is almost always one man's psychic and spiritual dilemma, and we invariably feel that Updike himself is that man. That his stories seem fuller than his novels may be due to the fact that he puts fewer documentary details in his stories—he goes straight for the dilemma. . . .

He has always wanted to describe the muffled and unstated connections between people—how people unconsciously hurt, or draw strength from, each other. In his earlier work, though, particularly in the stories about his parents and grandparents and his home town, the remembered details seemed to come to him faster than he had time to organize them, and his scenes were crowded and brimming. His themes have not changed, but, increasingly now, the details seem arbitrary, and there's something schematic in the way he shows those muffled connections.

Certainly no one thing explains the fuzziness at the core of Updike's work, but in his early stories, especially those set in a small Pennsylvania town, we feel we're seeing the dilemmas in his own life that first pulled him in opposite directions and left him with his sense of the unresolvable-ness of things. Some of the most intense, packed stories—"The Alligators," "A Sense of Shelter," "Flight," "The Happiest I've Been"—involve the courtship rites of teen-agers. The stories aren't about sex, though. They're about a character (his name is always different) who courts because he feels he ought to, and who is often most at peace when circumstances let him off the hook. . . .

There's a European, nineteenth-century note to Updike's early Pennsylvania stories. They form one long tale of a provincial teacher's son, a gifted, questioning, and kind young man, a prince by nature, who grows up knowing that he will never be a true prince and that, no matter how much he accomplishes when he goes away, he will always be the teacher's son when he comes back to his town. The stories are moving but they aren't cathartic, because the young man never consciously decides to risk isolation and face the fact of his superiority. We're never sure which role he most wants. What he settles for is a priestly, in-between role. Though he doesn't put his future course of action in words, it's clear that he will leave, and live up to his brilliant promise, but he won't let himself fly. He'll be like a man who, ashamed of his inherited riches, develops a limp, when there is actually nothing wrong with his legs, so the world will realize that, in some way, he has paid his dues. . . .

The Pennsylvania stories present a picture of an only child who continually watches, and tries to account for, two mighty figures—his mother and father. They are the only people in his numbingly ordinary world who are as sensitive and perceptive as he is. Though he finds his guileless father an embarrassment, and there is always a gulf between him and his mother, he wants to keep them, and their past, on a pedestal, and the reader understands why: if not for his parents, there would be nothing for Updike's young protagonist to believe in. He seems to make a religion out of being an average kid, even of being a proud son and celebrator of his state of Pennsylvania, because it keeps him, in his mind, from outgrowing his parents; if he outgrew them he'd be truly alone.

R. B. Larsen

The often acerbic critical controversy over the stature of John Updike continues, unabated by the publication of *Rabbit Redux*. It is still too early to tell, of course, how durable will be the total work of a writer so surprisingly fertile and inventive. One thing seems indisputable even now, though: his mastery of the short story form. . . .

Even after the strikingly modish *Rabbit Redux*, the short story seems as significant a part of Updike's achievement as it was for Hemingway and Fitzgerald. Many of Updike's efforts bear the hallmarks of good short fiction in America since Poe: discipline, structural soundness, a unity of theme or effect, a sense of wonder at life—all results of the "care and skill" which, Poe said, the form demands.[1] Yet they do not follow the direction taken early by Poe and almost universally since World War II, the depiction of brooding psychomachia that seems in our time to have transfixed the epigoni of Lawrence and Faulkner. Rather they are content to portray, if not (to borrow Howell's phrase) "the more smiling aspects of life," then at least those nonviolent, sublunary events that form the backbone of contemporary American experience. If Updike's characters are not happy, their frustrations drive them neither to madness nor to morbidity. The intelligent, rational, yet sensitive minds of the protagonists preclude psychopathic behavior merely as a function of their (albeit sometimes hypertrophic) observation of life's stable minutiae.

It is in the lyrical meditation that Updike allows precise intelligence and linguistic *delicatesse* their greatest play. The *lyrical* (meaning imaginative and image-filled subjective prose-poetry) *meditation* (meaning contemplation of large, problematic areas of human experience) is not a story in the conventional sense: it bears only vestigial "characterization" and makes no concessions to standard devices of "plot." It is more closely related to Hawthornes "pure essays" (our guide Poe's term for such pieces as "Snow-Flakes" and "The Sisters Years") or Washington Irving's sketches (both Updike and Irving had intensive art training and

Reprinted by permission of the Department of English of Syracuse University.

hence exhibit the painterly eye) than it is to something out of *Dubliners* or *Go Down, Moses.* Ranging uninhibitedly but always anchored to a central image or concept, it is often incremental in manner: meaning accrete through small revelations as the story works toward making concrete one or more monadic abstractions. In arriving at illumination it employs what Northrop Frye calls *"dianoia,* the idea or poetic thought (something quite different, of course, from other kinds of thought) that the reader gets from the writer."[2] In arriving there, too, it often requires of the reader a greater mental involvement than he is accustomed to giving the A+B+C plotted story. Yet it is typically neither an exhibition of stylistic dandyism nor the type of solemn lucubration that the word *meditation* sometimes implies: it is, metaphorically, a miniature geography of a region of human experience, elaborated with erudition and wit and a full measure of the author's renowned verbal magic, often partly parodic. Drawing upon story and essay and poem for its form, it succeeds in overcoming the usual limitations of its models: the storyline of the story, the prosaic logic of the essay, the often obscure ellipticality of the poem. It is a sophisticated writer's most sophisticated accomplishment. . . .

Ambiguity itself is one of the many delights of the lyrical meditation. Subsuming whole worlds of experience under the abstractions it engages, it ensures against facile exhaustion of meaning and thus more greatly rewards the sedulous reader. Ignoring what are often called the "conventions" of the short story, it is an autonomous form that arrogates to itself what it needs of poetry and the essay and offers, where appropriate, universal problems in place of plot and archetypes in place of character. And in celebrating the concrete and minute in experience as a vital aspect of the human condition, it becomes perhaps the most infrangible accomplishment of an author around whom critical whirlpools will, no doubt, continue to swirl.

Notes

1. "Review of *Twice-Told Tales,*" in *Discussions of the Short Story.* Hollis Summers, ed. (Boston: D. C. Heath, 1963), p. 3.

2. *Anatomy of Criticism* (Princeton: Princeton Univ. Press, 1957), p. 52.

Eileen Baldeshwiler

It seems clear that it is in the loosely structured, yet unified, sketches of Turgenev's *A Sportsman's Notebook*, with their subtle discrimination of shades of emotion, their famous "shimmering" tone and lovingly detached attention to the physical details of natural objects and scenes that the lyrical story first emerges as a distinctive form. Episodic in construction, few of the pieces revolve around a conventional plot; rather, more often than not, the author gently leads us through an interlude of time depicted by means of minute, impressionistic touches—not without occasional motifs or semi-symbolic figures—in such a way that the senses are alerted and the feelings softened and made reflective. . . .

Finally, in a discussion of the American lyrical short story, one would want to mention the work of a young writer of varied talents, John Updike. At a far reach from the expansive Olinger stories is the kind of achievement hinted at in "Sunday Teasing" (*The Same Door*) and brought much closer to fruition in the title story of *The Music School*, as well as in "Harv is Plowing Now" and "Leaves," from the same volume. In the latter story the reader is struck equally by the variety and disparity of the materials and by the faultlessness of their integration, a union created far below—or above—the level of story-line, theme, or motif. "Leaves" may best be described as a sophisticated quest story in the modern manner; at the same time it is an intense probing of the perennial question of moral guilt and of man's movement in and out of purely natural processes, and it is overlain with a profound sense of beauty, reflected or "expressed" in its own art. The manner is ostensibly descriptive and essayistic; details of action are presented in hints and indirections and kept carefully subordinated to an estimate of their effect and meaning. The issue of How to be gradually modulates to the question of What to say, thus the reflexive references to the writing of

Reprinted from "The Lyric Short Story: The Sketch of a History," *Studies in Short Fiction* 6 (1969): 443–53. Reprinted by permission of *Studies in Short Fiction*—Newberry College. Copyright © 1969 by Newberry College.

the story: "And what are these pages but leaves? Why do I produce them but to thrust, by some subjective photosynthesis, my guilt into Nature, where there is no guilt"? Updike's method of construction is to present isolated blocks of description that are yet joined by a continuity of persistent inquiry in the narrative voice. In "Leaves," the author also creates a unifying motif in the grape leaves, with their analogue in Whitman's "Leaves of Grass," to which Mr. Updike refers in the unexpectedly dramatic close of the story.

Raman Selden

Here is the opening of John Updike's story 'Should Wizard Hit Mommy?':

> In the evenings and for Saturday naps like today's, Jack told his daughter Jo a story out of his head. This custom, begun when she was two, was itself now nearly two years old, and his head felt empty. Each new story was a slight variation of a basic tale; a small creature, usually named Roger (Roger Fish, Roger Squirrel, Roger Chipmunk), had some problem and went with it to the wise old owl. The owl told him to go to the wizard, and the wizard performed a magic spell that solved the problem, demanding in payment a number of pennies greater than the number Roger Creature had but in the same breath directing the animal to a place where the extra pennies could be found. Then Roger was so happy he played many games with other creatures, and went home to his mother just in time to hear the train whistle that brought his daddy home from Boston. Jack described their supper, and the story was over.
>
> (From *Pigeon Feathers and Other Stories* [Alfred A. Knopf, New York, 1963, pp. 74–5])

The rest of the short story tells how on this occasion Jo steps out of her passive role as listener and begins to assert her own will over the story: she decides that the creature this time is going to be 'Roger Skunk'; she prompts Jack at the various stages in the tale (seeing the owl, being sent to the wizard); and finally she rejects Jack's version of the tale's ending. If we are reading the story for its psychological insights or its 'truth value', we might say that it illustrates the transition from innocence to experience; Jo is entering 'a reality phase' (as Jack—or the narrator— notes). She wants the story she is told to suit her own needs and desires, and therefore she rejects her father's version (which reflects *his* needs and desires). This account of the story is fine as far as it goes, but if we examine it from the point of view of narrative theory (and especially

Reprinted from *Practising Theory and Reading Literature: An Introduction*. © Copyright Raman Selden 1989. Reprinted by permission of the publisher.

structuralist types of theory) we will be able to give a fuller account in certain respects.

The structuralist assumption is that all stories can be reduced to certain essential narrative structures. This notion is based on the related idea that all particular linguistic utterances (spoken or written) are based upon a 'language system' or grammar which is capable of producing a virtually infinite corpus of utterances. The system itself does not have a separate existence, but is deducible from actual utterances. Ferdinand de Saussure, whose linguistic theories influenced structuralism, called the system 'langue' and utterance 'parole'. There are many aspects to a structuralist theory of narrative (and many versions). They include three main dimensions:

1. Thematic structure.

2. Linear structure (the sequence of actions).

3. The structure of narration (how the story is communicated).

If we consider the second for a moment, we can say that most structuralist theories try to reduce to a manageable size the number of narrative 'functions' which can be used in stories to form a sequence of actions. Vladimir Propp, in his *Morphology of the Folktale* (1928), found thirty-one 'functions' in the corpus of Russian tales he studied. He showed that all the tales used some of the functions, and always in the same order. The last two are 'The Villain is punished' and 'The Hero is married and ascends the throne'. Structuralists later tired to produce a typology of functions for more general use. The simplest formulation is that of Claude Bremond who describes the logical sequence of narrative functions as follows:

$$
\text{potentiality} \begin{cases} \begin{array}{l} \text{process of} \qquad\quad \text{success} \\ \text{actualisation} \overline{\qquad\qquad} \text{(objective reached)} \\ \text{(steps taken)} \\[1em] \text{non-actualisation} \quad \text{failure} \\ \text{(no steps taken)} \ \text{(objective missed)} \end{array} \end{cases}
$$

(objective defined)

Using Bremond's scheme (as modified by S. Rimmon-Kenan, *Narrative Fiction*, 1983, p. 22) we can see that Jack's stories always have the same structure:

objective (to solve 'problem')	— steps taken (consult wizard)	— success (problem solved)

The alternatives ('no steps taken' and 'failure') are not used. This analysis makes it clear that Jack's story formula with its exclusion of conflict is suited to very young children. This is also apparent if we use A. J. Greimas's well-known scheme which focuses on characters in narrative in terms of six *actants* as follows:

sender	— object	— receiver
helper	— subject	— opponent

Greimas developed what he called a 'structural semantics' which involved treating narratives as if there were sentences (see *Structural Semantics*, 1983). *Actants* work like nouns and are general categories which underlie all narratives. A character or an object may take on the role of one or more *actants*, and more than one character or object can function as one *actant*. In Jack's story formula Roger Creature is the Subject (hero), his Object is a solution to the 'problem', the Receiver is also Roger, the Helper is the Wizard (the owl is a subsidiary helper) and there is no Opponent (or villain).

The schemes of Bremond and Greimas require great elaboration to make them work sensitively, but their ambitious aim is clear—they try to show the underlying structure of all narratives. The danger of such approaches is that the results may seem obvious or banal. However, the analysis of Jack's story becomes more interesting when we consider the development of Updike's tale. Jack, having provided a basic story structure (what we might call an 'empty' structure to be filled with various contents), finds himself forced by Jo to fill it in a certain way. First, Jo repeatedly prompts Jack, starting by suggesting the name of the hero—'Roger Skunk'. Roger's problem is, of course, his smell which leaves him without playmates. Jo reminds Jack of the visits to the Owl and then to the Wizard. The cure is effected, payment is made and Roger, now smelling beautifully of roses, is able to have a wonderful time playing with friends. Jo is obviously satisfied and thinks the story is over, but Jack, not wanting her to take things for granted, inserts a new type of ending: back at home Mommy is very upset about Roger's transformation, drags Roger back to the Wizard, hits the Wizard on the head with her umbrella, and makes him restore Roger's skunk smell. The story then continues as usual with father's return from work and a lovely dinner. Jo is outraged and reminds her father that the other animals will now shun Roger; but Jack stubbornly defends Mommy against Jo's complaints ('That was a stupid mommy'), threatening her with a spanking if she doesn't settle down and go to sleep.

We can now see that the story of Roger Skunk can be analysed, using Bremond and Greimas, in two different ways. From Jo's viewpoint the movement from Objective through Actualisation to Success is reversed: the story ends with Roger facing the same problem and running the risk of having no playmates. In her version Mommy is the Opponent (villain). Jo's story is a sort of Tragedy. From Jack's viewpoint the plot ends happily: the Objective is harmony between Mommy (and Daddy) and Roger, and it is actualised by Mommy's action in returning to the Wizard; Mommy is the Helper, the Wizard the Opponent. From this we can see that the same story can be analysed in two quite different ways using the same structural scheme.

It seems to me that this narrative analysis is helpful in drawing attention to aspects of the story which go beyond narrative theory. We begin to see that Jack and Jo have some kind of emotional and psychological investment in their particular interpretations of the story. It might seem that Jack's interpretation must be right, since he is the storyteller. However, not only does Jo exercise a good deal of influence on the story but she seems perfectly aware of the *conventionality* of the story. She draws attention to her father's slip when he calls Roger 'Roger Fish' (she understands that each story is a retelling of the same story), and she responds to sad bits in the story with a conventional sadness: 'Jo made the crying face again, but this time without a trace of sincerity.' Because she is able to treat the story as a narrative structure and not as an absolute reality she is able to question the storyteller ('the source of truth') and to contradict his meaning. Her version of the meaning clearly relates to her need to be able to have friends. Jack's story asserts the primacy of the Mother–Child bond and the authority of the Father. Jo rejects this defiantly. Jack, it is clear, has a need to defend his own mother's behaviour (presumably in keeping *him* from his friends): "'That was a stupid mommy.' 'It was *not*,' he said with rare emphasis, and believed, from her expression, that she realized he was defending his own mother to her, or something as odd." From this we can see that Jack identifies with the role of Roger Skunk. Updike's story ends with Jack's sense of alienation from his wife, Jo's Mommy. He seems to feel sympathy with the child's unhappiness and dislike of the mother's role (even though he himself was responsible for this version of the story). It is clear that Updike's tale invites a *psychological* interpretation. However, our analysis of narrative structure has considerably assisted the process of interpretation by highlighting the narrative processes involved in the psychological games people play.

The Russian Formalists distinguished between 'story' (the events in abstract) and 'plot' (the literary deployment of the events). Genette suggests a more subtle tripartite division: 'story' (*histoire*), 'text' (*récit*) and 'narration'. 'Text' is the written or spoken form of the events, while 'narration' is the mode of writing or speaking used in the 'text' (see 'Frontiers of Narrative' in *Figures of Literary Discourse*, 1982). Consider the 'narration' of the Updike tale. A common-sense response would be to say that Updike is the narrator, but this would be to ignore entirely the fictional construction of the tale which must include the construction of the narrator. Various attempts have been made to describe the links in the chain of narration from the author through to the reader. Here is a typical formulation:

Actual	— Implied	— Narrator —/— Narratee —	Implied	— Actual
Author	Author		Reader	Reader

Structuralists exclude the actual author and reader from the textual level of a narrative. The sense of coherence or overall point of view we establish is not communicated directly to us by a narrative voice but is implied by a whole host of indirect signals. We call this coherence the 'implied author'. The term 'narrator' is reserved for the voice that communicates the story to us. The narrator can take many forms varying from a remote and godlike (omniscient) speaker to a totally unreliable and subjective speaker (see also section 3 on this). Updike's narrator is of the omniscient type; we are hardly aware of a narrator's presence. There are, however, a number of phrases which stand out as involving judgement or analysis which clearly do not emanate from Jack the fictional narrator of the Roger stories. Most of theses phrases are related to the tale's psychological level:

> Jack continued with zest, remembering certain humiliations of his own childhood . . . [he is telling Jo how the other animals shunned Roger Skunk]

> Jack didn't like women when they took anything for granted . . . [Jo thinks he has finished the story]

It is true that one could imagine Jack consciously having these thoughts, but we are aware of the implied author's focusing of a psychological perspective in the narrator's dwelling on these thoughts. It is therefore possible to distinguish between:

1. Jack's thoughts.

2. The narrator's voice.

3. The implied author's perspective.

The structuralist term 'focaliser' is a helpful addition to our repertoire. It refers to the agent whose perceptions shape the presentation of what is said (not necessarily from the author's viewpoint). The focaliser can be internal or external to the story. Focalising is external in Updike's story. To put it into other terms, the implied author's external perspective is expressed through the impersonal narrator's voice.

What of the reader? The actual reader can, of course, be any type of person you could imagine, from the scarcely literate to the sophisticated critic. The 'narratee' is the reader as represented within the fiction. For example, a narrator may directly address the narratee ('My dear reader' or 'Dear Madam'). There is no narratee in Updike's tale. The 'implied reader', like the implied author, is a more subtle presence, and represents the sort of reader assumed by the text in various indirect ways. When Jack acts out the wizard's role he is startled by his daughter's 'rapt expression' which reminds him of 'his wife feigning pleasure at cocktail parties'. The narrator implies a certain sort of reader for whom feigning pleasure at cocktail parties makes sense as a social sign. Such a reader would know what cocktail parties are and would understand why it might be necessary to feign enjoyment at them. This may seem a rather obvious sort of assumption. However, by drawing attention to this 'implied reader' we begin to see just how much construction goes into fictional narrative.

Albert E. Wilhelm

At several points in *Too Far To Go*, the collected stories dealing with Joan and Richard Maple, John Updike alludes to a motif used prominently in the tale of Hansel and Gretel. According to most European versions of the tale, when the two children attempt to follow their trail of bread crumbs back home after their second abandonment, they discover that all the markers have been consumed by birds of the forest. Similar tales containing this basic motif (designated R135 in Stith Thompson's *Motif-Index of Folk-Literature*) are widely distributed.[1] Indeed, Aarne and Thompson have cited analogs all over Europe, in Latin America, and even in Africa and Indonesia (see the discussion of Type 327 in Antti Aarne's *The Types of the Folktale*).[2] Perhaps this motif is pervasive because it is an effective device for introducing the theme of forced maturation. When the children cannot return home, they must walk further into the forest, outwit the cruel witch, and eventually win the treasure through their own ingenuity. When Updike alludes to the Hansel and Gretel story in *Too Far To Go*, he relies on the accumulated power of this trail-of-bread-crumbs motif to reinforce a similar truth about the necessity of growing up. Even though the Maples are nominally adults, they must still learn a basic lesson of maturing—that they must match their behavior to their season of life. Also, when their marriage eventually moves toward divorce, they must accept the course of events and embrace the future rather than flee into the past.

In "Snowing in Greenwich Village," the first story in the Maples chronicle, Joan and Richard have been married almost two years, but they frequently seem to be little more than children. Joan is still linked to her parents by strong bonds of emotional dependence. Before a round of drinks she always repeats her parents' "standard toast"[3] and, even in her own apartment, she sits "straight-backed on a Hitchcock chair from her parents' home in Vermont" (14). At one point a slight change in posture further emphasizes Joan's childlike nature. The back of the chair becomes much like the side of a crib as Joan winds "her hand

Reprinted by permission of *Studies in Short Fiction*—Newberry College.

207

through the slats like a child assuring herself that her bedtime has been postponed" (20–21). Earlier, on their wedding day, Richard appeared even more helpless. His parents drove him to the ceremony while he slumped with "his coat over his head, hoping to get back to sleep" (237). At the party in Greenwich Village he is still "so young-looking" that people do not normally ask him to assume "hostly duties" (13). Like Hansel and Gretel on their first trip into the forest, Joan and Richard are permitted at this stage in their marriage to revert to a more secure past. But the solid pebble trail that gleams in the moonlight will soon be gone, and they will be unable to turn back.

Updike's first explicit reference to Hansel and Gretel appears in "Giving Blood," the third story in the Maples collection. Now in the ninth year of their marriage, Joan and Richard face a new experience (giving blood for Joan's critically ill cousin) and new responsibilities to support each other emotionally in a relationship which has become strained. Richard notes their similarity to Hansel and Gretel as they wander along an ominous hospital corridor: "Up and down, right and left it went, in the secretive, disjointed way peculiar to hospitals that have been built annex by annex. Richard seems to himself Hansel orphaned with Gretel; birds ate the bread crumbs behind them, and at last they timidly knocked on the witch's door, which said BLOOD DONATION CENTER" (42). Just as the happenings at the witch's house constitute a test of maturity for Hansel and Gretel, so do the events at the hospital for Joan and Richard. At first Richard fears the blood sacrifice and even suggests that he will be "drained dry" (38). He bitterly resents the early morning drive into Boston and wants to return home to bed. Later, when the blood is freely given, his actions help to heal his marriage as well as the sick relative. Indeed, the Maples' shared experience becomes almost sacramental. As they lie on hospital cots in this "consecrated place," the technicians speak in whispers "as if not to disturb the mystical union of the couple sacrificially bedded together" (48–49). Hansel and Gretel responded to adversity by sharing their one remaining piece of bread. Richard imagines that he and Joan achieve an even closer communion: "Linked to a common loss, they were chastely conjoined; the thesis developed upon him that the hoses attached to them somewhere out of sight met" (49).

The next stories in *Too Far To Go* demonstrate, however, that the lessons of "Giving Blood" were poorly learned. The frantic movements in these intermediate stories suggest a desperate search for the trail that has vanished. In "Twin Beds in Rome" Joan and Richard are pilgrims seeking amidst the ruins of past civilizations the lost glory of their marriage. Joan wants to go "back to the way things were," but Richard protests: "No. I don't want to go back to that. I feel we've come very far and have only a little way more to go" (61). In "A Taste of Metal" the Maples try to make their way home from a late party over slippery roads. The reckless drive ends in a collision with a telephone pole and a quick liaison between Richard and another woman. Faced with these unexpected developments, Richard now wants desperately to turn back the clock—to retrace an elusive trail. Noticing the music which has been playing on the car radio, he thinks that, "if only the oboe sonata were played backwards, they would leap backwards from the telephone pole and be on their way home again" (97).

Updike's most prominent references to Hansel and Gretel appear in the final story of the collection. Here, when Richard remembers his and Joan's wedding day, he correctly sees it as a sharp break with the past: "Hand in hand, smaller than Hansel and Gretel in his mind's eye, they ran up the long flight of stairs into a gingerbread-brown archway and disappeared" (238–239). Now, twenty-two years later, the Maples have certainly gone too far to turn back. Though the story describes the end of their marriage, its title, "Here Come the Maples," suggests a new beginning. This legal phrase taken from the divorce documents conjures up in Richard's mind "a vision of himself and Joan breezing into a party hand in hand while a liveried doorman trumpeted their names" (236–237). To be sure, this story is full of metaphors of starting afresh. In the divorce court they are "sailing uncharted waters"; the no-fault procedure is a "tabula rasa" (254). For Richard this new beginning is possible because he now accepts responsibility. Earlier he had blamed Joan even for the petty annoyances in their marriage. Now, "he had set her free, free from fault. She was to him as Gretel to Hansel, a kindred creature moving beside him down a path while birds behind them ate the bread crumbs" (253). Once again the simple folklore motif helps to reiterate an important point of the stories. Joan and Richard can solve their problems not by retreating but only by walking on into the woods.

Notes

1. Stith Thompson, *Motif-Index of Folk-Literature*, rev. ed. (Bloomington: Indiana University Press, 1957), V, 281–282.

2. Antti Amatus Aarne, *The Types of the Folktale*, 2nd rev. ed., trans. Stith Thompson (Helsinki: Suomalainen Tiedeakatemia, 1964), pp. 116–119.

3. John Updike, *Too Far To Go* (New York: Fawcett, 1979), p. 16. Subsequent references are to this edition.

Erica Jong

That John Updike is the most skillful writer currently using the American language seems clear to me. He is the writer I read when I want to be reminded of the possibilities of language, a writer of prose who uses the language as carefully as any poet. The claim of some of his detractors—that he has *too* much technique—seems transparently envious to me. They know they will never write as well as he does, so they are saying, in effect, that he is too skilled and that this somehow stands in the way of "greatness." . . .

If the creation of a varied, sublimely literate, humorous, and intelligent *oeuvre* is an act of generosity (which I believe it is) then Updike is the most generous of artists. I have always particularly admired his adeptness in various forms—short stories, novels, literary essays (directed at the intelligent common reader rather than the PhD candidate), poems, light verse, even doggerel. . . .

I have also admired the ingenious way Updike both fragments and transforms his autobiographical experiences in his fiction, using different protagonists as the representatives of different aspects of his own complex and contradictory character. Henry Bech is the writer (though of a rather different sort than his creator—he is "blocked"); Richard Maple, the husband and father; Piet Hanema, the Dutchman (and builder—craftsman, maker); Rabbit Angstrom, the working man and political naif; and Thomas Marshfield, the unfrocked minister (a Chaucerian figure if ever there was one—praising the Lord with his trousers down). Of course it is true that every fictional character is an autobiographical projection of sorts (and this includes heroes and villains, major and minor characters), but it is particularly true in Updike's case that the protagonist of each of his major novels or groups of stories represents an aspect of self which he wishes to examine.

Although I admire *The Coup*, which contains some of the most dazzling writing by an always dazzling writer, I am even more drawn to the Updike who can write a story like "Separating" (in *Too Far To Go*), one

Reprinted by permission of THE NEW REPUBLIC, ©1979, The New Republic, Inc.

of the most extraordinarily honest stories about marriage ever written. In a curious way, I felt *The Coup* was a tour de force, a rebuke to those critics who doubted Updike's ability to journey to foreign lands and write of multi-colored peoples, murders, and political intrigues. Reading it, one was delighted by the humor, the beauty of the language, the ingenuity of construction; but upon reflection the book seemed less memorable than Updike's American stories and novels. . . .

What then do we find in *Too Far To Go*, Updike's collected Maples stories? Here is a writer writing about what is closest to home: a marriage, four children, a suburb of Boston to which husbands commute and wives are banished. Unlike the Africa of *The Coup*, nobody dies of hunger here, and men do not *legally* have four wives; but in truth the problems are not so different from those of Updike's Africa. Hunger is spiritual rather than physical; men long for more wives than one, though they can hardly cope with the multiple personalities of the singular wives they have; and the revolutions that are fought in bedrooms are not less painful for being bloodless than the revolutions fought in the third world.

It would be amusing to compare *Too Far To Go* with *The Coup*—amusing, but unfair, though the former book seems at times to adumbrate the latter. (In "Giving Blood" Richard Maple "nervously wonders" about meeting "the King of Arabia," who is ensconced in the hospital with four wives: "Only four? What an ascetic," he says.) But that is merely one of those spooky precognitions all novelists are familiar with: the ghost of a later book flitting through the pages of an earlier one.

Too Far To Go never meant to be a proper novel; it just grew, whereas *The Coup* was clearly conceived as a whole. Yet in both books the concerns are characteristically Updikean: how can man ever know woman—that mysterious other?; how can "mere" lust so discompose our lives?; how is it that men who long to be at peace with the spirit are always so enmeshed in things of the flesh—or can they somehow make spirit and flesh one?

Updike's characteristic protagonist is a man who would like to abolish the duality between matter and spirit but cannot because various insurmountable obstacles stand in his way. These obstacles are usually represented by women, though one suspects that Updike's women are at least partly symbols for the ineffability of the life force. But they are also real women. Both Joan Maple in *Too Far To Go* and Kadongolimi in *The Coup* represent that "continuum of women" which will always welcome the Updike hero "when all else crumbles." A feminist reading Updike cannot but envy that warm welcoming womb of women to which the

Updike hero always has access even when it clearly creates as many problems as it solves. . . .

The title of this collection might well be "No Fault." Updike says in his foreword that "the moral of these stories is that all blessings are mixed"; but we know that Updike is not a writer who likes stories with simplistic morals. As he says in "Why Write?" (originally a speech given in Australia in 1974 and collected in *Picked-Up Pieces*): "The absence of a swiftly expressible message is, often, *the* message; . . . reticence is as important a tool to the writer as expression. . . ." In fact his comments in that splendid address on the writer's craft constitute a better gloss on the Maple stories than any I might compose: "What the writer makes," says Updike, "is ideally as ambiguous and opaque as life itself."

So much for morals. The Maple stories *are* ambiguous and opaque, and so, ultimately, are the Maples. To the extent that they are like real people, life has no simple morals for them. . . .

Jane Barnes

Updike seems to write the way spiders spin: weaving his webs to catch life as it passes, spinning, spinning as much to survive as to astonish. He is probably the most prolific gifted writer of his generation, though the quality of his outpouring is uneven. The problem of picking and choosing between what is good and what is less good is related, I think, to his subject. As a rule, the stories about the particular narrator I have described seem to be better than Updike's other stories. These others fall into several categories: experimental ("Under the Microscope," "During the Jurassic"), descriptive ("The Indian," "Son"), and—for lack of a better word—journalistic ("When Everyone was Pregnant," "One of My Generation," "How to Love America"). All of these stories have in common the absence of such literary conventions as character, plot, or dialogue. They seem to serve the purpose of unburdening the author's receptive mind of all the different kinds of information that he breathes in from his environment.

What distinguishes the stories about the narrator is the emotion irradiating the finely spun structures. They are more truly felt than the experimental or journalistic stories which seem too much like demonstrations of the author's facility with language and data. At the same time, the stories about the narrator also vary; between the earliest stories and the most recent ones, while the narrator is struggling to come to terms with sex and love, the style is often puffy, sometimes it seems downright anxious—as though the author were really not sure of the material. In the course of Updike's development, the problem of meaning has been complicated by and interlocked with the problem of handling his talent. At moments, he seems to have been swept away by sheer youthful delight, as though his gift were a marvelous toy: other times a terrible piety seems to have possessed him, as though he could only live up to his promise by taking his Style seriously. And then his intelligence, along with his remarkable observing powers, presented real

Reprinted by permission of the *Virginia Quarterly Review*.

problems by crowding his attention with an embarrassment of impressions, details, facts.

These distractions get the upperhand when the author's moral grasp of his material is weakest. In "Packed Dirt, Churchgoing, A Dying Cat, A Traded Car," for instance, the overwriting goes hand in hand with the falsely ancient tone of the young man. He comes home to see his sick father in the hospital, his thoughts coated by a world weariness worthy of a very old person who'd seen nothing but war, torture, and death. In fact, the narrator is a young, suburban husband who's seen nothing but peace and domesticity, whose real problem (as he confesses to a hitchhiker) is that he doesn't see the point of his virtuous life. This is not quite the same thing as confronting the void, though there is a tendency in Updike's stories to inflate American boredom into French existentialist despair. At his worst, there is more sneakiness than evil in Updike, more opportunism than moral questing in his restless, curious narrator.

Then, too, though the narrator is clearly a self-centered person, it is not clear that his suffering is more than the pinch we all feel trying to live decently with others. His suffering sometimes seems like pure whining—his philosophizing nothing more than a complaint that spouses can cramp a person's sexual style. It is generally assumed that Updike's stories about domestic life are autobiographical. This assumption seems to be made out of a worldly wisdom which allows all sophisticated people to connect what is known about the author through articles (*i.e.*, that Updike has been married, divorced, and recently remarried) and what happens in the fictional life of his central hero (who has been married, divorced, and recently remarried). It *is* hard not to wonder if the narrator hasn't benefited from Updike's possible experience. At the start, the narrator is a timid, even a cowardly man. That he slowly, but surely has his way with women probably has less to do with a change in his personal charm and more with the unadmitted fact that the author's fame made him desirable and gave him unexpected opportunities, ones which Updike passed on to his narrator. There are times when the narrator's cheerlessness about his adulteries seems just insupportable, only explicable by something having been left out—such as the fact that this is not the typical experience of a lusty suburban male, but rather the typical experience of a celebrity who suddenly finds himself in sexual demand. The narrator's depression would be more believable if it *were* openly identified as the cynicism a famous author might feel towards a rise in his desirability that had nothing to do with his true human self.

Yet having made these criticisms, I want to disassociate myself from the knowing, wordly assumption that Updike's work must be autobiographical. I want to consider the role of autobiography in these stories, but I want to do it from the inside out. Instead of talking about them as reflections of the author's life, I want to discuss their importance in his development as a writer.

Updike himself makes the connection between the human content and the author's art. He speaks of his hero's sense of being the "creator" of both his parents and his mistress. From the start, we know the narrator regards women and art as equally mysterious, if not equivalents. We know that women have dominated his experience, that they are the media through which he comes to terms with the past, learns to love and begins to act for himself. When the author refers to the narrator's sense of himself as the artist of his private life, the association of women with art naturally teams up with Updike's identification with his hero. We can take this as the primary, the *essential* starting point of any discussion of the role of autobiography.

Having begun, there are several paths open to us, all leading to "Domestic Life in America" as a culmination of the art the author has evolved through his hero's quest. Through time, the resonance in these stories has deepened, the authorial voice has become true, simpler, wiser. As a collection, *Problems* is marked by the author's growth as a writer, but the best stories in the book are best because they are about the subject which is most crucial to Updike. In those, form and feeling are one; the problem raised and the problem solved matter because the human heart is at stake; the drama is literally tied to it like a creature punished in the flames.

The narrator is not that complicated a character, but he seeks complexity out. As he has explored the varieties of erotic experience and conflict, Updike's style has reflected the alteration in values and depths and types of feeling. The best Olinger stories provide us with a model of what Updike's recent stories have returned to. In "Flight," "Pigeon Feathers," "A Sense of Shelter," there is more fancy writing than there is in *Too Far To Go* or *Problems*, but in both groups of stories the writing all serves a purpose. In the long run, the unruly impulses in his style seem to have been brought under control by the same principle that liberates the narrator from the past.

"His life must flow from within." As the narrator clarifies his values, as he becomes his own man, free of his ties to the past, Updike's style becomes simpler again. In "Domestic Life in America," there are few unnecessary words, almost no irrelevant descriptions. There is a very clean-cut relationship between content and art, between the narrator's inner state and the story's language and design. In fact, it is a photograph of the narrator's feelings at this moment in his life, yet the story has more power than this description of stasis might imply. It has the power of Updike's best writing—his quick insight, wit, and catlike tread. I associate this purity of style with another source of power in the story: it reveals a new resolution of conflicts which the narrator has been wrestling with from the start. . . .

Originally, the narrator was paralyzed because every action involved a life-and-death struggle. He could not move without moving against someone else. For the young narrator, identification with one parent meant attacking the other. For Richard Maple, giving his wife her way meant giving up his own. Finally, however, the narrator is compelled to act because not acting hurts himself. No one else is going to act on his behalf; he has to. But for him to reach this point the problem has had to change. The extreme either/or that characterized the important people in his life has subsided. The narrator slowly but surely has incorporated into himself the parts of his parents which, at first, he served alternately as absolutes. He takes his own shape, and as he does, the opposing principles in the universe around him cease to clash so violently. The sense of futility so often present in the early stories is transformed, not because the problem goes away, but because the narrator has become engaged in it. "Domestic Life in America" is there as proof. The narrator is alive and well by virtue of his willingness to pursue what he wants. He has accepted the fact that this will hurt others, and does what he can to take responsibility for his part in the dog-eat-dog reality. He cannot change his feelings, but he does not hide or suppress them. While he also fulfills his obligations at the level of finances and work, the most important form his responsibility takes is acting on what he perceives to be "the real relation between things."

This last is from Marx, who also said that people would only know what these real relations were once they had rid themselves of their illusion. Through time, the narrator's illusions have worn away, allowing the difficult, tiring, moving human truth to emerge. The relationships which have had various kinds of power over the narrator turn out to be commanding for the simplest reason. These people, after all, are not the symbols he once envisioned. They are just the people he happened to know in life. He probably would have known them anyway, even if they had not fit into his sense of how the world was divided.

Division has haunted the narrator and informed the writer's art. It grew out of the boy's understanding of the differences between his parents and grew into his conflict between marriage and wife, on the one hand, and love and mistress, on the other. For some time, the division between parents and women was also between duty and self, morality and pleasure. In "Domestic Life in America," the element of compulsion, of one thing versus another, has fallen away. There is still strife and conflict, but it is between characters who are both good and bad, who are as mixed as the blessings they enjoy and the penalties they pay. The arguments which the narrator worked out through them were always only partially true about the human beings. And the real debate was always one the narrator was having with them about his own nature.

Chronology

1932	John Updike born in Shillington, Pennsylvania.
1936–1950	Attends Shillington public schools, where his father teaches math at Shillington High School.
1945	Moves with family to grandparents' old farm in Plowville, Pennsylvania.
1950	Enters Harvard University. Works on editorial board, Harvard *Lampoon*, until graduation.
1953	Marries Mary Pennington.
1954	Graduates *summa cum laude* (with a major in English) from Harvard; sells first story ("Friends from Philadelphia") to the *New Yorker*.
1954–1955	Attends Ruskin School of Drawing and Fine Arts in Oxford, England, on a Knox Fellowship. Daughter Elizabeth born. Offered a position with the *New Yorker* by E.B. White.
1955–1957	Returns to U.S. and becomes staff writer for the *New Yorker*, contributing regularly to the "Talk of the Town" column. While living in New York City, works on manuscript for an unpublished novel, "Home."
1957	Son David born; resigns position at the *New Yorker* and moves with family to Ipswich, Massachusetts.
1958	Collected poems, *The Carpentered Hen*.
1959	Son Michael born; *The Same Door*; *The Poorhouse Fair*, which receives the 1960 Rosenthal Foundation Award of the National Institute of Arts and Letters; Guggenheim Fellowship. "A Gift from the City" included in *Best American Short Stories 1959*.
1960	Daughter Miranda born; *Rabbit, Run*.
1961	"Wife-Wooing" included in *Prize Stories 1961*.
1962	*Pigeon Feathers and Other Stories*; "The Doctor's Wife" in-

cluded in *Prize Stories 1962*; "Pigeon Feathers" included in *Best American Short Stories 1962*.

1963 *Telephone Poles and Other Poems*; *The Centaur*.

1964 Receives National Book Award for *The Centaur*; elected member of the National Institute of Arts and Letters; *Olinger Stories: A Selection*.

1964–1965 Travels to Russia, Rumania, Bulgaria, and Czechoslovakia as part of U. S. U. S. S. R. Cultural Exchange Program.

1965 *Of the Farm*; *Assorted Prose*.

1966 *The Music School*; "The Bulgarian Poetess" receives First Prize in *Prize Stories 1966*; film adaptation of *Rabbit, Run*.

1967 "Marching through Boston" included in *Prize Stories 1967*.

1968 *Couples*; "Your Lover Just Called" included in *Prize Stories 1968*; Updike's "fretful face" peers from "*Time*'s grim cover" of April 26.

1969 *Midpoint and Other Poems*.

1970 *Bech: A Book*; "Bech Takes Pot Luck" included in *Prize Stories 1970*.

1971 *Rabbit Redux*.

1972 *Museums and Women and Other Stories*.

1973 Travels and lectures for three weeks as Fulbright lecturer in Ghana, Nigeria, Tanzania, Kenya, and Ethiopia.

1974 *Buchanan Dying* (play); "Son" included in *Best American Short Stories 1974*; separates from his wife Mary and moves to Boston; subsequently divorced.

1975 *A Month of Sundays*; *Picked-Up Pieces*; "Nakedness" included in *Prize Stories 1975*.

1976 *Marry Me: A Romance*; Special Award for Continuing Achievement in *Prize Stories 1976*, which includes "Separating"; "The Man Who Loved Extinct Mammals" included in *Best American Short Stories 1976*; film version of "The Music School"; moves to Georgetown, Massachusetts.

1977 *Tossing and Turning*; new edition of *The Poorhouse Fair* with an introduction by Updike; elected to the American Academy of Arts and Letters; marries Martha Bernhard.

1978 *The Coup.*

1979 *Problems and Other Stories*; *Too Far to Go: The Maples Stories*; *Too Far to Go* produced as a television drama.

1980 "Gesturing" included in *Best American Short Stories 1980.*

1981 *Rabbit Is Rich*, which receives Pulitzer Prize, National Book Critics Circle Award, and American Book Award; awarded Edward MacDowell Medal for literature; "Still of Some Use" included in *Best American Short Stories 1981.*

1982 *Bech Is Back*; moves to Beverly Farms, Massachusetts. Updike featured on the cover of *Time* for the second time on Oct. 18.

1983 *Hugging the Shore*, which receives National Book Critics Circle Award for Criticism; "Deaths of Distant Friends" included in *Best American Short Stories 1983*; "The City" included in *Prize Stories 1983.*

1984 *The Witches of Eastwick*; edits and writes introduction for *The Best American Short Stories 1984*; film version of "The Christian Roommates" (titled *The Roommate*).

1985 *Facing Nature* (poems); "The Other" included in *Prize Stories 1985.*

1986 *Roger's Version.*

1987 *Trust Me*; receives Elmer Holmes Bobst award for fiction; "The Afterlife" included in *Best American Short Stories 1987*; film adaptation of *The Witches of Eastwick.*

1988 *S.*; receives life achievement award from Brandeis University; "Leaf Season" included in *Prize Stories 1988*; film version of "Pigeon Feathers."

1989 *Self-Consciousness* (memoirs); *Just Looking: Essays on Art.*

1990 *Rabbit at Rest*, which receives the Pulitzer Prize and the National Book Critics Circle Award.

1991 *Odd Jobs: Essays and Criticism*; "A Sandstone Farmhouse" receives First Prize in *Prize Stories 1991* and is included in *Best American Short Stories 1991.*

Selected Bibliography

Primary Works

Collections of Short Fiction

Bech: A Book. New York: Knopf, 1970. "Rich in Russia," "Bech in Rumania," "The Bulgarian Poetess," "Bech Takes Pot Luck," "Bech Panics," "Bech Swings?," "Bech Enters Heaven."

Bech Is Back. New York: Knopf, 1982. "Three Illuminations in the Life of an American Author," "Bech Third Worlds It," "Australia and Canada," "The Holy Land," "Macbech," "Bech Wed," "White on White."

The Beloved. Northridge, CA: Lord John, 1982. Limited edition.

Couples: A Short Story. Cambridge, MA: Halty Ferguson, 1976. Limited edition.

Museums and Women and Other Stories. New York: Knopf, 1972. "Museums and Women," "The Hillies," "The Day of the Dying Rabbit," "The Deacon," "I Will Not Let Thee Go, Except Thou Bless Me," "The Corner," "The Witnesses," "Solitaire," "The Orphaned Swimming Pool," "When Everyone Was Pregnant," "Man and Daughter in the Cold," "I Am Dying, Egypt, Dying," "The Carol Sing," "Plumbing," "The Sea's Green Sameness," "The Slump," "The Pro," "One of My Generation," "God Speaks" [originally published as "Dues Dixit"], "Under the Microscope," "During the Jurassic," "The Baluchitherium," "The Invention of the Horse Collar," "Jesus on Honshu," "Marching Through Boston," "The Taste of Metal," "Your Lover Just Called," "Eros Rampant," "Sublimating."

The Music School. New York: Knopf, 1966. "In Football Season," "The Indian," "Giving Blood," "A Madman," "Leaves," "The Stare," "Avec la Bébé-sitter," "Twin Beds in Rome," "Four Sides of One Story," "The Morning," "At a Bar in Charlotte Amalie," "The Christian Roommates," "My Lover Has Dirty Fingernails," "Harv Is Plowing Now," "The Music School," "The Rescue," "The Dark," "The Bulgarian Poetess," "The Family Meadow," "The Hermit."

Olinger Stories: A Selection. New York: Vintage, 1964. "You'll Never Know, Dear, How Much I Love You," "The Alligators," "Pigeon Feathers," "Friends from Philadelphia," "Flight," "A Sense of Shelter," "The Happiest I've Been," "The Persistence of Desire," "The Blessed Man of Boston, My Grandmother's Thimble, and Fanning Island," "Packed Dirt, Churchgoing, A Dying Cat, A Traded Car," "In Football Season."

Pigeon Feathers and Other Stories. New York: Knopf, 1962. "Walter Briggs" [originally published as "Vergil Moss"], "The Persistence of Desire," "Still Life," "Flight," "Should Wizard Hit Mommy?," "A Sense of Shelter," "Dear Alexandros," "Wife-Wooing," "Pigeon Feathers," "Home," "Archangel," "You'll Never Know, Dear, How Much I Love You," "The Astronomer," "A & P," "The Doctor's Wife," "Lifeguard," "The Crow in the Woods," "The Blessed Man of Boston, My Grandmother's Thimble, and Fanning Island," "Packed Dirt, Churchgoing, A Dying Cat, A Traded Car."

Problems and Other Stories. New York: Knopf, 1979. "Commercial," "Minutes of the Last Meeting," "Believers," "The Gun Shop," "How to Love America and Leave It at the Same Time," "Nevada," "Son," "Daughter, Last Glimpses Of," "Ethiopia," "Transaction," "Separating," "Augustine's Concubine," "The Man Who Loved Extinct Mammals," "Problems," "Domestic Life in America," "Love Song, for a Moog Synthesizer," "From the Journal of a Leper," "Here Come the Maples," "The Fairy Godfathers," "The Faint," "The Egg Race," "Guilt-Gems," "Atlantises."

The Same Door. New York: Knopf, 1959. "Friends from Philadelphia," "Ace in the Hole," "Tomorrow and Tomorrow and So Forth," "Dentistry and Doubt," "The Kid's Whistling," "Toward Evening," "Snowing in Greenwich Village," "Who Made Yellow Roses Yellow?," "Sunday Teasing," "His Finest Hour," "A Trillion Feet of Gas," "Incest," "A Gift From the City," "Intercession," "The Alligators," "The Happiest I've Been."

Too Far to Go: The Maples Stories. New York: Fawcett, 1979. "Snowing in Greenwich Village," "Wife-Wooing," "Giving Blood," "Twin Beds in Rome," "Marching Through Boston," "The Taste of Metal," "Your Lover Just Called," "Waiting Up," "Eros Rampant," "Plumbing," "The Red-Herring Theory," "Sublimating," "Nakedness," "Separating," "Gesturing," "Divorcing: A Fragment," "Here Come the Maples."

Trust Me. New York: Knopf, 1987. "Trust Me," "Killing," "Still of Some Use," "The City," "The Lovely Troubled Daughters of Our Old Crowd," "Unstuck," "A Constellation of Events," "Deaths of Distant Friends," "Pygmalion," "More Stately Mansions," "Learn a Trade," "The Ideal Village," "One More Interview," "The Other," "Slippage," "Poker Night," "Made in Heaven," "Getting into the Set," "The Wallet," "Leaf Season," "Beautiful Husbands," "The Other Woman."

Novels

The Centaur. New York: Knopf, 1963.
The Coup. New York: Knopf, 1978.
Couples. New York: Knopf, 1968.
Marry Me: A Romance. New York: Knopf, 1976.
A Month of Sundays. New York: Knopf, 1975.

Selected Bibliography

Of the Farm. New York: Knopf, 1965.
The Poorhouse Fair. New York: Knopf, 1959.
Rabbit at Rest. New York: Knopf, 1990.
Rabbit Is Rich. New York: Knopf, 1981.
Rabbit Redux. New York: Knopf, 1971.
Rabbit, Run. New York: Knopf, 1960.
Roger's Version. New York: Knopf, 1986.
S. New York: Knopf, 1988
The Witches of Eastwick. New York: Knopf, 1984.

Poetry

The Carpentered Hen. New York: Harper, 1958.
Facing Nature. New York: Knopf, 1985.
Midpoint and Other Poems. New York: Knopf, 1969.
Telephone Poles and Other Poems. New York: Knopf, 1963.
Tossing and Turning. New York: Knopf, 1977.

Drama

Buchanan Dying. New York: Knopf, 1974.

Collected Prose

Assorted Prose. New York: Knopf, 1965.
Hugging the Shore. New York: Knopf, 1983.
Just Looking: Essays on Art. New York: Knopf, 1989.
Odd Jobs. New York: Knopf, 1991.
Picked-Up Pieces. New York: Knopf, 1975.

Autobiography/Memoirs

Self-Consciousness. New York: Knopf, 1989.

Uncollected Stories

"The Afterlife." *New Yorker* 15 Sept. 1986: 34–41.
"Aperto e Chiuso." *Playboy* Jan. 1991: 82–84, 178–82.
"Bech in Czech." *New Yorker* 20 Apr. 1987: 32–49.
"Brother Grasshopper." *New Yorker* 14 Dec. 1987: 40–46.
"The Burglar Alarm." *New Yorker* 9 March 1987: 30–31.
"Conjunction." *New Yorker* 27 July 1987: 29–32.
"First Wives and Trolley Cars." *New Yorker* 27 Dec. 1982: 36–39.
"Homage to Paul Klee; or, A Game of Botticelli." *Liberal Context* 12 (Fall 1964): 8–12.

"The Journey to the Dead." *New Yorker* 23 May 1988: 26–34.

"The Man Who Became a Soprano." *New Yorker* 26 Dec. 1988: 28–35.

"Morocco." *Atlantic* Nov. 1979: 45–48.

"The Other Side of the Street." *New Yorker* 28 Oct. 1991: 34–48.

"The Rumor." *Esquire* June 1991: 121–24.

"A Sandstone Farmhouse." *New Yorker* 11 June 1990: 36–48.

"Short Easter." *New Yorker* 27 March 1989: 38–42.

"Spat: [An Architectural Fiction]." *Architectural Digest* March 1989: 26–29.

"Tristan and Iseult." *New Yorker* 3 Dec. 1990: 42–43.

"Wildlife." *Esquire* Aug. 1987: 62–66.

Other Writings

Afterword to "Made in Heaven." In *New American Short Stories: The Writers Select Their Own Favorites*. Ed. Gloria Norris. New York: New American Library, 1986: 25–26.

"The Artist and His Audience." *New York Review of Books* 18 July 1985: 14–18.

"Being on TV Is Like Being Alive . . . Only More So." *TV Guide* 23 Nov. 1985: 7–8.

"The Cultural Situation of the American Writer." In *Arab and American Cultures*. Ed. George N. Atiyeh. American Enterprise Institute for Public Policy Research, 1977.

"Embarrassed." *TV Guide* 6 Dec. 1986: 7–8.

"The Golden Age of the 30 Second Spot." *Harper's* June 1984: 17.

"The Illustrative Itch." *New York Review of Books* 10 April 1986: 35–36. Rpt. as Foreword. *Doubly Gifted: The Author as Visual Artist*. Ed. Kathleen G. Hjerter. New York: Harry N. Abrams, 1986.

"The Importance of Fiction." *Esquire* August 1985: 61–62.

"In Appreciation of Women." *Cosmopolitan* Nov. 1985: 394, 401.

Introduction. *Best American Short Stories 1984*. Eds. John Updike and Shannon Ravenel. Boston: Houghton Mifflin, 1984.

"Tuning Out the Inner Critic." *New York Times Book Review* 21 June 1987: 29.

"Twisted Apples." *Harper's* March 1984: 95–97.

"Why Couples Fall Apart." *Harper's Bazaar* Feb. 1984: 180.

"Why Rabbit Had to Go." *New York Times Book Review* 5 Aug. 1990: 1, 24–25.

"The Writer Lectures." *New York Review of Books* 16 June 1988: 23–26.

"Writers on Themselves: Magic, Working Secrets." *New York Times Book Review* 23 Feb. 1986: 3, 28–29. Rpt. as Introduction. *Writers at Work: The Paris Review Interviews, Seventh Series*. Ed. George Plimpton. New York: Viking, 1986.

Secondary Works

Interviews

Banker, Stephen. Interview with John Updike. Tapes for Readers. Washington D.C., 1978.

Bech, Henry [pseud. John Updike]. "Henry Bech Redux." *New York Times Book Review* 14 Nov. 1971: 3.

———. "Updike on Updike." *New York Times Book Review* 27 Sept. 1981: 1, 34–35.

Boyers, Robert, et al. "An Evening with John Updike." *Salmagundi* 57 (1982): 42–56.

Burgin, Richard. "A Conversation with John Updike." *John Updike Newsletter* 10, 11 (Spring–Summer 1979): 1–11. Rpt. from *New York Arts Journal* nos. 9, 11, 1978.

Campbell, Jeff. Appendix: "Interview with John Updike." *Updike's Novels: Thorns Spell a Word*. Wichita Falls, TX: Midwestern State UP, 1987.

DeVine, Lawrence. "Updike: Life Meets Paper." *Detroit Free Press* 26 June 1983: 1C, 4C.

Findlay, William. "Interview with John Updike." *Cencrastus* 15 (New Year 1984): 30–36.

Gado, Frank. "A Conversation with John Updike." *The Idol* 47 (1971): 3–32. Rpt. in *First Person: Conversations on Writers and Writing*. Schenectady, NY: Union College Press, 1973: 80–109.

Greiner, Donald J. "Updike on Hawthorne." *Nathaniel Hawthorne Review* 13.1 (Spring 1987): 1–4.

Howard, Jane. "Can a Nice Novelist Finish First?" *Life* 4 Nov. 1966: 74–82.

Kakutani, Michiko. "Turning Sex and Guilt into an American Epic." *Saturday Review* Oct 1981: 14–15, 20–22.

MacDonald, Craig. "A Chat with John Updike." *Writer's Digest* Sept. 1977: 5.

Nichols, Lewis. "Talk with John Updike." *New York Times Book Review* 7 April 1968: 34–35.

Raymont, Henry. "John Updike Completes a Sequel to *Rabbit, Run*." *New York Times* 27 July 1971: 22.

Reilly, Charlie. "A Conversation with John Updike." *Canto* 3 (1980): 148–78. [Excerpt rpt. as "Talking with John Updike." *Inquiry Magazine* 11 Dec. 1978: 14–17.]

Rhode, Eric. "John Updike Talks to Eric Rhode about the Shapes and Subjects of His Fiction." *Listener* 81 (19 June 1969): 862–64. [Excerpt reprinted as "Grabbing Dilemmas: John Updike Talks about God, Love, and the American Identity." *Vogue* 1 Feb. 1971: 140, 184–85.

Rothstein, Meryvn. "In *S.*, Updike Tries the Woman's Viewpoint." *New York Times*: 2 March 1988: C21.

Rubins, Josh. "Industrious Drifter in Room 2." *Harvard Magazine* 76 (May 1974): 42–45, 51.

Samuels, Charles. "The Art of Fiction XLIII: John Updike." *Paris Review* 12 (Winter 1968): 84–117. Rpt. in *Writers at Work: The Paris Review Interviews, Fourth Series*. New York: Viking, 1976. 427–54.

Sanoff, Alvin P. "Writers 'Are Really Servants of Reality.'" *U.S. News and World Report* 20 Oct. 1986: 67–68.

Seib, Philip. "A Lovely Way through Life: An Interview with John Updike." *Southwest Review* 66 (1981): 341–50.

Suplee, Kurt. "Women, God, Sorrow & John Updike." *Washington Post* 27 Sept. 1981: F1–F3, F8–F9.

Vendler, Helen. "John Updike on Poetry." *New York Times Book Review* 10 April 1977: 3, 28.

Bibliographies

DeBellis, Jack. "Updike: A Selected Checklist 1974–1990." *Modern Fiction Studies* 37 (1991): 129–56.

Gearhart, Elizabeth. *John Updike: A Comprehensive Bibliography with Selected Annotations*. Norwood, PA: Norwood Press, 1978.

Greiner, Donald J. "John Updike." *Contemporary Authors: Bibliographical Series*. Vol. 1. Detroit: Gale Research, 1986. 347–82.

———. "Selected Checklist" in *The Other John Updike: Poems/ Short Stories/ Prose/ Play*. Athens: Ohio UP, 1981.

Meyer, Arlin G., and Michael A. Olivas. "Criticism of John Updike: A Selected Checklist." *Modern Fiction Studies* 20 (1974): 121–33.

Olivas, Michael A. *An Annotated Bibliography of John Updike Criticism 1967–1973, and A Checklist of His Works*. New York: Garland, 1975.

Roberts, Ray A. "John Updike: A Bibliographical Checklist." *American Book Collector*, new series, 1.1 (Jan.–Feb. 1980): 5–12, 40–44, 1.2 (Mar.–Apr. 1980): 39–47.

Sokoloff, B. A., and David E. Arnason. *John Updike: A Comprehensive Bibliography*. Norwood, PA: Norwood Editions, 1972.

Taylor, C. Clarke. *John Updike: A Bibliography*. Kent, OH: Kent State UP, 1968.

Critical Studies

Bloom, Harold, ed. *John Updike*. New York: Chelsea House, 1987.

Burchard, Rachel C. *John Updike: Yea Sayings*. Carbondale: Southern Illinois UP, 1971.

Campbell, Jeff. *Updike's Novels: Thorns Spell a Word*. Wichita Falls, TX: Midwestern State UP, 1987.

Detweiler, Robert. *John Updike*. 1972. Rev. ed. New York: Twayne, 1984.

Greiner, Donald. *John Updike's Novels*. Athens: Ohio UP, 1984.

———. *The Other John Updike: Poems, Short Stories, Prose, Play*. Athens: Ohio UP, 1981.

Hamilton, Alice, and Kenneth Hamilton. *The Elements of John Updike*. Grand Rapids, MI: William B. Eerdmans, 1970.

———. *John Updike: A Critical Essay*. Grand Rapids, MI: William B. Eerdmans, 1967.

Hunt, George. *John Updike and the Three Great Things: Sex, Religion, and Art*. Grand Rapids, MI: William B. Eerdmans, 1980.

Macnaughton, William R., ed. *Critical Essays on John Updike*. Boston: G. K. Hall, 1982.

Markle, Joyce B. *Fighters and Lovers: Theme in the Novels of John Updike*. New York: New York UP, 1973.

Newman, Judie. *John Updike*. New York: St. Martin's, 1988.

Ristoff, Dilvo I. *Updike's America: The Presence of Contemporary America in John Updike's Rabbit Trilogy*. New York: Peter Lang, 1988.

Samuels, Charles Thomas. *John Updike*. Minneapolis: U of Minnesota P, 1969.

Tallent, Elizabeth. *Married Men and Magic Tricks: John Updike's Erotic Heroes*. Berkeley: Creative Arts, 1981.

Taylor, Larry E. *Pastoral and Anti-Pastoral Patterns in John Updike's Fiction*. Carbondale: Southern Illinois UP, 1971.

Thorburn, David, and Howard Eiland, eds. *John Updike: A Collection of Critical Essays*. Englewood Cliffs, NJ: Prentice Hall, 1979.

Uphaus, Suzanne Henning. *John Updike*. New York: Ungar, 1980.

Vargo, Edward P. *Rainstorms and Fire: Ritual in the Novels of John Updike*. Port Washington, NY: Kennikat Press, 1973.

Vaughn, Philip H. *John Updike's Images of America*. Reseda, CA: Mojave, 1981.

Articles, Parts of Books, Selected Reviews

Adams, Robert Martin. "Without Risk." *New York Times Book Review* 18 Sept. 1966: 4–5.

Allen, Mary. "John Updike's Love of 'Dull Bovine Beauty.'" In *The Necessary Blankness: Women in Major American Fiction of the Sixties*. Urbana: U of Illinois P, 1976. 97–132. Rpt. in Bloom. 69–95.

Amis, Martin. "Updike: A Rabbitland and Bechville." In *The Moronic Inferno*. New York: Viking, 1987. 155–59.

Atlas, James. "John Updike Breaks Out of Suburbia." *New York Times Sunday Magazine* 10 Dec. 1978: 60–76.

———. "Languid, but Never Dull." *Atlantic* Oct. 1982: 103–4.

Banks, R. Jeff. "The Uses of Weather in 'Tomorrow and Tomorrow and So Forth.'" *Notes on Contemporary Literature* 3.5 (1973): 8–9.

Barnes, Jane. "John Updike: A Literary Spider." *Virginia Quarterly Review* 57 (1981): 79–98.

Blechner, Michael Harry. "Tristan in Letter: Malory, C. S. Lewis, Updike. *Tristania* 6.1 (1980): 30–37.

Broyard, Anatole. "All the Way with Updike." *Life* 19 June 1970: 12.

———. "Falling in Love." *New York Times* 17 March 1979: 17.

Cameron, Dee Birch. "The Unitarian Wife and the One-Eyed Man: Updike's *Marry Me* and 'Sunday Teasing.'" *Ball State University Forum* 21 (1980): 54–64.

Cassidy, Thomas E. "The Enchantment of the Ordinary." *Commonweal* 11 Sept. 1959: 499.

Chanley, Steven M. "Quest for Order in 'Pigeon Feathers': Updike's Use of Christian Mythology." *Arizona Quarterly* 43 (1987): 251–63.

Chester, Alfred. "Twitches and Embarrassments." *Commentary* 34 (July 1962): 77–80.

Cochran, Robert W. "The Narrator Then and Now in Updike's 'Flight.'" *Rendezvous* 10 (Fall 1975): 29–32.

Conn, Sandra M. "Do Not Go Gentle: Visions of Death in John Updike's 'Pigeon Feathers' and 'Packed Dirt. . . .'" *Publications of the Mississippi Philological Association* 1985: 25–32.

Crowley, Sue Mitchell. "The Rubble of Footnotes Bound into Kierkegaard." *Journal of the American Academy of Religion* 45.3, Supplement (1977), H: 1011–35.

Culbertson, Diana. "Updike's 'The Day of the Dying Rabbit.'" *Studies in American Fiction* 7 (1979): 95–99.

De Bellis, Jack. "The Group and John Updike." *Sewanee Review* 72 (1964): 531–36.

Dessner, Lawrence Jay. "Irony and Innocence in John Updike's 'A & P.'" *Studies in Short Fiction* 25 (1988): 315–17.

Detweiler, Robert. "John Updike's Sermons." In *Breaking the Fall: Religious Readings of Contemporary Fiction*. San Francisco: Harper, 1989. 91–119.

Dinnage, Rosemary. "At the Flashpoint." *Times Literary Supplement* 4 May 1973. 488. Rpt. in Thorburn and Eiland.

Doyle, Paul. "Updike's Fiction: Motifs and Techniques." *Catholic World* Sept. 1964: 356–62.

Edelstein, J. M. "The Security of Memory." *New Republic* 14 May 1962: 30–31.

Edwards, A. S. G. "Updike's 'A Sense of Shelter.'" *Studies in Short Fiction* 8 (1971): 467–68.

Emmet, Paul J. "A Slip that Shows Updike's 'A & P.'" *Notes on Contemporary Literature* 15 (1985): 9–11.

Enright, D. J. "Updike's Ups and Downs." *Holiday* 38 (Nov. 1965): 162–66. Rpt. as "The Inadequate American: John Updike's Fiction" in *Conspirators and Poets*. Chester Springs, PA: Dufour, 1966. 134–40.

Epstein, Joseph. "John Updike: Promises, Promises." *Commentary* 75 (1983): 54–58.

Fisher, Richard E. "John Updike: Theme and Form in the Garden of Epiphanies." *Moderna Sprak* 56 (Fall 1962): 255–60.

Friedman, Ruben. "An Interpretation of John Updike's 'Tomorrow and Tomorrow and So Forth." *English Journal* 61 (1972): 1159–62.

Galloway, David D. "The Absurd Man as Saint: The Novels of John Updike." In *The Absurd Hero in American Fiction: Updike, Styron, Bellow, Salinger.* 1966. 3rd ed. Austin: U Texas P, 1981. 17–80.

Gerlach, John. "The Practice of Openness: Updike's "Ace in the Hole." *Toward the End: Closure and Structure in the American Short Story.* University, AL: U of Alabama P, 1985. 124–28.

Gingher, Robert S. "Has Updike Anything to Say?" *Modern Fiction Studies* 20 (1974): 95–105.

Goss, Marjorie Hill. "Widening Perceptions in Updike's 'A & P'" *Notes on Contemporary Literature* 14 (1984): 8.

Gray, Paul. "Perennial Promises Kept." *Time* 18 Oct. 1982: 72–81.

Greiner, Donald. "John Updike." In *Broadening Views: 1968–1988.* Vol. 6 of *Concise Dictionary of American Literary Biography.* 6 vols. Detroit: Gale, 1989. 276–97.

Griffith, Albert J. "Updike's Artist's Dilemma: 'Should Wizard Hit Mommy?'" *Modern Fiction Studies* 20 (1974): 111–15.

Gullette, Margaret Morganroth. *Safe at Last in the Middle Years: The Invention of the Midlife Progress Novel: Saul Bellow, Margaret Drabble, Anne Tyler, and John Updike.* Berkeley: U California P, 1988.

Hamilton, Alice, and Kenneth Hamilton. "Metamorphosis Through Art: John Updike's *Bech: A Book.*" *Queen's Quarterly* 77 (1970): 624–36. Rpt. in Macnaughton.

Hamilton, Kenneth. "John Updike: Chronicler of the Time and of the 'Death of God.'" *Christian Century* 84 (7 June 1967): 745–48.

Hardwick, Elizabeth. "Citizen Updike." *New York Review of Books* 18 May 1989: 3–8.

Harper, Howard M., Jr. "John Updike: The Intrinsic Problem of Human Existence." In *Desperate Faith: A Study of Bellow, Salinger, Mailer, Baldwin and Updike.* Chapel Hill: U North Carolina P, 1967. 162–90.

Hart, Elizabeth A. "John Updike's 'A Sense of Shelter.'" *Studies in Short Fiction* 26 (1989): 555–57.

Hendin, Josephine. "The Victim Is Hero." In *Vulnerable People: A View of American Fiction Since 1945.* New York: Oxford UP, 1978. 88–99.

Hicks, Granville. "John Updike." *Literary Horizons.* New York: New York UP, 1970. 107–33.

Hoagland, Edward. "A Novelist's Novelist." *New York Times Book Review* 17 Oct. 1982: 1, 30–32.

Hunt, George W., S.J. "Bech Is Back!" *America* 20 Nov. 1982: 314–16.

————. "Kierkegaardian Sensations into Real Fiction: John Updike's 'The Astronomer.'" *Christianity and Literature* 26.3 (1977): 3–17.

————. "The Problems of John Updike." *America* 8 March 1980: 187–88.

————. "Reality, Imagination, and Art: The Significance of John Updike's 'Best' Story." *Studies in Short Fiction* 16: 219–29. Rpt. in Macnaughton.

Hurley, C. Harold. "Updike's 'A & P': An 'Initial' Response." *Notes on Contemporary Literature* 20.3 (1990): 12

Jong, Erica. Rev. of *Too Far to Go* by John Updike. *New Republic* 15 Sept. 1979: 36–37.

Kauffman, Stanley. "Onward with Updike." *New Republic* 24 Sept. 1966: 15–17.

Kazin, Alfred. "Professional Observers: Cozzens to Updike." In *Bright Book of Life: American Novelists and Storytellers from Hemingway to Mailer.* Boston: Little, Brown, 1973. 95–124.

Kinsela, Rebbie. "Pigeon Feathers and Witches." *Christianity Today* 7 Mar. 1986: 60.

Klinkowitz, Jerome. "John Updike." *American Novelists Since World War II.* Vol. 2 of *Dictionary of Literary Biography.* 5 vols. Detroit: Gale, 1978. 484–92.

————. "John Updike's America." In *Literary Subversions: New American Fiction and the Practice of Criticism.* Carbondale: Southern Illinois UP, 1985. 59–69. Also in *North American Review* Sept. 1980: 68–71.

————. "John Updike since *Midpoint.*" In *The Practice of Fiction in America: Writers, from Hawthorne to the Present.* Ames: Iowa State UP, 1980. 85–97.

La Course, Guerin. "The Innocence of John Updike." *Commonweal* 88 (7 Dec. 1962): 512–14.

Larsen, R. B. "John Updike: The Story as Lyrical Meditation." *Thoth* 13.1 (1972–73): 33–39.

Lesser, W. Rev. of *Trust Me. Hudson Review* 40 (Winter 1988): 661–68.

Lurie, Alison. "The Woman Who Rode Away." *New York Review of Books* 12 May 1988: 3–4.

Luscher, Robert M. "John Updike's *Olinger Stories*: New Light among the Shadows." *Journal of the Short Story in English 11 (1988): 99–117.*

Lyons, E. "John Updike: The Beginning and the end." *Critique* 14.2 (1972): 44–59.

McCoy, Robert. "John Updike's Literary Apprenticeship on *The Harvard Lampoon.*" *Modern Fiction Studies* 20 (1974): 3–12.

McFarland, Ronald E. "Updike and the Critics: Reflections on 'A & P.'" *Studies in Short Fiction* 20 (1983): 95–100.

Mann, Susan Garland. *The Short Story Cycle: A Genre Companion and Reference Guide.* Westport, CT: Greenwood P, 1988.

Markle, Joyce B. "On John Updike and 'The Music School.'" In *The American Short Story.* Ed. Calvin L. Skaggs. New York: Dell, 1979. 389–94.

Mienke, Peter. "Yearning for Yesteryear." *Christian Century* 7 Dec. 1966: 1512.

Miller, Miriam Youngerman. "A Land Too Ripe for Enigma: John Updike as Regionalist." *Arizona Quarterly* 40 (1984): 197–218.

Mizener, Arthur. "Behind the Dazzle Is a Knowing Eye." *New York Times Book Review* 18 Mar. 1962: 1, 29. Rpt. in Macnaughton.

Muradian, Thaddeus. "The World of John Updike." *English Journal* 54 (1965): 577–84.

Murphy, Richard W. "John Updike." *Horizon* 4 (March 1962): 84–85.

Nadon, Robert J. "Updike's Olinger Stories: In the Middle Landscape Tradition." *Perspectives on Contemporary Literature* 5 (1979): 62–68.

Novak, Michael. "Updike's Quest for Liturgy." *Commonweal* 10 May 1963: 192–95. Rpt. in Thorburn and Eiland.

Overall, Nadine. "John Updike's *Olinger Stories: A Selection.*" *Studies in Short Fiction* 4 (1967): 195–97.

Overmeyer, Janet. "Courtly Love in the 'A & P.'" *Notes on Contemporary Literature* 2.3 (1972): 4–5.

Ozick, Cynthia. "Bech, Passing." In *Art and Ardor: Essays.* New York: Knopf, 1983. 114–29.

Peden, William. *The American Short Story: Continuity and Change 1940–1975.* Boston: Houghton Mifflin, 1975. 47–53.

———. "Minor Ills That Plague the Human Heart." *New York Times Book Review* 16 August 1959: 5.

Petry, Alice. "The Dress Code in Updike's 'A & P.'" *Notes on Contemporary Literature* 16.1 (1986): 8–10.

Pinsker, Sanford. "John Updike and the Distractions of Henry Bech, Professional Writer and Amateur American Jew." *Modern Fiction Studies* 37 (1991): 97–112.

Podhoretz, Norman. "A Dissent on Updike." In *Doings and Undoings: The Fifties and After in American Writing.* New York: Farrar, Straus, 1964. 251–57.

Porter, M. Gilbert. "John Updike's 'A & P': The Establishment and an Emersonian Cashier." *English Journal* 61 (1972): 1155–58.

Raban, Jonathon. "Talking Head." *New Statesman* 16 Oct. 1970: 494.

Regan, Robert A. "Updike's Symbol of the Center." *Modern Fiction Studies* 20 (1974): 77–96.

Reising, R. W. "Updike's 'A Sense of Shelter.'" *Studies in Short Fiction* 7 (1970): 651–52.

Richardson, Jack. "Keeping Up With Updike." *New York Review of Books* 22 Oct. 1970: 46–48. Rpt. in Thorburn and Eiland.

Robinson, James C. "1969–1980: Experiment and Tradition." In *The American Short Story, 1945–1980: A Critical History.* Ed. Gordon Weaver. Boston: Twayne, 1983. 106–8.

Robinson, Marilynne. "At Play in the Backyard of the Psyche." *New York Times Book Review* 26 April 1987: 1, 44–45.

Romano, John. "Updike's People." *New York Times Book Review* 28 Oct. 1979: 1, 44–45.

Rosa, Alfred F. "The Psycholinguistics of Updike's 'Museums and Women.'" *Modern Fiction Studies* 20: 107–11.

Rowland, Stanley J. "The Limits of Littleness." *Christian Century* 4 July 1962: 840–41.

Rupp, Richard H. "John Updike: Style in Search of a Center." *Sewanee Review* 75 (1967): 693–709. Rpt. in *Celebration in Postwar American Fiction*. Coral Gables: U of Miami P, 1970 and in Bloom.

Samuels, Charles T. "A Place of Resonance." *Nation* 3 Oct. 1966: 328–29. Rpt. in Thorburn and Eiland.

Sant'Anna, Norma. "Some Considerations on John Updike's 'Music School.'" *Estudos Anglo–Americana* 3–4 (1979–80): 200–205.

Schwartz, Sanford. "Top of the Class." *New York Review of Books* 24 Nov. 1983: 26–30+.

Searles, George J. "The Mouths of Babes: Childhood Epiphany in Roth's 'Conversion of the Jews' and Updike's 'Pigeon Feathers.'" *Studies in Short Fiction* 24 (1987): 59–62.

Selden, Raman. "Narrative Theory: John Updike." *Practising Theory and Reading Literature: An Introduction*. Lexington: U of Kentucky P, 1989. 61–66.

Shaw, Patrick W. "Checking Out Faith and Lust: Hawthorne's 'Young Goodman Brown' and Updike's 'A & P.'" *Studies in Short Fiction* 23 (1986): 321–23.

Shreve, Anita. "The American Short Story: An Untold Tale." *New York Times Magazine* 30 Nov. 1980: 136–44.

Shurr, William H. "The Lutheran Experience in John Updike's 'Pigeon Feathers.'" *Studies in Short Fiction* 14 (1977) 329–35.

Sissman, L. E. "John Updike: Midpoint and After." *Atlantic* Aug. 1970: 102–4.

Smith, Ron. "John Updike." In *Critical Survey of Short Fiction*. Ed. Frank N. Magill. Vol. 6. Englewood Cliffs, NJ: Salem P, 1981. 2366–76.

Spectorsky, A. C. "Spirit under Surgery." *Saturday Review* 22 Aug. 1959: 15, 31.

Strandberg, Victor. "John Updike and the Changing of the Gods." *Mosaic* 12 (1977): 157–75. Rpt. in Macnaughton.

Suderman, Elmer F. "Art as a Way of Knowing." *Discourse* 12 (1968): 3–14.

Sullivan, Walter. "Updike, Spark, and Others." *Sewanee Review* 74 (1966): 709–16.

Sykes, Robert H. "A Commentary on Updike's Astronomer." *Studies in Short Fiction* 8 (1971): 575–79.

Tanner, Tony. "A Compromised Environment." In *City of Words: American Fiction, 1950–1970*. New York: Harper, 1971. 273–94.

———. Rev. of *Museums and Women and Other Stories*. *New York Times Book Review* 22 Oct. 1972: 5, 24. Rpt. in Macnaughton.

Theroux, Paul. "A Marriage of Mixed Blessings." *New York Times Book Review* 8 April 1979: 7. Rpt. in Macnaughton.

Todd, Richard. "Updike and Barthelme: Disengagement." *Atlantic* Dec. 1972: 126–32. Rpt. in Thorburn and Eiland.

Towers, Robert. "Cuisine Minceur." *New York Review of Books* 8 Nov. 1979: 18.

Tracy, Bruce H. "The Habit of Confession: Recovery of the Self in Updike's 'The Music School.'" *Studies in Short Fiction* 20 (1983): 95–100.

"*The Universe Today.*" *Esquire* August 1987: 51–55.

Verduin, Kathleen. "Fatherly Presences: John Updike's Place in the Protestant Tradition." In McNaughton 254–68.

"View from the Catacombs." *Time* 26 April 1968: 66–75.

Walkiewicz, E. P. "1957–1968: Toward Diversity of Form." In *The American Short Story, 1945–1980: A Critical History*. Ed. Gordon Weaver. Boston: Twayne, 1983. 40–44.

Walters, Ray. "Paperback Talk." *New York Times Book Review* 11 March 1979: 33.

Ward, J. A. "John Updike's Fiction." *Critique* 5 (1962): 27–40.

Waxman, Robert E. "Invitations to Dread: John Updike's Metaphysical Quest." *Renascence* 29 (1977): 201–10.

Wilhelm, Albert E. "Narrative Continuity in Updike's *Too Far to Go.*" *Journal of the Short Story in English* 7 (1986): 87–90. "Rebecca Cune: Updike's Wedge between the Maples." *Notes on Modern Literature* 7 (1983): Item 9.

———. "Three Versions of Updike's "Snowing in Greenwich Village.'" *American Notes and Queries* 22 (1984): 80–82.

———. "The Trail-of-Bread-Crumbs Motif in Updike's Maples Stories." *Studies in Short Fiction* 25 (1988): 71–73.

Wood, Ralph C. *The Comedy of Redemption: Christian Faith and Comic Vision in Four American Novelists*. Notre Dame, IN: U of Notre Dame P, 1988.

———. "Updike's Problems / And Ours." *Cross Currents* Spring 1980: 71–74.

Yates, Norris. "The Doubt and Faith of John Updike." *College English* 26 (1965): 469–74.

Index

Index

The Author

Robert M. Luscher is an Associate Professor of English and Director of the Honors Program at Catawba College, where he teaches American literature. His articles on Mark Twain, Emily Dickinson, Mary Wilkins Freeman, J. D. Salinger, and John Updike have appeared in *American Literary Realism*, *ESQ*, *ATQ*, *Resources for American Literary Study*, and the *Journal of the Short Story in English*, respectively. Recently, he travelled to Angers, France, to present a paper on Ernest Gaines at the Colloquium on the Short Story in the American South. A portion of his work on the short story sequence appears in *Short Story Theory at a Crossroads* (1989), published by LSU Press. He also serves as a contributing editor of the journal *Short Story*. He lives in Salisbury, North Carolina, with his wife, Diana, and his two daughters, Aurora and Julia.

The Editor

General Editor Gordon Weaver earned his B.A. in English at the University of Wisconsin-Milwaukee in 1961; his M.A. in English at the University of Illinois, where he studied as a Woodrow Wilson Fellow, in 1962; and his Ph.D. in English and creative writing at the University of Denver in 1970. He is author of several novels, including *Count a Lonely Cadence*, *Give Him a Stone*, *Circling Byzantium*, and most recently *The Eight Corners of the World* (1988). Many of his numerous short stories are collected in *The Entombed Man of Thule*, *Such Waltzing Was Not Easy*, *Getting Serious*, *Morality Play*, *A World Quite Round*, and *Men Who Would Be Good* (1991). Recognition of his fiction includes the St. Lawrence Award for Fiction (1973), two National Endowment for the Arts Fellowships (1974, 1989), and the O. Henry First Prize (1979). He edited *The American Short Story, 1945–1980: A Critical History*, and is currently editor of *Cimarron Review*. He is professor of English at Oklahoma State University. Married, and the father of three daughters, he lives in Stillwater, Oklahoma.